Customs and Traditions of the Canadian Navy

Customs and Traditions of the Canadian Navy

Lt.(N) Graeme Arbuckle

NIMBUS PUBLISHING LIMITED

Published by
Nimbus Publishing Limited
P.O. Box 9301, Station A
Halifax, N.S. B3K 5N5

Printed and bound in Canada

Typesetting: McCurdy Printing & Typesetting Limited, Halifax
Printing and binding: John Deyell Company

Canadian Cataloguing in Publication Data

Arbuckle, Graeme, 1953-
    Customs and traditions of the Canadian Navy

Bibliography: p.
Includes index.
ISBN 0-920852-38-6

1. Naval ceremonies, honors, and salutes — Canada.
2. Canada. Canadian Armed Forces. Maritime Command — Flags. 3. Canada. Canadian Armed Forces. Maritime Command — Insignia. I. Title.
V310.A72 1985   359.1'0971   C85-098327-4

Photo & illustration credits

The Arms, Flags & Emblems of Canada, 1978 ed., (Ottawa, DSS, 1978)
1.28, 1.29

The Book of Flags, Gordon Campbell & I.O. Evans, (London, Oxford University Press, 1960) 4th ed.
1.06, 1.07, 1.08, 1.09, 1.30, 1.31

Canada's V.C.'s, George C. Machum, (Toronto, McClelland & Stewart, 1956)
3.29, 3.30, 3.31, 3.32, 3.33

The King's Flags and some others, Cecil King, Mariner's Mirror, (St. Albans, Staples Printers, 1952)
1.17, 1.18

Ribbons and Medals, Taprell H. Doring, (London, George Phillip and Son, Ltd., 1957)
3.34-3.45

RN 1937 Dress Regulations
5.05-5.08

Uniform Instructions for the RCN, (Ottawa, Queen's Printer, 1956)
5.09-5.14, 5.16-5.22

Cover illustration courtesy of George Quigley

Photos from Department of National Defence, Ottawa

Plate no.	File no.	Plate no.	File no.
1.02	HS61822	2.32	E 70793
1.03	AL644	2.33	E 70825
1.04	AL63	2.34	E 70824
1.05	4014	2.35	No. Neg. No.
2.05	013782	2.36	No. Neg. No.
2.07	013776	2.38	HS58434
2.08	013785	2.40	HS58421
2.09	013794	2.41	HS58416
2.14	013783	2.42	HS58431
2.15	013795	2.45	HS58425
2.16	013778	2.47	HS58429
2.18	013781	2.48-2.53	No. Neg. No.
2.19	013804	2.54	DNS 24015
2.20	013775	2.55	DNS 23974
2.21	013784	2.56	ET 82 693
2.22	013780	2.57	ET 82 699
2.23	013792	2.58	ET 82 707
2.25	ET81-3089	2.59	ET 82 695
2.26	ET81-3050	2.60	ET 82 721
2.27	E 59735	2.61	ET 82 713
2.28	E 59720	2.62	ET 82 716
2.29	E 59721	3.46-3.55	No. Neg. No.
2.30	E 59719	4.01	No. Neg. No.
2.31	E 59725		

Contents

Foreword 8

Preface 9

1 Naval Ceremonial 11

I Salutes and Marks of Respect 11
The Hand Salute 11
  Deportment 12
Gun Salutes 13
  Deportment 15
Ceremonies When Two Ships Pass 16
  Deportment 17
Manning and Cheering Ship 17
  Deportment 17

II Visits to HMC Ships by VIPs 18
Arrival from Shore 18
Arrival at the Brow 19
Arrival by Air 19
Honours and Marks of Respect 19
  Piping the Side 20

III The Ship's Boats 20
  Deportment 21

IV Mustering by the Open List 22
  Deportment 23

V Flags and Pennants 23
Origins and History 23
The Royal Standard 23
The Royal Union Flag 25
The Flag of St. George 25
The Flag of St. Andrew 26
The Cross of St. Patrick 26
England and Scotland 26
The Union Jack 27
The Union Flag 27
  Deportment 28
Flag of the Lord High Admiral 28
  Deportment 29
Canadian Naval Board Flag 29
Ensigns Used by the RCN 29
  The White Ensign 29
  The Blue Ensign 30
  The Red Ensign 30

The National Flag of Canada 30
  Deportment 32
  HMC Ship's Ensign: Deportment 32
  Boat's Ensigns: Deportment 33
The Naval Jack 33
  Deportment 33
Personal Flags 34
The Queen's Personal Canadian Flag 34
  Deportment 34
The Governor General's Flag 34
  Deportment 34
Standards of Members of the Royal Family 35
Distinguishing Flags 35
  Deportment 37
The Commissioning Pennant and Church
Pennant 39
  Deportment 40
The Squadron Command Flag 41
  Deportment 41
SCOPA Pennant 41
  Deportment 41
Queens Harbour Master Flag 42
  Deportment 42

VI The Origins of Naval Signalling 42

VII Ceremonial Anchorage 46
  Deportment 46

VIII The Ship's Bell 46

2 Naval Ceremonies 48

I Colours, Halfmasting and Sunset in HMC Ships 48
Colours 48
  Deportment 48
Half-masting 49
Sunset 51

II Tattoo, Retreat and Sunset Ceremony 51
  Deportment 51
  Phase One: The Ceremony 53
  Phase Two: The Tattoo 54
  Phase Three: Retreat 54
  Phase Four: Subsection Drill 59

Phase Five: Proving Rifles 59
Phase Six: The Evening Hymn 60
Phase Seven: Sunset 60
Phase Eight: Moving Off 60

III Divisions and Evening Quarters 62
Divisions — The Ship's Company 62
Evening Quarters 65

IV The Launching of a Ship 65
Keel Laying Ceremony 66
  Deportment 66
Naming a Ship 66
Launching a Ship 69
  Deportment 71

V The King's and Queen's Colours 74
Formation of the Parade 77
Sequence of Events 77

VI Fleet Reviews 85

VII Paying Off 86

VIII Change of Command 87

IX Religious Services 89
Baptisms 89
Weddings 89
Burial at Sea 90
Laying Up of Colours 91

X The Naval Gun-Afloat and Ashore 92

XI Crossing the Line 96
Crossing the Line: The Equator 96

XII Christmas and New Year's Day 101
Christmas Day 101
New Year's Day 102

3 Miscellaneous Naval Customs 103

I The Bo's'n's Call and it's Use 103
Pipes on the Bo's'n's Call 105

II Grog and the Splicing of the Mainbrace 106
Grog in the Making 106
Splicing the Mainbrace 109

Navy Rum Terminology 109
  Drink Measures 109
18th Century Royal Navy Drinks 109
Modern Pusser's Drinks 110

III Naval Commissions and Warrants 111
The "Commission" and the "Commissioned Officers" 111
The "Warrant" and the "Warrant Officers" 113

IV Naval Decorations and Medals 115
The Naval General Service Medal (1793-1840) 116
The Conspicuous Gallantry Medal (Royal Navy, 1855) 116
The Victoria Cross (1856) 116
The Distinguished Service Cross (Late Conspicuous Service Cross) 119
The Distinguished Service Medal (RN) 119
Navy Gold Medals (1794-1815) 119
Naval General Service Medal (1915) 119
1914-1915 Star 120
British War Medal (1914-1920) 120
Victory Medal 120
1939-1945 Star and Atlantic Star 121
Defence Medal (1939-1945) 121
Canadian Decorations, Medals and Awards 121
Canada General Service Medal (1866-70) 121
The Canada Medal 121
Canada Volunteer Service Medal 122
Decorations for Bravery 122
Cross of Valour 122
Star of Courage 122
Medal of Bravery 123
The Order of Canada 123
Companions of the Order of Canada 124
Officers of the Order of Canada 124
Members of the Order of Canada 124
The Order of Military Merit 124
Commanders of the Order 125
Officers of the Order 125
Members of the Order 125
The Canadian Forces Decoration 126
Chief of the Defence Staff Commendation 126
The Maritime Commander's Commendation 126

Orders, Decorations and Medals   127
   Precedence   127
   Occasions for Wearing   127

V The Canadian Touch **128**
HMCS and Their Forebears   128
The Barber Pole Brigade   129
Battle of the Atlantic   129
Trafalgar Day   131

VI And What About . . .? **132**
Nail the colours to the Mast   132
The Hammock   132
The First Woman in the Navy?   132
Some Old Beliefs and Superstitions   133
Warming the Bell   134
Dead Horse Ceremony   134
The Jaunty   134
Shore Leave   135
The Luck Coin in Ships   135
General Drill   136

4   The Wardroom   137

I Humble Beginnings   **137**

II The Purpose of the Wardroom   **137**

III Dining in the Wardroom   **138**
General   138
Terminology   138
Dress   138
The President and Vice-President   138
Before Dinner   139
   Arrival   139
   Seating Plan   139
   Entry   139
Dining   139
   Grace   139
   The Menu   139
Service   140
   Table Settings   140
   Table Manners   140
Rules of Order   140
   Discipline   141
Toasts   141
   Passing the Port   141
   The Loyal Toast   142

Toasts to Other Nations   142
Toasts of the Day   143
Other Toasts   143
Wine Guardians   143
Adjournment   144

5   Naval Uniforms   145

I Naval Swords   **145**

II Distinction Colours   **148**

III No Baton for the Admiral   **150**

IV Ranks and Badges of Rank   **152**
Volunteer Officers   152
The Naval Cadet   152
Midshipmen   153
The Master and His Mate   153
The Sub-Lieutenant   154
The Lieutenant   154
The Commander and the Lieutenant
Commander   154
The Captain   155
The Admiral   155
Ratings   156
Seamen   157
The Petty Officer   158
Branch Badges   159

V The Sailor's Collar   **160**

6   Badges and Insignia   161

I Ships' Badges: Their Origins and Use   **161**
Ships' Mottoes   164
Battle Honours   164
The Maple Leaf   165
The Foul Anchor   165
The Naval Crown   165

*II Reproductions of Selected HMCS
Badges*   **166**

Bibliography   **178**

Foreword

In 1985, the Canadian Navy marks its Seventy-Fifth Anniversary with a cross-Canada celebration. The pride of those of us who presently serve is shared by Canadians from every walk of life. It marks an important milestone in history, and records for posterity our deep appreciation of the contributions made by our predecessors in the service of Crown and Country.

The Navy spirit has grown strong, nurtured by the customs and traditions of the sea, and will remain strong so long as each of us bears a full knowledge and understanding of our heritage.

Customs and Traditions of the Canadian Navy is another contribution to this heritage. Within its pages is recorded the development of the ceremonies and ceremonial which belong traditionally to "the Fleet in which we serve." It is a most welcome addition to our Naval literature and all who read this book will be well served by it.

J.C. Wood
Vice Admiral

Preface

Before the meaning of tradition to the Navy can be fully appreciated one must be aware of what the Navy meant in the early days. There is no more appropriate phrase for describing the nature of the "Old Navy" than the one used in Mediaeval England: "All English shipping and seamen." Although initially the Navy was a temporary force, used only in emergency situations, in point of fact, all state seamen and ships could (and can) be called upon to play their part in a nation's conflict. Dunkirk provides a perfect example of the far-reaching use of men and ships. The "New Navy" was formed three centuries before Dunkirk and the country had good reason to be pleased with the variety and complexity of tasks it could perform. However in 1940, with its ships spread over half the world, the Navy simply could not provide the deck space needed to evacuate the hundreds of thousands of soldiers waiting on the French beaches. The "Old Navy" all but forgotten, was again called to serve, and the fleet which appeared off Dunkirk demonstrated that in war the Navy of a country is, in fact, all her ships and seamen.

"Tradition" can briefly be described as the transmission of knowledge, opinions and practices from ancestor to posterity by word of mouth. "Customs" are long established practices which from long consent have become unwritten laws.

For the Navy, the customs and traditions of the sea have evolved over many hundreds of years and embody that spirit of courage and adventure strangely unique to seafaring history. Some of these customs, such as 'saluting the quarterdeck,' trace their origins back to the early Greeks and Romans; some, like the symbol of the fouled anchor, so contradictory of the high reputation for seamanship, have no logical explanation; others, like continuing to refer to a rating as a 'tar' have simply become a habit. Collectively though, they form an indelible bond between those "that go down to the sea in ships; and occupy their business in great waters."

There is no question that the spirit of adventure, courage, determination and pride, which has characterized naval services since Alfred the Great, is the true foundation of the Navy's greatness and strength. This tradition of spirit has been passed on by all the great leaders of naval activities as well as by the countless courageous men who have served at sea for a thousand years. As Mahan in his essay on military obedience expressed it:

"The value of tradition to the social body is immense. The veneration for practices or for authority consecrated by long acceptance, has a reserve of strength which cannot be obtained by any novel device. Respect for the old customs is planted deep in the hearts as well as the intelligence of all inheritors of English speaking policy."

Today, we can look back on a history which reflects the Canadian Navy's contributions around the world. It has striven for and achieved distinction - distinction which is the demonstrated combination of seventy five years of contributions by Canadian sailors. It is the courage of the Battle of the Atlantic — the stamina and determination of the "Corvette Navy." It is the 'ceremony of the flags' where old and new meld into a uniquely Canadian demonstration of parade colour and precision. It is a loyalty to the Sovereign and country expressed by each of "His" or "Her Majesty's Canadian Ships," both past and present members of the "Fleet in which we serve."

Each generation, bred in the tradition of struggle and victory have accepted the responsibility of keeping these traditions alive. This is undertaken today through study, uniform, ceremonial and other outward signs, yet even so, few of the many individuals working in the naval environment realize that the varied and interesting activities they now perform have been repeatedly performed by others for hundreds of years.

There is a wealth of information recorded in the Navy's history from its inception to the present day. This book adds to that information by providing a wide selection of those customs and traditions practiced in the Canadian Navy today, as well as an insight into their beginnings and the evolution that each has undergone.

Since 1967, when the armed forces were unified it has become increasingly tenuous to rely on word of mouth to maintain an awareness of naval customs and traditions among the officers and men who now serve in the Canadian Navy. This book has been written to help ensure that the senior service maintains its unique identity.

Publication of this book would not have been possible without the assistance of the Maritime Command Museum, Ms. M. Smith and her staff; Dr. W.A.B. Douglas, head of the Directorate of History, NDHQ and his staff; Mr. F.D.H. Nelson and the CFB Esquimalt Historical Society, who provided a great deal of historical material from their personal files; the Commanders of Maritime Command, Vice-admiral J.L. Fulton (RETD) and Vice-admiral J.C. Wood, as well as the Commanders of Maritime Forces Pacific, Rear-admiral W.A. Hughes (RETD) and Rear-admiral G.L. Edwards, for their support of the project as a Command undertaking; the Canadian Forces Photographic Unit, Rockcliffe, for their assistance in procuring the majority of the photographs; Mrs. P. Jean White of Westcoast Writing and Research, who was invaluable in editing the original manuscript; and finally, to Commodore W.J. Draper, Captain(N) J.R. Anderson and Lieutenant-Commander M.L. Crofton, whose unflagging enthusiasm and support throughout the past five years has, I hope, been rewarded.

J. Graeme G. Arbuckle
Lieutenant(N)

1 Naval Ceremonial

I
Salutes and Marks of Respect

The Hand Salute

Use of the hand salute began as a gesture of peaceful intention and mutual respect; it remains so today. There are many theories about the origin of the salute. One is that the open hand was a sign that no weapon was being concealed; another that the palm of the hand was turned down to conceal a dirty hand; and yet another refers to the age of chivalry when a knight would raise his right hand to his visor in quiet assurance that he would not un-horse his approaching rival.

It is not possible to substantiate these theories; documentary evidence, if it ever existed, has been lost. There are, however, examples throughout history of practices that were everyday occurrences yet were never recorded, and the hand salute could very well be one of them.

It is generally agreed that the hand salute is the first part of the movement to uncover the head. There is evidence that, in the Royal Navy of the eighteenth century, both officers and men removed their head-dress when being addressed. (This was also done in civilian life ashore.) An example of the custom is illustrated in the following account of the battle at Trafalgar:

"...when steering for the enemy's fleet, Sir Horatio Nelson hailed HMS *Zealous* and asked Captain Hood if he thought he might venture to bear up round the shoal. The answer was: "I cannot say Sir, but if you will allow me the honour of leading into action, I will keep the lead going."

"You have my permission, and I wish you good luck" was the reply; and as Nelson said this, he took off his hat. Captain Hood, in his hurry to return the courtesy of his Admiral, dropped his hat overboard."[1]

It is also clear from paintings, etc., that by Nelson's time the practice had developed, at least at sea, to the point that occasionally the hat was not removed but only seized between the thumb and index finger as a gesture of removal. However, up to the end of the last century, the cap or hat was fully removed on more formal occasions. This form of salute is still observed when the Articles of War are read, as a mark of respect to the Queen and Parliament as governing authorities.

The salute was described as follows in the Training Ship Regulations of 1882:

"Touching the hat or cap, or by taking it off, always looking the person saluted in the face. By touching the cap is meant holding the edge with the forefinger and thumb."

This regulation was applied to the whole Navy in 1883 and was amended in 1888 as follows:

"The Naval salute is made by touching the hat or cap or taking it off, looking the officer saluted in the face. Admirals, captains, officers of the same relative rank, and the officer commanding the saluter's ship of whatever rank, are on all occasions saluted by the hat being taken off. The hat is to be taken off by the right hand taking hold of it by the right side except when passing, when it is taken off with the off hand."

In 1890 Queen Victoria completely regulated hand saluting in the Royal Navy. These regulations are found in the "King's Regulations and Admiralty Instructions of 1908," Article 145. The reasons for the Queen's actions are not clear but it is said that she did not like to see men in uniform with their heads uncovered. Another explanation is that the 1888 Regulations were too general and resulted in a variety of salutes ranging from removal of the cap to simply touching the peak. During a visit to Osborne, the German Emperor is said to have commented to the Prince of Wales that no two officers saluted alike!

At the Queen's direction, the Admiralty discontinued the removing of hats or caps and introduced the present hand salute. Salutes to the right were made with the right hand and salutes to the left were made with the left hand. The salute with the left hand was abolished in the Navy in 1923 to bring Royal Navy custom into line with their allies and to conform to the practice in the Indian Army. Both on the continent, and among Indian and African troops, a salute given with the left hand was considered an insult.

When the Royal Canadian Navy was established in 1910, most of the methods and customs of the Royal Navy were brought to the new Service by Article 48 of the Naval Service Act:

"The Naval Discipline Act, 1866, and the Acts in amendment thereof passed by the Parliament of the United Kingdom for the time being in force, and the King's Regulations and Admiralty Instructions, insofar as the said Acts, Regulations and Instructions are applicable and except insofar as they may be inconsistent with this Act or with any regulations made under this Act, shall apply to the Naval Service and shall have the same force in Law as if they were formed as part of this Act."[2]

Although many civilians still raise or remove their hats as a mark of respect, naval officers and ratings salute instead. However, when a civilian removes his hat for more than a short time officers and ratings may remove head-dress.

The hand salute is a personal salute of officers and ratings. It is a symbolic movement having several meanings: a greeting; a mark of mutual respect, trust, and confidence; an act of courtesy and good manners; a mark of loyalty; a recognition of the authority vested in the Queen's Commission and the responsibility and status of the bearer of that Commission. It also demonstrates the willingness and the obligation, to accept direction. There is no servility or loss of dignity in a salute. Everyone in the Service has a superior and receives direction, right up to the Chief of the Defense Staff and Her Majesty The Queen, who exercise their various authorities by the powers vested in them by the Act of Parliament. The hand salute of the Canadian Forces is the naval salute in which the palm of the hand is turned slightly down and inwards and is not seen, unlike the flat open-palmed salute of the Army and Air Force tradition. It was adopted when the forces were unified in 1968. Historically, the hand salute was used in the British Army long before it was used in the Royal Navy.

The hand salute has, of course, a much wider application than a mark given and returned by individuals. It is also the expression of loyalty when the National Anthem is played; of respect for the flag and what it stands for; of respect at 'colours' and 'sunset'; and for the Queen's colour, and the standards, colours and guidons of specific units.

The origin and precise meaning of the 'salute to the quarterdeck' has long been debated. Some claim that it is a mark of respect for the place of command and the Royal authority from which the command, the Captain's Commission, is derived. But many historians believe, without solid evidence, that the salute evolved from the custom of paying obeisance to a shrine or crucifix which was thought to have been housed aft. It may even be related to religious observances of pre-Christian times. Certainly, for centuries, the quarterdeck has been almost hallowed territory—respected as the place of honour in the ship; the seat of authority and command; an area restricted for use only by certain members of the ship's company and requiring a standard of dress and decorum not demanded for other parts of the ship.

Deportment

Officers and men salute all other officers who are senior to them in rank. Officers also salute others of the same rank who, by nature of their appointments, are senior. For example, a lieutenant attached to a minesweeper should salute the ships commanding officer even though that officer is also a lieutenant. The latter is addressed as "Sir" by the former when on duty.

In the Canadian Navy acting sub-lieutenants salute sub-lieutenants who in turn salute lieutenants.

The officer-of-the-'watch' or 'day' is entitled to a salute by any officer who approaches him on a matter concerning his office since he is the captain's representative.

Seniors are always saluted by juniors when they pass in barracks or on shore. When on board ship, juniors only salute when meeting seniors for the first time in the morning and thereafter when addressing or being addressed by them. The reason for this is obvious: when ashore members meet infrequently, but in the close confines of a ship they frequently meet.

The significance of the salute would be destroyed if it were carried to ridiculous lengths. Nevertheless, salutes must be returned, with one exception: the senior does not return the second salute of a junior when the latter, having made a report is departing.

On the first meeting in the morning the junior salutes his superior in silence. The senior will return the salute and may say "Good morning." When and if he does, the juior responds. This ritual may sound trite but it is based on good sense and helps maintain discipline—an officer may not always feel up to responding to a junior's greeting and a silent salute puts no pressure on him to do so. Petty officers salute the captain, the executive officer, the heads of departments, their divisional officers and all other officers with whom they have close contact.

While men are expected to rise and stand at attention when their officers pass and where applicable, salute, sometimes during non-working hours, an officer passing a group of men will remove his cap as a signal that he desires no other attention than to have a gangway made for him. Officers only extend this courtesy when they are sure that, if it were not given, the men would observe the rules of good behaviour. In fact, it is a recognition of good discipline. If an officer or man is not wearing a hat and wishes to salute he comes to attention or executes a smart 'eyes left' or 'eyes right.' Good manners require that the junior makes way for his senior; they also require that everyone should give the gangway to a man carrying a load, regardless of rank.

The officers of the other two Services and of all foreign Armed Services who are senior are always accorded the courtesy of being saluted by Navy juniors.

When 'colours' or 'sunset' is sounded, individuals face aft and salute, regardless of the fact that the ensign may be invisible to them or that the quarterdeck of another ship is near and is visible. If one is standing on the forecastle and the 'still' or other call for attention is sounded on the quarterdeck of the ship ahead, one faces in that direction and stands at attention.

Members stand at attention and salute when any national anthem is played.

Members in uniform salute when the National Anthem is played in places such as arenas, where civilians normally keep their hats on. Situations also arise in HMC ships when it is necessary to salute between decks. Individuals remove their caps when entering any of the following spaces:
(a) An officer's cabin;
(b) An officer's office;
(c) An officer's mess;
(d) An enclosed mess.
The cap is removed in these spaces even when making rounds, with the possible exception of an officer's office. It is considered good manners to remove the cap when entering the main cafeteria to speak to someone.

Except when reporting rounds, salutes are not made between decks. The junior comes to attention when addressing or being addressed by a senior, just as he would anywhere else, except in a mess or cafeteria where a more relaxed atmosphere prevails.

When a space between decks is used in lieu of the upper deck for such events as 'requestmen,' 'defaulters' or 'general payment,' the cap is worn and behaviour is exactly the same as if the event were taking place on the upper deck. That is, on these occasions, members do salute between decks.

Members salute when going on board a ship in commission, whether boarding over the quarterdeck or not, and whether or not they are greeted by the officer-of-the-watch or another member of the quarterdeck staff. If one is in civilian dress he comes to attention at the head of the brow or the gangway. The hat is raised as he comes to attention. In some Navies such as the United States Navy, a person pauses at the ship's side, faces the stern (where the ensign and quarterdeck are located) and then salutes. It should be noted that this is not normal practice in HMC ships. When going ashore a salute is not given except to return that of the officer-of-the-watch or other officer or man who salutes.

The 'still' is piped if a flag officer or other dignitary passes in a boat or is seen walking or driving past a ship on the jetty — everyone comes to attention facing him and the officer-of-the-watch salutes.

Ships at sea salute each other when passing and the junior ship asks permission to proceed. If it is necessary or advisable for a junior to cross a senior's bow, he is expected to ask permission.

One always salutes when stepping onto the quarterdeck but does not salute when stepping off, except to return the officer-of-the-watch or quartermaster salutes.

If one happens to be standing by the gangway when an officer or an officer's guest comes aboard, a salute is in order even if one is not the officer-of-the-day.

The members of the quarterdeck staff are assistants to the officer-of-the-day; they are not required to do any duty for anyone else without his prior consent.

Gun Salutes

Gun salutes like hand salutes were a sign of peaceful intentions. In the early days guns were kept shotted, and after firing a salute an appreciable time elapsed before the guns could be fired again. A gun fired twice in an hour was an average time during Henry VIII's reign.

Written records of the use of gun salutes between ships at sea, and ships and shore establishments, are sketchy. Sir William Monson noted in his book *Naval Tracts* that:
> "The saluting of ships by another at sea is both ancient and decent though in this latter time much abused..."[3]

It seems that at that time, around 1600, certain Admirals had begun altering the old tradition. Custom dictated that ships fired a salute of three, five or seven pieces according to the rank of the Admiral being saluted; it required the Admiral not to answer with more than one or three pieces. Sir William's complaint was that Admirals were exceeding the number, thinking that many pieces added extra honours to the salutation. He was strongly in favour of staying with the old tradition!

In a letter dated 6 May, l663, James, Duke of York, laid down the following regulations for the ceremony of 'honours' in salutes:

"1. That no Commander of a ship of the second rank, (being neither Admiral, Vice-Admiral, or Rear-Admiral) at the first coming, and saluting his Admiral, give to his Admiral above eleven pieces, his Vice-Admiral nine, and Rear-Admiral seven, and the rest proportionally less by two, according to their ranks; and the Commander of any ship is not to salute his Admiral after he hath been absent from the flag two months.

2. That when any Admiral of a foreign nation is met withal he be answered by a like number, by all ships that he saluted. If a Vice-Admiral, then the Admiral to answer him with two less; that the Vice-Admiral, Rear-Admiral, and as many of the rest as he shall salute are to give him a like number. If a Rear-Admiral, then the Admiral and Vice-Admiral are to answer with two less, but if he salutes the Rear-Admiral, or any other ship, they are to return the like number.

3. That in case a ship of the second rank shall carry any Ambassador, Duke, or Nobleman, he shall fire the ordinance following, viz. at his coming on board, seven guns; and at their landing, eleven. And the other ships by two less, according to their ranks and numbers of ordinance.

4. That when any man-of-war, merchantman of a foreign nation, or of our own, salutes any of the King's ships, he is to be answered by two less.

5. That when any of His Majesty's ships shall have occasion to salute any of the King's castles, they are to give two guns less than they are directed to give when they salute the Admiral as aforesaid."[4]

By an Order in Council dated l3 July, 1668, James ll approved what was probably the first set of rules for gun salutes. They were entitled "An Establishment Touching Salutes by Guns" and were probably meant to save powder, since among other instructions is one forbidding the firing of salutes during the drinking of healths, and another regulating the frequency of salutes to the same officers. Salutes were to be fired on the anniversary of the King's birthday and Coronation, and on Restoration Day (29 May), the number of guns being as "shall be judged proper." (The Gunpowder Plot was evidently added later to the list of anniversaries since there is a record of such a salute being fired in 1716.) The Royal Family were saluted on embarking or landing with a number of guns which was to be at the discretion of the Commander-in-Chief.

Salutes between naval officers depended both on the rank of the officer saluted and on the rate of the vessel saluting. They varied between twenty-one for the Lord High Admiral, when saluted by a first rate, to three guns for a captain saluted by a sixth rate. Flag officers returned with four less and private ships with two. A merchant vessel saluting was returned with six less guns. All salutes were odd numbers.

Obviously there was no concern for powder aboard the *Centurion* when news of the death of Charles ll reached her at Cadiz on 5 March, 1684. The following entries are recorded in the Master's Log:

"6 Mar: We put our ship in mourning for ye death of our Soveraign ye King and fired 120 guns each marcht being all in mourning and fired guns likewise we fired in all 1140 guns. We began at noone and fired until ll at night."

"7 Mar: We put out our mourning coulers again and kept them out till 11 in ye forenoone, then we took them in and brought out our other coulers and fired l23 guns in all ye merchant ships firing all the guns they had three times over to ye proclaiming of His Royal Highness James Duke of York King of England."[5]

The relevant chapter of the 1731 "Regulations and Instructions Relating to His Majesty's Service at Sea," (which developed into the modern Queen's Regulations and Admiralty Instructions), is obviously based on the Order-in-Council of 1688. The number of guns to be fired for Royal salutes was still at the discretion of the Commander-in-Chief, and those for anniversaries were to be "as the Chief Officer shall think proper, not exceeding twenty-one." Salutes between officers now depended on their relative rank and not upon the rates of the ships. The largest salute became seventeen guns from a captain to an Admiral who was Commander-in-Chief, and the smallest thirteen from a captain to a Vice- or Rear-Admiral, or between two flag officers neither being Commander-in-Chief.

These regulations were still unchanged in the 13th edition of the Regulations, dated 1790. In the 1806 edition Royal salutes but not anniversary salutes had been settled at twenty-one guns. In l808 the question of who fired the salute became irrelevant, although it did affect return salutes which are four less to a captain and two less to another flag officer. The salutes to naval officers became seventeen for an Admiral, Commander-in-Chief; fifteen for other Admirals and thirteen for Vice- and Rear Admirals.

Of all the salutes, the origin of the twenty-one gun salute, or Royal Salute, is the most difficult to identify. In 1951 the *Canadian Military Journal* gave the following theory based on material at the Historical Research Section, War Office, Whitehall, London, England.

"Before 1865, the Royal Salute was thirty-five

guns. In the year of 1865 Queen Victoria perceived the idea of changing the salute to twenty-one guns. Her Majesty's idea was based upon the following: the number seven is the perfection of the Bible, the Holy Trinity is made up of three. Three times seven is twenty-one. The battleships of that time carried seven heavy guns and three salvoes would be twenty-one."[6]

The new Regulations dated 1806, however, show that even then the Royal Salute was none other than twenty-one guns.

It is an ancient superstition that gun salutes should be an odd number. In *Boteler's Dialogues* published by the British Naval Records Society in 1685, the Captain, (referring to a distinguished visitor on board),states that he:

"...had his farewell given him with so many guns as the ship was able to give; provided that they always be an odd number."

Admiral: "And why odd?"

Captain: "The odd number in ways of salute and ceremony is so observable at sea that, whensoever guns be given otherwise, it is taken for an expression that either the Captain, or Master, or Master Gunner is dead in the voyage."

During the Coronation of King George VI, a Royal Salute of forty-one guns, one for each complete year of His Majesty's life, was fired at St. James Park. At the moment he received the Crown a sixty-two gun Royal Salute, the Age Salute with the twenty-one gun Royal Salute added, was fired at the Tower of London. A British Army officer in a letter to *The Times* recalled the ancient custom of odd and even guns and continued:

"It may be foolish superstition to regard the firing of an even number of rounds in a salute to a live person as ominous, but it is a pity that old custom should be neglected in such an important ceremony."

The Regulations of the Tower of London, dated 1951, states that salutes to sixty-two guns were to be fired on the following occasions:

(a) The birthday of His Majesty the King;
(b) The birthday of Her Majesty the Queen;
(c) The birthday of Her Majesty Queen Mary;
(d) The anniversary of the Coronation;
(e) The day appointed as the official birthday of His Majesty, The King; and

That salutes of forty-one guns were to be fired on the occasions of State opening of Parliament and special occasions such as a Royal birth.

It used to be the custom to fire the salutes with the guns shotted. When news of the Declaration of King Charles II reached the fleet which was then anchored in the Downs, Samuel Pepys, the noted military historian, recounted that:

"The General began to fire his guns which he did, all that he had in the ship, and so did the rest of the Commanders, which was very gallant, and to hear the bullets go hissing over our heads as we were in the boats!"

An Admiralty prohibition against firing salutes above Gravesend coincides closely with the date a shot, fired during a salute from a man-of-war off Greenwich, went unpleasantly close to Greenwich Palace, where Queen Elizabeth l then resided.

An anecdote is told of an unfortunate birthday salute which occured on 1 May, 1834. The frigates *United States* and *Constellation* were lying in the Harbour of Toulon preparing to fire a twenty-one gun Royal Salute in honour of the birthday of Louis Phillipe, King of France. Gunners mate Samuel Setty of the *United States*, prepared twenty-four guns, twenty-one of which were to be fired in the noon salute. The salute went off smoothly until the firing of the eighteenth gun which sounded like a shot had been fired. The gunner assured the lieutenant all guns were unshotted and the salute was allowed to continue. When the twentieth gun had been fired, however, the lieutenant was convinced that a shot had been fired and suspended the remainder of the salute. It soon became evident that the last three guns fired had not been unshotted. The eighteenth gun hit a shore battery knocking off part of the embrassure. The nineteenth sent a solid shot into the side of the French ship *Suffren*, killing several sailors and causing considerable damage. The *Suffren* immediately beat to quarters, double shotted her guns, and was about to fire a broadside into the *United States* when a boat was sent over to explain the accident.[7]

The interval between successive rounds in a salute is five seconds. Before stop watches were invented the gunner timed the interval by repeating the couplet, "If I wasn't a gunner I wouldn't be here, No. 2, No. 3, etc. gun Fire!"[8]

Gun salutes executed by the Canadian Forces today are fired from the guns of HMC ships and by batteries of the Royal Canadian Artillery Regiment at designated saluting stations across Canada.

Deportment

Gun salutes are salutes with cannons given to: Royalty,(Royal salutes); Nations,(national salutes); and Individuals, (personal salutes).

All ships larger than destroyers and with a saluting armament of QF guns, are designated as saluting ships. National Defence Headquarters may designate destroyers to act as saluting ships on special occasions.

The national anniversaries on which salutes are fired in Canada are:

(a) Monday immediately preceding 25 May at 1200 local time. (The official birthday of the

1.01 Saluting guns at Esquimalt, B.C.

1.02 Arrival of USS *Essex* in Halifax Harbour, July 1960.

Sovereign);
(b) 1 July at 1200 local time. (Dominion Day);
(c) 11 November at 1100 local time. (Remembrance Day). This salute is one of 21 minute guns.

Dates for salutes in other countries are determined locally. The Royal Navy pamphlet entitled "Cermonial-National Anniversaries and Festivals" (DC1 RN 761) is an excellent guide, as is "The Manual of Ceremonial—HMC Ships."

As a general rule, salutes are only to be fired between 0800 and sunset. A salute fired by a ship-of-war of another nation outside these times, however, is to be returned. In foreign waters, the custom of the individual country is followed.

If the date of a salute falls on a Sunday, provisions are made as follows:
(a) When the date of an anniversary requiring a salute falls on Sunday, the salute is to be fired on the following day.
(b) Other salutes are not to be fired on Sunday between the hours of 1030 and 1300. If a salute is delayed on this account, it is to be explained that the salute was delayed due to divine service.

Ceremonies When Two Ships Pass

The salute to vessels flying the English flag started when the waters from the coast of Norway to Cape Finistere were claimed as "English Seas." It is known that before Norman days, sails of foreign vessels were lowered in these waters as a mark of respect to English sovereignty. This mark of respect rendered the vessel unmanoeuverable for a time. Because the ship had no appreciable way on after the sails were lowered, and the decks were cluttered with rigging and sails, the one saluted feared no attack. From this old custom grew the present regulations of 'tossing oars,' 'lying on oars,' 'stopping engines' and in sail boats 'letting fly the sheets' in order to render honours to superiors. The practice of 'striking' dates from a remote period, and the English claim to it was not abandoned until after Trafalgar. The rules of etiquette regarding the ceremony of 'striking' are described by Captain Nathanial Butler, writing in 1634:

"When any inferior shyp or fleete being to come upp, and passe within reache of the cannon of some of the fleete more eminent in any respect than ittselfe, that then all the fleete does not only take in all their flaggs, but that every particular shyp besides belonging to that fleete as they come up even with the Admiral of the other by way of acknowledgement and submission, do strike all their topsayles, upon the bunk, that is, doe hale them doun, att the least halfe mast highe. This complement is requirable from all shyps whatsoever not being of His Majesty's owne."

Extracts from the Duke of York's Instructions around 1673 regarding enforcing the salute are as follows:

"Article 22: Upon your meeting with any ship or ships within His Majesty's seas belonging to any foreign state or Prince, you are to expect that, in their passing by you, they strike their topsails, and take in their flag, in acknowledgement of His Majesty's sovereignty in those seas. And if any shall refuse to do it or offer to resist, you are to use your utmost endeavours to compel them thereunto, and in no wise to suffer any dishonour to be done to His Majesty. And in any case if His Majesty's subjects shall be so far forgetful of their duty as to omit striking their topsails as they pass by you, when it may be done without any loss of the voyage you are to bring them to the flag, to answer his contempt, or otherwise to return the name of the ship and the Master unto me, as also of the place from whence, and the port to which she shall be bound; and you are to make the Master of her pay charge of what shot you shall make at her. And you are further to notice, that in His Majesty's seas, His Majesty's ships are in no wise to strike any, and that in other parts no ship of His Majesty's is to strike her flag or topsail to any foreigner, unless such foreigner shall have first struck, or at the same time strike her flag or topsail to His Majesty's ship, except in the harbour of some foreign Prince, or in the road within shot of cannon of some foreign fort or castle, where the Captains of His Majesty's ships are to conform to the custom of the place, and to salute the forts in such manner as is usual and customary for the ships of war of His Majesty or other princes in that place. And for your better guidance in this article you are to take notice that His Majesty's Seas do extend to Cape Finisterre."[9]

At one time, when England maintained by force her proud title of "Mistress of the Seas" it was customary for the Kings of foreign states to salute the English flag on the seas. This, of course held particularly in the Narrow Seas, for England claimed both sides of the Channel. In fact, one of King John's titles was Duke of Normandy. Sovereigns who were compelled to salute the English flag by cannon were King Phillip of Spain, on his visit to Queen Mary in 1554, and the King of Denmark on his return from an official visit to King James l in London. Foreign ambassadors and captains sometimes were called before a Court of Admiralty for failure to salute.

The tradition of rendering salutes to another flag has not changed appreciably from the form laid out in the Duke of York's instructions of 1673. Merchantmen still dip their ensigns to warships, although this is no longer a requirement but simply a mark of respect. Salutes to flags and shore establishments are still made by gun salute from ships entering ports, and salutes between warships on the high seas are now usually conducted with the use of the 'pipe,' although there are still occasions when ships fire gun salutes.

Deportment

The ceremony observed by two warships passing between sunrise and sunset is in keeping with the general practices of other maritime nations.

When warships pass one another (whether both are underway or not), the junior sounds the 'still.' The senior does likewise and after a short interval sounds the 'carry on.'

When ships are nested, the out-board ship pipes on behalf of the senior officer of the nest.

When a foreign warship passes and there is doubt as to seniority, HMC ships are to be prepared to pipe first, and are to do so in sufficient time to avoid failure to pipe at all.

When a ship is alongside or at anchor, the officer-of-the-day/watch normally salutes from the gangway area. When underway or maintaining an anchor watch on the bridge, an officer on the bridge area salutes. Personnel on the upper deck are brought to attention and are to face in the direction in which the honours are being exchanged.

Certain auxiliary forces of other countries (for example the U.S. Coast Guard) have similar customs. While they are not entitled to the same marks of respect accorded warships, HMC ships are to return such salutes when received, as a matter of courtesy.

Manning and Cheering Ship

'Manning and cheering ship' is a very old custom. It is more than a mark of respect; it is an expression of esteem and affection by the whole ship's company for a particular person or another ship's company. This drill is invariably carried out with spirit and enthusiasm when Her Majesty the Queen or her representative, the Governor General visit or make their departure from units of the Fleet; when HMC ships enter harbour after an engagement or victory at sea; and when one of HMC ships sails to her new home port or to 'pay off.' Sometimes a departing flag officer or other senior officer is so honoured.

In the days of sail, 'manning and cheering ship' was a remarkable sight as each ship of the squadrons vied with the other in smartness and speed to man the yards and rigging clear up to the mastheads.

Deportment

Today, the ship's company lines the rails on the upper deck and led from the bridge, give three mighty cheers.

On the command "Fall in for manning ship," the ship's company falls in as for divisions. The divisions are divided up to ensure that there is an equal number of men on each side of the ship.

On the order "Stand by to man ship," divisions take up pre-assigned positions so that each man is one pace clear of the guard rail and at arm's length from his neighbour. Dressing is from forward, care being taken that no unnatural 'holidays' (gaps) appear due to obstructions such as fan trunkings or superstructure; personnel are at attention.

At the order "Man ship," each man takes one pace forward and grasps the guard rail with both hands, crossing hands with the man adjacent to him while doing so.

The executive officer orders "Stand by to

cheer: Ship's company... Attention."

On the command "Remove head-dress; Three cheers for:...; Hip,hip, hurray," the head-dress is held at the full extent of the right arm and circled clockwise during the "Hurray," keeping the crown outboard. On completion of the three cheers, the order "Replace head-dress," is given. The ship's company however, is not dismissed from 'manning ship' until the ship is well clear of the reviewing area.

The ship's company may then be ordered to dismiss by one of the following methods:
(a) The 'disperse' is sounded on the bugle;
(b) The 'carry on' is piped; or
(c) The command "Dismiss" is given by the executive officer.
Upon being dismissed, the ship's company turns forward prior to moving off.

II
Visits to HMC Ships by VIPs

The following is a general description of the ceremonial for the reception of personages onboard one of HMC ships.

Arrival from Shore

Fifteen minutes before the expected arrival of the VIP, the ceremonial side party, guard and the band (if appropriate) muster in the vicinity of the brow.

The ceremonial side party consists of:
(a) The ship's cox'n, chief bo's'n's mate, and at least two senior men from the BOSN 181 trade. They take a position aft of the brow, facing forward, in order of seniority from outboard in.
(b) The officer-of-the-day/watch, who may take either of two positions. The "Manual of Ceremonial" for HMC ships states that the OOD/OOW should take up a position forward of the brow facing aft. This allows the CO/XO to stand and greet the VIP at the head of the brow. However some commanding officers think that the OOD/OOW, as the captain's representative, should stand at the head of the brow when VIPs arrive, thus demonstrating his overall control of the evolution on behalf of his captain. The CO/XO moves forward as the guest clears the brow area. The captain, in this instance, has discretion.
(c) The commanding officer and executive of-

ficer stand either six or eight feet from the end of the brow facing outboard. (It should be noted that at least two extra brow staff are required to handle boat ropes and to assist the dignitary to disembark from his boat).

The stage set, the reception of the VIP proceeds in this manner:

The OOD/OOW takes a preliminary position at the top of the accommodation ladder, from where he can observe the approach of the VIP boat. The 'still' or 'alert' is sounded when the boat is still several lengths away from the lower platform. The first 'piping of the side' is made as the boat approaches, timed so that it finishes as the boat stops alongside the lower platform; the second piping is timed so that it finishes as the dignitary reaches the upper platform.

As the dignitary reaches the inboard end of the upper platform and steps on board, the guard is brought to the 'present' and the band plays the appropriate musical salute. After the salute, the guard is returned to the 'shoulder.' The VIP is welcomed on board by the senior officer.

1.03 Commander-in-Chief Mediterranean greeted by Captain (N) Hennessy, July 1952.

The guard is then reported to the VIP, who inspects them (unless he is junior to the host officer, in which case the guard will not be reported to him. The visitor's retinue proceeds to an area clear of the brow and the inspections area. After the official party has had sufficient time to leave the upper deck the 'carry on' is sounded.

The ceremonial for departure is almost the reverse of that on arrival. In particular the 'still' is sounded as the dignitary emerges from the superstrucure. The accompanying retinue pre-

1.04 Commander-in-Chief Mediterranean inspects guard in HMCS *Algonquin*, July, 1952.

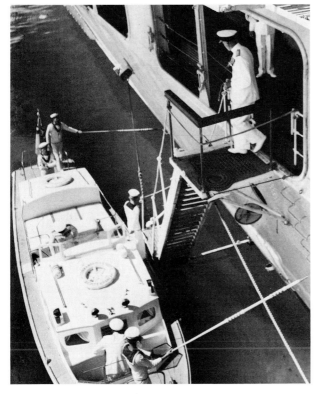

1.05 Commander-in-Chief Mediterranean departs HMCS *Magnificent*.

cedes the dignitary into the boat before piping. The first 'piping of the side' takes place as the dignitary steps on to the upper platform; the second, as the boat leaves the accommodation ladder.

The 'carry on' is not sounded until the boat clears either the stem or the stern of the ship.

Arrival at the Brow

The same procedures as those followed for arrivals from shore are followed, except that as the automobile carrying the VIP reaches the jetty, the 'still' is piped; and as the dignitary crosses the gangway, the 'side' is piped.

Arrival by Air

Because of the peculiarities of helicopter-carrying ships suitable procedures which take the circumstances into account are followed. Safety of personnel is the main consideration.

Honours and Marks of Respect

Members of the Royal Family boarding one of HMC ships are received by a Royal guard commanded by a lieutenant-commander or a lieutenant(N) with arms presented. The bugle sounds the 'alert' and the band plays "God Save The Queen." If a band is not available, the 'general salute' is sounded on the bugle. When more than one member of the Royal Family is present, the 'musical salute' is played only for the senior personage, although each is received on board as described above. The entire score of "God Save The Queen" is used for the reception of Her Majesty the Queen, HRH The Duke of Edinburgh and HRH Queen Elizabeth, the Queen Mother. The first six bars of "God Save The Queen" are played at the reception of other members of the Royal Family.

When the Governor General or Lieutenant-Governor boards one of HMC ships he/she is received by a Royal guard, commanded by a lieutenant-commander or lieutenant(N), with arms presented. The bugle sounds the 'alert' and the band plays the vice-regal salute. If a band is not available, the 'general salute' is sounded on the bugle.

The Prime Minister and the Minister of National Defence, when visiting HMC ships in an official capacity, are received by a guard commanded by a lieutenant(N), and the bugle sounds the 'alert.'

All officers of the Canadian Diplomatic Corps who are entitled to a salute of eleven guns or more are received on board HMC ships with the 'alert' sounded on the bugle.

The Chief of the Defence Staff and officers of the rank of commodore or higher, when flying their command flags, are received on board HMC ships by a guard commanded by a lieutenant(N) with arms presented, the bugle sounds the 'alert' and the band plays the musical salute. If a band is not available, the bugle sounds the 'general salute.' Flag officers not entitled to fly distinguishing flags when paying formal visits, or attending as a president or member of a court martial, are received as above with the exception of the musical salute.

Captains(N) in command when paying official visits to HMC ships are received on board by a guard under the orders of a petty officer, with arms presented. Captains(N) and commanders attending a court martial as members are to be received by a petty officer's guard. The guard is, however, to present arms only to the president of the court.

Foreign officers are paid similar honours and marks of respect as those accorded Canadian officers under similar circumstances.

When civic dignitaries pay official visits to HMC ships they are received with respect and attention due their position, but inappropriate honours such as military guards are not accorded them.

Piping the Side

'Piping the side' is a form of salute honouring certain personages as they board or leave HMC ships. If the person boards from a boat he is piped twice; once as the boat approaches the ship and again as the person mounts the accommodation ladder. If the arrival is over the brow or gangway, he is piped once.

In the days of sail, captains often visited other ships in company, perhaps for a counsel of war or to repair on board the flagship 'booted and spurred,' that is, with swords and medals, to 'collect a bottle' for some misdemeanour such as needlessly crossing his Admiral's bow, or simply to dine with a brother captain. Certain members, such as flag officers and captains, were lowered into their barges or hoisted on board in a contrivance not unlike a bo's'n's chair suspended from a ship at the yardarm. This spared them the exertion of climbing the accomodation ladder. 'Piping the side' today sounds very much like the notes which meant 'hoist away,' 'handsomely' and 'avast hoisting.'

Over the years the ceremony had been considered purely nautical, that is, the honour was accorded exclusively to the Sovereign; a member of the Royal Family in naval uniform; flag officers; captains of HM ships and foreign naval officers. Some changes have been introduced in recent years regarding 'piping the side.'

The 'side' is piped when the following personages/personnel come on board or depart HMC ships in commission, between 'colours' and 'sunset':
(a) Her Majesty the Queen (the reigning Sovereign is the only personage who is entitled to receive a pipe when not wearing a uniform);
(b) His Royal Highness Prince Philip, Duke of Edinburgh when in naval uniform;
(c) Members of the Royal Family when in naval uniform or having the rank of naval captain and above;
(d) The Governor General of Canada, Lieutenant Governors of provinces within provincial jurisdiction, and when in uniform, the incumbent naval officer having the rank of commodore or above;
(e) Chief of Defense Staff and all Canadian naval officers of the rank of commodore and above are piped when in uniform;
(f) Flag officers and commodores and above of Commonwealth Navies when in uniform;
(g) All officers in uniform holding an appointment in command of a ship or formation of ships;
(h) Naval members of a court martial in uniform, when attending or leaving the court; and
(j) The officer of the guard when flying his pennant.
The 'side' is piped between 'colours' and 'sunset' when the blessed water from the baptismal font is returned to the sea.

The 'side' is piped at all times when the following come on board or depart a ship:
(a) All naval officers of other than Commonwealth Navies when in uniform; and
(b) A body, including remains or ashes. The 'side' is also piped during a burial at sea when the remains or ashes are committed.

The 'side' is piped when the personage/officer arrives and again when he departs, provided that conditions of time and uniform are still met.

When arrival or departure is by boat, the 'side' is piped as the boat arrives at, or departs from, the ship's ladder.

The 'side' is normally piped for an officer entitled to it even though he may be in the company of an officer who is senior to him but who is not himself entitled to receive the 'side.'

The 'side' is never piped except in HMC ships in commission.

III
The Ship's Boats

For centuries, warships have carried small boats for a variety of uses. These boats are to a ship what transport is to an Army — they ply along the lines of communication. Without her boats, a ship could be without food, ammunition, relief or reinforcement; without correspondence, orders or instructions, and without stores of all descriptions.

Records show that boats were carried as early as 1521, when an inventory of the gear of the *Mary Rose* was made. Ships of the Royal Navy at that time probably carried three boats, one with a maximum length of about 35 feet which was not carried on board but towed astern, and two smaller ones which were hoisted in, not by means of davits, but by tackles on the main and foremast shrouds.

The Battle Orders of Alonso de Chave, an Admiral of the Spanish fleet around 1530, confirms that small boats were employed during the Tudor Period. The Order read:

"The boats...should not close in till they see the ships grappled and then they should come up on the opposite side in the manner stated above, and carry out their special duties as occasion arises either with their bases (breech loading pieces of the secondary armament used for arming boats), of which each shall carry its own, and with harquebuses, or else by getting close in or by leaping in upon the enemy, so they can climb in without being seen, or from outside by setting fire to them, or by scuttling them with augers."

This curious duty of the armed boats was more fully explained in a later section on single ship actions:

"The ships being grappled, the boat ready equipped should put off to the enemy's ship under her poop, and get fast hold of her and first cut away her rudder, or at least jam it with half a dozen wedges cut in such wise it cannot steer or move, land if there is a chance for more, without being seen, bore a dozen auger holes below the water-line, so that the ship founders."[10]

During the battles with the French in 1345, the RN made use of "armed boats and row-barges" when the lack of wind rendered their ships unmanoueverable. Again, in 1690, at the battle of Beachy Head, the French center squadron used its boats to get more ships into action by towing them towards the allies when the fleets were becalmed.

By 1799 the use of fireships had become popular. Admiral Lord Howe, in his Fighting Instructions of that same year recorded:

"XXI: The ships appointed to protect and cover fireships, when ordered on service, or which, without being appointed, are in a situation to cover and protect them, are to receive on board their crews, and keeping between them and enemy, to go with them as near as possible to the ships they are directed to destroy. All the boats of those ships are to be well armed, and to be employed in covering the retreat of the fireship's boats, and in defending the ships from any attempts that may be made on her by the boats of the enemy."[11]

In addition to the above duties the boats were used for life saving and laying out hawsers. Today they are used for securing to buoys, and for the ordinary duties of embarking and disembarking officers and men, as well as for patrolling and other particular services. They are also used for disembarking armed parties directly on to beach or jetty.

Deportment

Juniors enter a boat first and leave it last. When going over a brow or gangway with a senior, the junior takes care to go well in advance so that there is no embarrassment or jostling. If there is a mistake in timing, the junior does as best befits the situation. Seniors are expected to take care to show their intentions clearly by waiting at the head of the brow or gangway for the junior to go down first, or by proceeding but giving the junior a clear lead. The drill for going over a brow onto a jetty is the same as going over a gangway into a boat, although the use of this drill is disputed. Seniors disembark from a boat first and go first over a brow to the ship.

Permission must always be obtained from the cox'n before crossing a boat to reach a destination. The usual request is, "May I cross your boat Cox'n?" This custom developed out of consideration for the safety of men and gear — there may be good reason for not crossing a boat.

If the cox'n of a non-routine boat gives anyone passage, he is thanked for his assistance.

The cox'n of a boat always salutes officers and their guests when they embark in, disembark from, or cross his boat. Officers ensure the cox'n does so. Cox'n's often help each other in this respect by holding up the number of fingers equalling the number of stripes worn by the senior officer in their boats. One finger does duty for cadets and midshipmen as well as for sub-lieutenants. Two fingers do duty for lieutenants and lieutenant-commanders. If there is no officer in the boat the cox'n holds his hand low and moves it back and forth at the wrist as an indication that no salute is required. All salutes are returned by the senior officer in the boat.

When embarked in a boat the appropriate miniature standard, distinguishing flag, or pennant is displayed in the bow of a boat, between the hours of dawn and dusk, for:

(a) The Sovereign or any member of The Royal Family: Their personal Standards;

(b) Foreign Royalty or Head of State: The appropriate standard or ensign of that country;

(c) The Governor General of Canada: The Governor General's personal flag;

(d) The Lieutenant Governor of a province, within the limits of his jurisdiction: The appropriate Lieutenant Governor's flag;

(e) The Prime Minister; The national flag of Canada;

(f) The Minister of National Defence; The national flag of Canada;

(g) The Chief of the Defence Staff: The Canadian Forces ensign;

(h) Flag officers in command of a ship or formation of ships: The appropriate distinguishing flag;

(i) Squadron commanders and commanding officers of HMC ships when proceeding on official business: The commissioning pennant;

(j) Members of a court martial when proceeding to and from the court: A commissioning pennant;

(k) The guard officer: A commissioning pennant.

The personal or distinguishing flag or pennant is flown when the personage for whom it is authorized is actually in the boat. The flag or pennant is removed or hooded when the person is not in the boat.

When passing a boat carrying a senior officer, and at other times when a salute is called for, the officer in charge of the saluting boat or its cox'n gives the hand salute, and the senior officer or his cox'n returns the salute.

Boats carrying officers of equal rank do not salute; all officers are saluted by the cox'n or by the officer in charge as they enter and leave the boat.

Salutes are also required to be made during the ceremony of 'colours' and 'sunset'; when passing a boat carrying a funeral party with a body; and during the firing of gun salutes.

During salutes, seated personnel sit at attention. Standing personnel face in the direction of the boat saluted. A boat's cox'n takes the following action (weather and circumstances permitting) during the salutes outlined above: power boats stop engines; boats under oars 'order oars'; boats under sail 'let fly the sheets.'

The cox'n salutes if wearing a cap; otherwise he sits or stands at attention.

A boat approaching a ship at night is hailed with "Boat ahoy."

The officer-of-the-watch should always be on the gangway when a boat is coming alongside and while it is there. No boat should ever leave the ship without permission of the officer-of-the-watch, even if there is an officer in the boat who is senior to the OOW. If the senior officer in the boat greatly out-ranks the OOW, he should as a courtesy, ask the cox'n if he is ready to proceed. The cox'n, however receives this order only from the OOW.

Boats for loading or unloading passengers or gear are never left lying alongside an accommodation ladder longer than is absolutely necessary. If a boat is required to wait it is told to "Lay off."

Although the cox'n of a boat receives his orders from the OOW, he must, while at a landing place, ask the permission of the senior officer present from his own ship, and who is taking passage in the boat, for permission to carry on. This officer, as a courtesy, asks the permission of any other officer in the boat senior to him before he accedes. The individual ship's officer, however is in charge, and his orders must be obeyed by all others. If there is no officer belonging to the ship present the cox'n asks permission from the next senior officer before proceeding. Officers must remember that the cox'n has already received orders from the OOW, who is the captain's representative, and that these orders must not be changed unless it is necessary, at which point the cox'n and the OOW must be so informed.

IV
Mustering by the Open List

Originally, the 'muster by the open list' was a surprise muster of the ship's company, where every man reported his name, rank, and his duties onboard. It was implemented to prevent unscrupulous officers from lining their pockets at the expense of the Crown.

It appears that at the time certain commanding and supply officers lacked the sense of integrity and honesty that prevails today. During long absences from the home port a number of men would be lost through various reasons: battles, illnesses, storms, etc. Their names were illegally kept on the ship's books for victuals and pay, and the value of these items were drawn each month and shared by the captain and the purser. Another ruse was to pad the ship's book by adding a few more names, for the same purpose. Both practices were long overlooked.

When it was at last brought to the attention of the Lord Commissioners of the Admiralty they introduced the scheme of 'mustering by the open list' even though in their ealier years they had probably shared a few golden sovereigns or guineas the same way.

The scheme required a senior officer to muster the ship's company and cause each man to pass before him. In doing so, the man would come to a halt, salute the inspecting officer and state his name, rating, non-substantive rates, and his number on the ship's book or list. This information would be checked against the entries in the book and the next man would present himself. In this way any surplus was easily identified.

Deportment

Today a 'muster by open list' is sometimes used by a senior officer, when taking up a new appointment, to meet and assess the people in his command. Procedures vary with actual circumstances.

Normally the ship's company falls in by divisions, with the senior man of the division on the left hand of the front rank. The remainder are fallen in, in order of seniority down the front rank from left to right, in the second rank and similarly in the third.

Each man marches up to the captain or senior officer and salutes. He reports his SIN number, rank, name, states his trade and the date a qualification was last received. (For example: 111 222 333 Leading Seaman Brown, J.F., weapons surface, qualified TQ 4, April 1979.)

He salutes, turns right, and marches off the quarterdeck/flightdeck. This procedure continues until all members of the ship's company or command have presented themselves to the reviewing officer.

Order of divisions commences with the division formed up on the forward side of the starboard side of the quarterdeck and continues in a clockwise manner until all divisions have been presented. Officers report on completion; divisional officers report to the reviewing officer before their divisions.

V
Flags and Pennants

Origins and History

The use of standards or flags in battle, dates back to antiquity. It is believed that the ancient Egyptians used a standard displaying the body of an animal held aloft on a spear point. The Roman's eagles and their various other ensigns are well known, while their barbian opponents adopted the dragon as their emblem. The earliest banners were usually hung from a cross-rod, suspended like a ship's yard from the pole, but the Moors, when they invaded Europe in 711, introduced the modern form of flag.

The crusader Richard I appears to have taken a considerable interest in naval affairs and in his time the use of the Royal or 'national arms' became more accepted. The two golden lions increased to three, and the St. George's Cross, still the distinctive flag of many Commonwealth Navies was also introduced. The Cross is thought to have derived from the white red-crossed surtouts or 'jacks' worn by the English crusaders to distinguish them from their foreign allies. For instance the French crusaders were dressed in blue jacks with white crosses, and, as in England, this design was soon adopted as a national banner or 'jack'. These rival jacks were likely present in large numbers at the battles of the Damme, on the canal near Bruges; at the victory of Hubert de Burgh, governor of Dover Castle, over a French fleet of superior force commanded by the dreaded sea captain Eustace the Monk in 1217; and again some years later, during the fight in mid-channel, when the French were again defeated. In the latter battle, the blue lily-starred banner of St. Louis probably figured prominently on the defeated side. In 1345, the year before the great victory of Sluys, 160 'pencils' 'pennoncels' or 'pennants', as we now call them, are said to have been ordered specially for the fleet, as well as distinctive banners for the various ships.[12] Each ship, emblazoned with designs emblematical of the ship's name, (frequently that of a saint), would be similar to one of the present day regiments with its Queen's or national colour, and its regimental colour. The matter of colours was obviously receiving attention and a certain organization and uniformity was being achieved.

The Royal Standard

Probably every Londoner has seen the Royal Standard flying over Buckingham Palace showing that Her Majesty the Queen is in residence. Its rich heraldic colours of red, gold, and blue, and the graceful curves of its design — the three lions, the rampant lion and the harp — distinguish it from the plainer colours and patterns of our flags.

It is the Royal Coat of Arms, which also appears on some British coins and Government documents. The Standard is the Queen's official banner, and is an indication of her presence ashore or afloat. It is broken at the masthead the moment she crosses the brow.

At one time the standard was worn by the Lord High Admiral, when afloat, as representative of the Crown. It also used to be hoisted over ships of the Royal Navy on the Sovereign's birthday and on other state occasions, but this custom is no longer observed. The Queen may, however, appoint a member of the Royal Family to represent her — for example, on a state visit — and authorize them to fly their personal standard, instead of the Royal Standard.

The design of the Royal Standard has changed dramatically over the centuries, but one emblem has long been part of it. The use of one, two or three lions (or leopards) as the Arms of the King of England dates back to the times of King Richard the Lion-Hearted, and possibly to William the Conqueror. At Sluys, where King Edward III commanded in person, the cog *Thomas* flew his Royal banner, the earliest recorded instance of a special banner being used by a monarch at sea. After the battle, King Edward claimed not only the title "King of the Seas," but also "King of France." He may have considered France the most important part of his kingdom, for he gave the French emblem, the fleur-de-lis, the place of honour in the first quarter of his newly designed Royal banner. He also placed it in the fourth quarter, leaving the second and third quarters for the three lions of England.

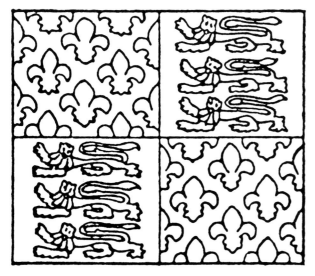

1.06   Standard of Edward III.

The fleur-de-lis were, as the heraldic description would read, "powdered," that is, some of the flowers appeared in halves on the edge of the banner, giving the impression that it had been cut from a larger flag. King Edward III used this style in his standard. However, the French King improved the appearance of his flag by reducing the number of lilies to three, each complete and all arranged in a triangle. Henry IV copied this alteration on the English Royal Standard, to show that he claimed France as it was then, and not as it had been.

King Henry VIII flew a 'double Royal Ensign,' in which the quarterings are eight instead of four, when he was present in his ship *Subtile*. He also flew several other smaller flags to denote his presence, most notably a flag with the initials "R.H." (Rex Henricus), another with the letter "H" and a fleur-de-lis, and several flags of green and white horizontal strips, which were the Tudor colours.

Queen Elizabeth I preferred the plain standard of Henry IV. She did, however, make use of several other forms of ensign, one of which bore the three golden lions of the English arms and the initials "E.R." below the George Cross. She also adopted a personal badge in the shape of a phoenix, adding her initials and the motto "The banner of our pride."

When King James I of Scotland became King James I of England, he naturally wished to acknowledge both countries on his flag. Since at least the thirteenth century the Royal banner of the King of Scots had been the emblem previously used by King William the Lion — a 'lion rampant' (standing erect as though about to fight). It was surrounded by a double framework, called a 'tressure,' ornamented with heraldic lilies, perhaps a token of the ancient friendship between Scotland and France. Like the lion, it was red on a gold field. James placed this Scottish emblem in the second quarter of his banner, while in the third quarter he placed that of Ireland, which he also claimed to rule. The Irish emblem had been chosen by Henry VIII and was a gold harp with silver strings on a blue field.

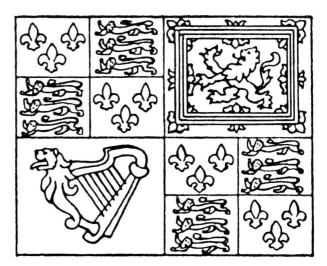

1.07   Standard of James I.

The Royal Standard went out of use during the Commonwealth era, and its place was taken by the Protector's Standard. The same standard was also flown by James II, but after his abdication it was doubled. William III and Mary, who succeeded him, were joint sovereigns, and their standard therefore bore their arms impaled (side by side) on one flag. Both were Stuarts and so flew the James Standard. In the hoist, William's flag bore his father's arms, the 'lion rampant' of

Nassau, gold on blue, on a small shield at its centre; Mary's, in the fly, was simply the James flag which was removed after her death.

When England and Scotland were merged into Great Britain, Queen Anne had the James flag, which she had previously flown, redesigned. The English lions and the Scottish lion rampant, which now kept only half its tressure, were impaled in the first and fourth quarters. The Irish harp remained in the third quarter but the French lilies lost the place of honour and were relegated to the second quarter.

King George I removed the arms of Great Britain from the fourth quarter of Queen Anne's flag, leaving them in the first quarter, and substituted those of Hanover, of which he was elector. Its arms included two golden lions on red (for Brunswick), another blue lion (for Lunenburg), and a white horse for Westphalia. At its centre was the Crown of Charlemagne which showed the ruler's rank.

1.08   Standard of George I.

When the United Kingdom of Great Britain and Ireland was formed, it seemed inappropriate to give as much space to Ireland as to England and Scotland combined. George III accordingly made changes in the Standard. He placed the Lions of England in the first and fourth quarters, the rampant lion and tressure of Scotland in the second, leaving the harp of Ireland in the third. The arms of Hanover went on a large shield at the centre of the banner, with an electoral cap, later replaced by a Royal Crown, above it. The lilies of France no longer appeared in the Standard as King George III formally renounced all claim to the French throne.

The 'Salic Law' in force on the continent forbade a woman to rule Hanover, and when Queen Victoria came to the throne, the arms of that state disappeared from her Royal Standard which now represented the four countries of the

United Kingdom. Except for a few changes of detail introduced more recently, it had come to its present form. It is described heraldically as: Quarterly. First and fourth gules, three lions passant gardant in pale or (England); Second, or a lion rampant within a double tressure flory counterflory gules (Scotland); third azure, a harp or, stringed argent (Ireland).

1.09   Royal Standard.

The Royal Union Flag

The Royal Union Flag (the flag of the British Commonwealth of Nations) comprises the flags of St. George of England, St. Andrew of Scotland, and St. Patrick of Ireland.

The Flag of St. George

The actual date when the flag of St. George, a red cross on a white field, was adopted as the national flag of England is unknown. There were a number of legends of St. George during the Middle Ages, but the accounts of his life and death vary considerably. It has been said that he

1.10   English Flag, before 1603.

became especially popular among the Crusaders because of the miraculous intervention accredited to him in bringing them victory on several occasions during the reigns of Richard I and Edward

I. There is no doubt that the Cross of St. George was in use in England as a national emblem in 1277. The flag of St. George was a flag of battle and it can be seen represented in the old prints and drawings that deal with military operations both on land and sea. "St. George's banner broad and gay" was the flag under which the great seamen of Queen Elizabeth I traded, explored and fought. It was the flag that Drake bore round the world, and to this day the flag of a British Admiral is the same simple device, while the White Ensign of the Royal Navy is the old flag which includes the Union flag displaying prominently the red cross of the warrior saint.

The Flag of St. Andrew

St. Andrew has been the patron saint of Scotland since the eighth century. The cross of St. Andrew is a saltire, that is, it is shaped like the letter "X" representing the two pieces of timber to which the saint was tied. According to legend, the saint believed it too great an honour to be crucified like Christ, and received permission from his persecutors for these concessions. For two days he continued to preach and instruct "the surrounding populace in that faith which enabled him to sustain his sufferings without a murmur." It is said that this form of cross appeared in the sky to Achaius, King of the Scots, the night before a great battle with Athelstan. Being victorious, he went barefoot to the Church of St. Andrew, and vowed to adopt this cross as the national symbol.

In 1513, the Scottish Crown owned a number of ships, notably the *Great Michael*, a contemporary of the *Grande Francoise*. Historical records indicate that *Great Michael* employed the red lion of Scotland and the white saltire of St. Andrew but there is no clear indication that St. Andrew's cross was used as freely as was the cross of St. George in English ships.

The national flag of Scotland comprises the white saltire of St. Andrew on a blue field.

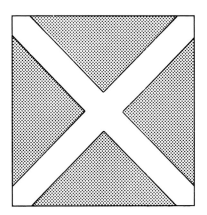

1.11   Scots Flag, before 1603.

The Cross of St. Patrick

St. Patrick was neither crucified nor martyred (he died in his bed at the age of ninety), so the Cross of St. Patrick is not found among the emblems of saints, and its use is in defiance of all tradition and custom. The saltire rouge on a field of argent was the heraldic device of the Geraldines dating from at least 1169, when Maurice Fitzgerald, the grandson of Rhys the Great, King of South Wales, landed in Ireland.

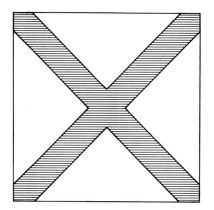

1.12   Irish Flag of St. Patrick.

England and Scotland

England and Scotland were united into the United Kingdoms of Great Britain, under the sovereignty of King James, in 1603. It was therefore necessary to design a new flag that would typify the union, and blend together the emblems of the two patron saints. This was not an easy task since there is no way of creating, in heraldic terms, two places of equal value on a flag. The position next to the staff is more honourable than the corresponding position in the fly; in the same way the upper part of the flag is more honourable than the lower. However, a Royal Ordnance dated 12 April, 1606, dealt with the problem as follows:

"Whereas some difference hath arisen between our subjects of South and North Britain, travelling by seas, about the bearing of their flags, for the avoiding of all such contentions hereafter we have, with the advice of our council, ordered that from henceforth all our subjects of this isle and kingdom of Greater Britain, and the members thereof, shall bear in their maintop the Red Cross, commonly called St. George's Cross, and the White Cross, commonly called St. Andrew's Cross, joined together, according to a form made by our heralds, and sent by us to our Admiral to be published to our said subjects; and in their foretop our subjects of South Britain shall wear the

Red Cross only, as they were wont, and our subjects of North Britain in the fore-top the White Cross only, as they were accustomed. Wherefore we will and command all our subjects to be comparable and obedient to this our order, and that from henceforth they do not use or bear their flags in any other sort, as they will answer the contrary at their peril."[13]

The Scots objected to the new combined flag and protested against using it, devising a Union flag of their own, in which the saltire passed over the Red Cross. But their protests had little effect and the authorized version remained in use for nearly two hundred years.

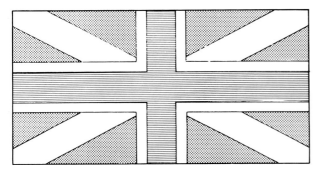

1.13   Union Flag, as ordered in 1606.

The Union Jack

It is well known that Mediaeval and Renaissance ships flew flags or streamers at the bow-sprit end and later on national, port and corporation flags. Such a "smawle little flagg with a red crosse" was advocated, if not adopted, as a national distinction on the Cadiz expedition of 1596. It is not possible to establish what flag was officially accepted between 1606, when the Union flag was first introduced, and the proclamation of 5 May 1634, which forbade its use by all but HM ships. Such vessels were "enjoined to wear one of these as a small volume in her bowsprit's top." The flags thus worn, are termed 'jacks,' and ships of the Royal Navy continued to be recognized by that emblem until the Interregnum of 1649.[14]

The Union Flag

The composition of the new national flag was first made known in the Order of the King in Council on 5 November, 1800, and its immediate use was required by the following proclamation on 1 January, 1801:

"Whereas by the first article of the Articles of Union of Great Britain and Ireland it was declared: That the said kingdoms of Great Britain and Ireland should upon this day, being the First day of January, in the Year of our Lord One Thousand Eight Hundred and One, for ever after be united into one kingdom, by the name of the United Kingdom of Great Britain and Ireland and that the Royal Style and Titles apertaining to the Imperial Crown of the said United Kingdom and its Dependencies, and also the Ensigns Armorial, Flags and Banners thereof, should be such as we, by our Royal proclamation under the Great Seal of the said United Kingdom, should appoint: ... That the Union flag shall be azure, the crosses saltire of St. Andrew and St. Patrick quarterly, per saltire counterchanged argent and gules: the latter fimbriated of the second, surmounted by the Cross of St. George of the third, fimbriated as the saltire."[15]

The diagonals in the new flag were counterchanged, that is, on one half of the flag they are of the same colour (red) and metal (argent, that is, white) but reversed in the other. The effect is that on each half of the flag one cross appears higher than the other and the red bars are not in the middle nor do they continue straight across.

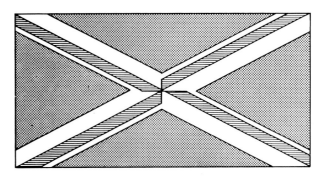

1.14   Arms counterchanged.

1.15   Union Flag of 1801.

In the Royal Proclamation of 1801, it was laid down that the Union flag should be displayed on all His Majesty's forts and castles, and in all His Majesty's ships, but not by all His Majesty's subjects. Although this proclamation has never been amended, the Union has, in the course of time, come to be regarded by all as the national flag. On at least two occasions, once in the House of Lords in 1908 and again in 1933 by the Home

Secretary in the House of Commons, Parliament has expressed the opinion that the Union may be flown 'on land' by any of His Majesty's subjects.

Deportment

The circumstances in which the plain Union flag (i.e. without a badge in the centre) is displayed by HM ships 'afloat' are limited to the following:

(a) As one of the three flags which indicate the presence of the Sovereign onboard;

(b) At the jackstaff when at anchor, or, when underway and dressed with masthead flags;

(c) At the trunk of the main, or of the principal mast, as a command flag on those rare occasions when an Admiral-of-the-Fleet embarks; and

(d) At the peak of the gaff (or yardarm, if there is no gaff) to denote that a court martial is being held. (This is why the Union is sometimes incorrectly referred to as the "Court Martial Jack.")

The Royal Union Flag was approved by Parliament on 18 December, 1964 for continued use as a symbol of Canada's membership in the Commonwealth of Nations and of her allegiance to the Crown.

Where physical arrangements make it possible, the Union flag is flown in addition to the National flag, ensign, ship's ensign, and jack, as appropriate at defence establishments, and in HMC ships within Canada or Canadian waters. It is worn:

(a) On the Queen's official birthday (the Monday immediately preceding 25 May);

(b) On the anniversary of the Statute of Westminster (11 December); and

(c) When instructed by Defence Headquarters on the occasion of Royal visits and certain Commonwealth gatherings within Canada.

The Union flag is worn in HMC ships as follows:

(a) Ships with more than one mast wear it at the main and the national flag at another position;

(b) Ships with one mast wear it at the masthead;

(c) On the anniversary of the Statute of Westminster, ships dress with masthead flags only and gun salutes are not fired; and

(d) In single masted ships the Royal Union Flag does not displace a distinguishing flag or pennant already flying.

Flag of the Lord High Admiral

The flag of the Lord High Admiral or 'Admiralty Flag,' was introduced by James, Duke of York, (afterward James II), as Lord High Admiral and General of the Navy. It was adopted by the Lord

Commissioners in 1725 and showed the cable twisted around the anchor, in the 'foul anchor' design. This was altered on the flag in 1815, when the cable passed through the ring and hung loosely about the anchor.

The anchor is a well-known charge or badge of heraldry. The earliest example of the foul anchor in a command flag was discovered in the Cluny Museum in Paris, and dates back to the sixteenth century. It is a white guidon, bearing a fouled anchor in blue. It was carried by one of Admiral Coligny's horsemen at Jarnac in 1569.

The earliest example of an anchor and cable as the emblem of an English naval commander appears in a triptych (a picture or carving on three panels with folding sides) in the Church of the Order of St. John of Jerusalem, in Clerkenwell. The picture refers to the Grand Prior of the 'Langue' at Rhodes and one of the panels displays a golden anchor on a red shield, with a black cable.

1.16   Coligny "Guidon".

1.17   Standard of the Lord High Admiral, 1634.

Whether or not these flags were used to indicate the presence of the Lord High Admiral is not known. However, during the seventeenth century the fouled anchor was displaced on their flags or, in its place, a shield of arms, with or without supporters. Such flags, for example the fleur-de-lis powdered on a field of blue, (the French 'Pavillon Royal'), were in use in other countries. Admiralty writings of 1634 indicated that in a fleet, "wheresoever the Prince is there in person, or his High Admiral in his room, there is then carried ... in the main top of the ship ... the Standard Royal, that is the Arms and Escutcheon of the Kingdom."[16]

Deportment

The current Admiralty flag has been hoisted over the Admiralty building in London since 1850. It is flown continuously, the only exception being that it is struck temporarily on those very rare occasions when the board, as a whole, is absent afloat. There is only one occasion when it is half-masted ... at the death of a Sovereign. The Admiralty flag does not return salutes, but whenever their Lordships think it necessary, orders are given by signal or otherwise for some other ship in company to return the salute of a foreign warship, gun for gun. The flag is hoisted when any two or more of the Lords of the Admiralty are embarked. It is displayed on the foremast head of the Royal yacht whenever the Sovereign is onboard. The Sovereign is head of the Navy, with the Lords Commissioners next, so the Royal Standard flies at the main, since heraldically, the main is more honourable than the fore.

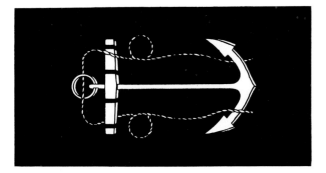

1.18   Lord High Admiral's or Admiralty Flag.

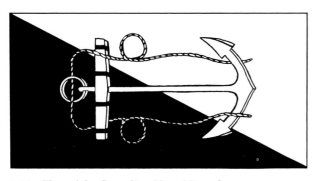

1.19   Flag of the Canadian Naval Board.

Canadian Naval Board Flag

The flag used by the Naval Board of Canada, when it existed, was "a golden anchor on a diagonally divided flag, blue to the hoist and red to the fly." This is a variation on the flag of the Admiralty. It was broken when two or more members of the Naval Board were embarked. It was last worn for the commissioning of HMCS *Nipigon* on 30 May, 1960; the Naval Board was dissolved in August of that same year.

Ensigns used by the RCN

The White Ensign

The White Ensign was used by the RCN until the advent of the new Canadian national flag, and remains in use by the Royal Navy.

When the three Royal Navy squadrons were combined the need arose for a single ensign for all HM ships.

It is probable that flags for national distinction were flown during the Armada campaign of 1588, and there is little doubt that in the expedition to Cadiz in 1596, when the English force was divided into four squadrons, each with three flagships, the Vice/Rear-Admirals of the fleet wore the national flag at the fore and mizzen. Striped squadronal flags, bearing the Cross of St. George, were also flown on that occasion. Others were of red, white and blue — probably the first time these memorable colours appeared.

Of the line flags worn on the expedition of 1627, the senior was the Royal Standard entrusted to the Duke of Buckingham, Lord High Admiral, who, as "Admiral particular of the bloody colours," also commanded the Red Squadron. The Vice- and Rear-Admirals in addition to their blue and white squadronal flags, wore the 'King's usual colours,' the Union flag of 1606.

The division of the Royal Navy squadrons, and their use of coloured ensigns to distinguish them, lasted for two hundred years. The order of precedence place the Admiral of the Red as the commander of the centre and most senior squadron, the Admiral of the Blue as the commander of the fore and second senior squadron, and the Admiral of the White as the commander of the van (rear) and most junior squadron. This division required that each ship carry three complete sets of colours, in case it should change squadrons. An order of Queen Anne, requiring merchant ships to wear the Red Ensign, added to the confusion. The most serious problems arose during battles, when it became nearly impossible to distinguish red from blue in the smoke and fire of the fight, as well as distinguishing them from those of the enemy. At Trafalgar, Admiral Nelson ordered his entire fleet to hoist the White Ensign since it was more distinguishable from the French flag in action. An order in Council, dated 9 July 1864, resolved the problem. The three squadrons were dissolved, the squadronal colours withdrawn, and the fleet directed to fly the White Ensign, which later became the Royal Navy's only ensign.

The White Ensign is charged with the Red Cross of St. George and the Union Flag in the upper canton next to the hoist.

In a letter to the High Commissioner for the Dominion of Canada in London, dated 1 June, 1910, the Deputy Minister for the Naval Service of Canada requested information on the proper flag to be flown by the ships of the Naval Service. Many letters were exchanged before specific action was taken by an Order in Council.

The following is an excerpt taken from PC 289, dated 3 March, 1911:

"...states that the Minister of the Naval Service concurs in the suggestion that His Majesty's Canadian Ships *Niobe* and *Rainbow* shall fly the White Ensign and pendant, with the Canadian flag at the stem, this being a temporary measure pending an arrangement being arrived at after consultation between representatives of the Admiralty and the Canadian Government, or at the next Imperial Conference, and that instructions have been issued to the ships accordingly."

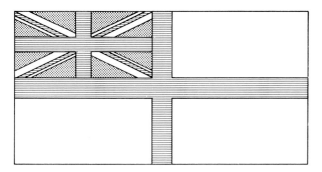

1.20   White Ensign.

The 'temporary arrangement' was ratified at the Imperial Conference of 1911, when it was ordered on 16 December, 1911, that:

"All ships and vessels of the Royal Canadian Navy shall fly at the stern the White Ensign as the symbol of authority of the Crown, and at the jack staff the distinctive flag of the Dominion of Canada, such distinctive flag being the Blue Ensign with the arms of the Dominion set in the fly. The White Pendant will be flown at the masthead."

A Colonial Office dispatch on 15 October, 1910 had requested that the White Ensign be defaced with the Coat of Arms of Canada, but the Admiralty adamantly refused to give permission.

The Blue Ensign

The distinctive flag of Canada was the Blue Ensign with the arms of the Dominion inset. The arms were different from today's, although the original design, approved by a Royal warrant dated 26 May, 1868, consisted of the quartered arms of the four original provinces. From time to time other provinces joined the Confederation and it became the common practice to add their arms to the original design. The present basic design was approved by the Minister of National Defence in October 1960. The design of the shield came from the New Coat of Arms of Canada, which had been approved in 1957.

The Red Ensign

Canada was the first Commonwealth Dominion to possess a distinctive merchant flag, since in 1892 permission was granted for the Canadian Coat of Arms of 1869 to be placed in the fly of the Red Ensign. The authority to display the Canadian Red Ensign ashore, (but only outside Canada) originated with an Order-in-Council, PC 134 dated 26 January, 1924, which declared that the Canadian Red Ensign was to be displayed on "suitable occasions from all buildings owned or occupied by the Canadian Government and situated without Canada." During World War II, the Canadian Red Ensign came to the forefront and was used extensively by the Canadian Army overseas.

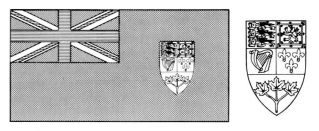

1.21   Canadian Blue Ensign.

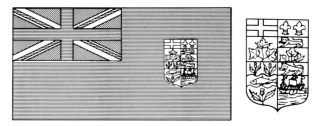

1.22   Dominion Red Ensign.

The National Flag of Canada

It is probable that the first flag to fly over what is now Canadian soil was the English flag of the fifteenth century, the St. George's Cross. It was carried by John Cabot, a Venetian sailing under

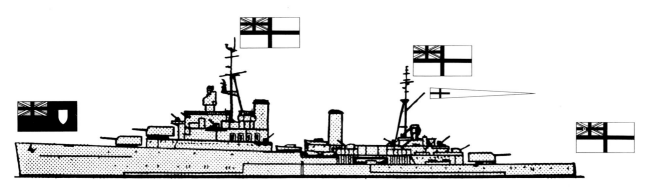

1.23 1911-1961. White Ensign at stern; White Ensign at mastheads; White Commissioning Pennant; Blue Ensign at jackstaff as jack.

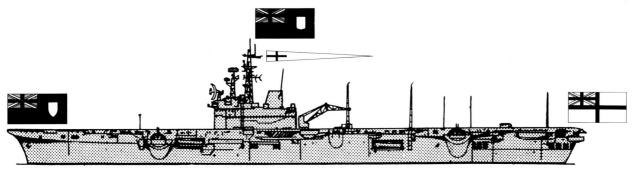

1.24 1961-1965. White Ensign at stern; Red Ensign at masthead; White Commissioning Pennant; Blue Ensign at jackstaff as jack.

English colours, who reached North America in the last years of the fifteenth century.

The honour of being the first flag to fly over settlements in Canada, however, goes to the Flag of Royal France, which was raised by Jacques Cartier at his first landing at Gaspe Harbour in 1534.

Created in 1606 as a Royal symbol, the Union Flag probably was flown shortly afterwards at early settlements in Newfoundland. It came into use with British settlements in Nova Scotia after 1621. The present Union Flag was proclaimed in 1801 for use in His Majesty's forts and castles and ships, although in the years that followed it had a wider display, in Canada as elsewhere. The Red Ensign may have been used fairly widely in Canada from Confederation, but after 1904 Parliament approved a resolution recognizing the continued use of the flag as a symbol of Canada's membership in the Commonwealth of Nations and of her allegiance to the Crown.

The National Flag adopted by Parliament was proclaimed by Her Majesty the Queen on February 15, 1965. It is a red flag of the proportions two by length and one by width, containing in its centre a white square the width of the flag, with a single red maple leaf in its centre. The proclamation read:

ELIZABETH THE SECOND

By The Grace Of God Of The United Kingdom, Canada

And Her Other Realms And Territories Queen

Head Of The Commonwealth, Defender Of The Faith

To All To Whom These Presents Shall Come Or

Whom The Same May In Anywise Concern, GREETING:

A Proclamation

WHEREAS the Senate of Canada, by resolution dated the 17th day of December, in the year of Our Lord one thousand nine hundred and sixty four, has recommended that there be designed, as the National Flag of Canada, the flag hereinafter described:

AND WHEREAS the House of Commons of Canada, on the 15th day of December, in the year of Our Lord one thousand nine hundred and sixty four, did concur with the recommendation, made on the twenty-ninth day of October, in the year of Our Lord one thousand nine hundred and sixty-four by a Special committee thereof, that the flag, hereinafter described as the National Flag of Canada:

NOW KNOW YE that by and with the advice of Our Privy Council for Canada, We do by this Our Royal Proclamation appoint and declare as the National Flag of Canada upon, from and after the fifteenth day of February, in the year of Our Lord one thousand nine hundred and sixty-five, a red flag of the proportions two by length and one by width, containing in its centre a white square the width of the flag, bearing a single red maple leaf, or, in heraldic terms, described as gules on a Canadian pale a maple leaf of the first.

ALL OF WHICH Our Loving Subjects and all others whom these Presents may concern are hereby required to take notice and to govern themselves accordingly.

IN TESTIMONY WHEREOF We have caused these Our Letters to be made Patent and the Great Seal of Canada to be hereunto affixed. Given the 28th day of January in the Year of Our Lord One Thousand Nine Hundred and Sixty-Five and in the thirteenth Year of Our Reign

By Her Majesty's Command

Lester B. Pearson

Prime Minister of Canada.

Red and white are the colours for Canada, as officially declared and appointed by King George V on November 21, 1921, in a proclamation of Canada's Coat of Arms recommended to His Majesty by the Canadian Government.

The maple leaf, as noted earlier, has been regarded as a Canadian emblem as early as 1700. It was used for decorative purposes during the visit of the Prince of Wales to Canada in 1860; it appeared in the Coats of Arms granted to Ontario and Quebec in 1868 and, as the distinctively Canadian symbol, in the Coat of Arms of Canada granted in 1921. For many years the maple leaf has also been used extensively as a symbol and mark of identity by the Canadian Armed Forces.

The leaf in the flag design is stylized or in conventional form, as is usual when nature's gifts are incorporated into flags, banners or arms.

Deportment

The National Flag of Canada is:
(a) Flown or displayed superior to all other flags, banners, or pennants, with the exception of the Queens personal Canadian flag or the Governor General's flag;
(b) Flown on the main flagpole at all defence establishments inside Canada;
(c) Worn at the ensign staff of all HMC ships in commission;
(d) Not allowed to touch the ground, floor or deck.

On ceremonial parades, including guards of honour, the National flag is carried (usually by a senior non-commissioned officer) if consecrated colours are not being carried. Only one National flag is carried, and it is not necessarily attended by an armed escort. The National flag is saluted as for consecrated colours, but is not accorded the honours associated with these colours when marched on or off parade. It must not be dipped or lowered by way of salute or complement. The Canadian Forces ensign may be carried with the National flag.

During courts martial the National flag is mounted on a staff and placed behind the president of the court.

The National flag must not be used as a cover for a box, table, desk, podium, or other objects, nor draped except on a casket.

It is customary for the National flag, if available, to be broken at the appropriate masthead by other Commonwealth and foreign ships of war when:
(a) Salutes are exchanged with Canadian ships, forts, or batteries;
(b) Salutes to senior Canadian officers and personal salutes are fired. The National flag is worn when HMC ships are dressed. It must not displace a distinguishing flag or masthead pennant.

On all occasions when the National flag of Canada is worn, displayed, or handled, it should be treated with dignity and respect.

HMC Ship's Ensign: Deportment

The National flag of Canada is currently worn as the ship's ensign by HMC ships in commission. It is worn:
(a) When in a Canadian port from 'colours' to 'sunset';
(b) When under way at all times by day and night;
(c) When in foreign ports according to local regulations; and
(d) On seeing another warship under way, irrespective of nationality.

The ship's ensign must be worn at the ensign staff when a ship is in harbour or under way in pilotage waters. At sea, it is worn as follows:
(a) In ships fitted with more than one mast: at a small gaff fitted on the main mast.
(b) In ships with one mast: at a suitable prominent position on that mast or at a staff on the superstructure.

The ship's ensign is to be shifted from its harbour position to its sea position or to its harbour position as appropriate while crossing harbour limits. Ensigns are worn at the ensign staff in special circumstances at the discretion of the ship's commanding officer or the senior officer of the ships in company.

The ship's ensigns must not touch the deck, be wrapped around guardrails, pipes, or fittings, or be handled in any manner that could be construed as being in any way disrespectful. To this end, the ship's ensign when 'bent on' is to be 'in hand' as befits the commencement of a military ceremony.

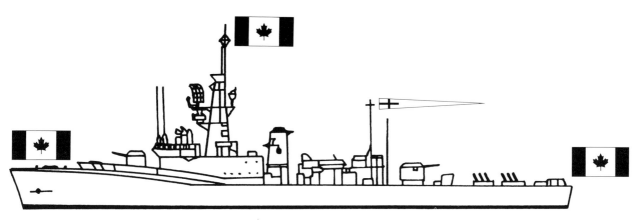

1.25   1965. Canadian National Flag as an ensign, a jack and at masthead; White Commissioning Pennant.

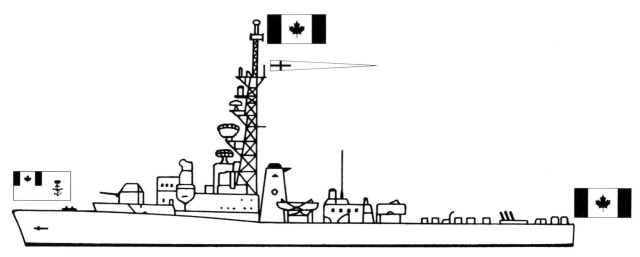

1.26   1968. Canadian National Flag as an ensign and at masthead; White Commissioning Pennant; Distinctive Naval Jack at jackstaff.

Boat's Ensigns: Deportment

Boats belonging to HMC ships wear the National flag of Canada as their boat's ensign. It is worn:

(a) In Canadian and Commonwealth waters from 'colours' to 'sunset' when ships are dressed either overall or with masthead flags;

(b) In other than Canadian and Commonwealth waters between dawn and dusk when away from their ships; and

(c) On all other occasions, both day and night, when going alongside a warship of a nation outside the Commonwealth. It is not, however, worn by boats under sail.

The Naval Jack

The Naval Jack is the flag authorized for wear at the jack-staff in HMC ships.

Deportment

The Naval Jack is worn by HMC ships as follows:

(a) At anchor or alongside from 'colours' to

1.27   The Naval Jack.

'sunset';

(b) When under way and dressed with masthead flags;

(c) Both day and night when under way and wearing or escorting another ship of war or merchant vessel, wearing:

1. The Queen's personal Canadian flag or Royal standard.

2. A foreign Royal or Imperial standard.

3. The flag of a head of state.

4. The flag of His Excellency the Governor General of Canada.

5. At all ship launching, commissioning or naming ceremonies. It should be noted, however, that the Jack shall not be worn by ships in dock, refit, or out of routine except on the occasion of 'dressing ship,' nor by ships which have been commissioned but not officially accepted.

The Naval Jack may be paraded ashore by units of Maritime Command within the following guidelines:
(a) It may be paraded with the national flag;
(b) It must not be attended by an armed escort; and
(c) It may be carried on ceremonial parades or paraded with guards of honour.
Compliments must not be paid to the Jack.

The Jack, when flown at the jack-staff, is fitted with a 'headstick' and is 'tracked.' The Jack, when 'bent on' is to be 'in hand' as befits the commencement of a military ceremony.

Personal Flags

The order of precedence for personal and distinguishing flags and pennants is:
(a) The personal Canadian flag of the Sovereign;
(b) The personal flag of the Governor General;
(c) The personal flag of a head of state;
(d) The personal flag of a member of the Royal Family;
(e) The personal flag of a lieutenant governor;
(f) A personal flag of a head of state of a foreign state or national diplomatic post;
(g) The distinguishing flag of the Chief of the Defence Staff;
(h) The distinguishing flag of a flag officer;

The Queen's Personal Canadian Flag

The Queen has adopted a personal flag specifically for use in Canada. The design comprises the Arms of Canada charged in the centre with Her Majesty's own symbol in gold on a blue background, the initial "E" surmounted by the St. Edward's Crown within a chaplet of roses.

Deportment
The Queen's personal Canadian flag is:
(a) Flown day and night at any building in which the Sovereign is residing;
(b) Flown day and night at defence establishments, on board ship, and on aircraft or other vehicles when the Sovereign is present or onboard;
(c) Displayed in the bow of the boat between dawn and dusk when the Sovereign is being transported by boat;

1.28   HM Queen Elizabeth's personal Canadian Flag.

(d) Displaces all other personal and distinguishing flags and pennants, and is:
Not flown on the same halyard with other flags.
Broken immediately on arrival and lowered immediately on departure of the Sovereign.
(e) Broken with other flags when the Sovereign embarks in a ship, as follows:
The Queen's personal Canadian flag at the main, the National flag at the fore, and the Royal Union flag at the mizzen.
In ships with two masts: the Queen's personal Canadian flag at the main, the National flag at the fore, and the Royal Union flag at the starboard yard.
In ships with only one mast: the Queen's personal Canadian flag at the masthead, the National flag at the starboard yard, and the Royal Union flag at the port yard.
(f) At the masthead when the Sovereign goes onboard for a short visit (the National flag and the Royal Union flag are not then broken).

The Governor General's Flag

The flag of the Governor General is dark blue with the Royal crest in its centre, consisting of a gold, jewelled St. Edward's crown surmounted by a crowned gold lion. Beneath the crest is a gold scroll inscribed with "Canada" in blue letters.

Deportment
The Governor General's flag is:
(a) Flown day and night at any building in which he resides;
(b) Flown day and night at defence establishments, onboard a ship and on aircraft or other vehicles when the Governor General is actually present or onboard;
(c) Given the same precedence and honours as the Queen's personal Canadian flag. (If the Governor General is visiting at the same time as the Sovereign, his flag is not flown.)
(d) Displayed at the main and the National flag at the fore when His Excellency embarks in a

1.29 Personal flag of the Governor General.

ship. In single-masted ships, the Governor General's flag only is displayed at the masthead.

(e) Displayed on the bow of the boat between dawn and dusk when His Excellency is being transported by boat;

(f) To displace all other distinguishing flags and pennants already displayed in the ship.

Standards of Members of the Royal Family

When a member of the Royal Family, other than the Sovereign, is present on an official visit to a defence establishment or one of HMC ships, or is being transported in an aircraft or vehicle, his or her personal standard is flown in the manner prescribed for the Queen's personal Canadian flag.

If more than one member of the Royal Family is present on an official visit, only the standard of the member taking precedence is flown.

The standards of members of the Royal Family take precedence over, but do not displace, other personal or distinguishing flags and pennants.

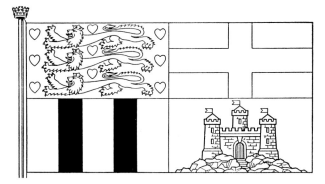

1.30 Standard of HRH Prince Phillip, Duke of Edinburgh.

1.31 Standard of HRH Queen Elizabeth, the Queen Mother.

On occasions of informal visits to ships or defence establishments by a member of the Royal Family, the personal standard is hoisted.

Distinguishing Flags

The use of distinguishing flags for 'flag officers' can be traced at least as far back as 1545. At that time, the Admiral used, as was his right as an Admiral-of-the-Fleet, the Royal standard as his distinguishing flag. He also made use of the early national flag, the cross of St. George, which was hoisted at the fore.

The two junior Admirals flew two St. George crosses, the Vice-admiral from the fore and the Rear-admiral from the mizzen. This form of distinction remained in force until the appearance of the Royal Union flag. By the time of the expedition to Cadiz in 1596, Vice and Rear-admirals still used the cross of St. George as their personal distinguishing flags, while new squadronal colours were used to distinguish their commands.

Following the Proclamation of 1606, the Cross of St. George was replaced by the new Union flag as the distinguishing flag for Admirals. Seniority could be distinguished by the colour and location of the squadronal colours and the Admiral's distinguishing flag. The squadronal colours shown were: red at the main for the centre squadron; blue at the fore for the van squadron; and white at the mizzen for the rear squadron.

During the Interregnum of 1649, the Cross of St. George was again the flag of Vice and Rear-admirals. In 1653, the van and rear squadrons changed colours. Blue became the junior, or rear colour, and remained so until the colours were discontinued in 1864. The Union flags (or their precursors in a national sense, the red crosses of St. George) were freely used before the Restoration as command flags in English fleets. But after the Restoration their use for indicating the presence of British officers of high rank was narrowly restricted.

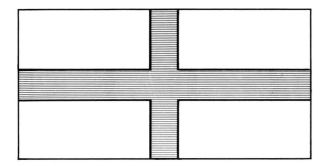

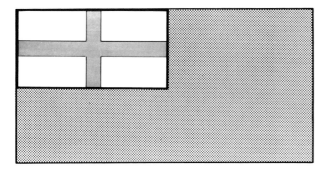

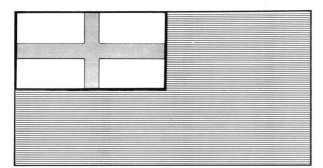

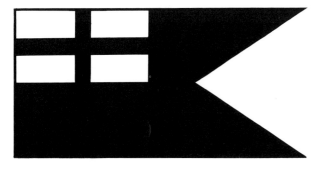

1.32　Top to bottom: George Cross; Red Ensign; Blue Ensign; Broad Pennant.

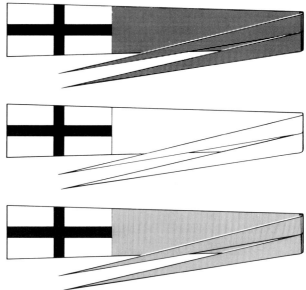

1.33　Squadronal Colours. Top to bottom: Red Squadron; White Squadron; Blue Squadron.

In the list drawn up by Pepys around 1686, the Royal standard was still mentioned as the proper flag of the Lord High Admiral, and the Union flag (over a distinction pennant) as that of the Vice-and Rear-admirals of England. Union flags are mentioned as proper to a naval force in which only three flags were necessary. But in a fleet of three squadrons, with nine flags, the recognized squadronal flags (of red, white and blue) took

their usual place unless the Admiral-of-the-Fleet was present. Throughout such a fleet the ensigns were to agree in colour with the normal command colours of red, white and blue.

The commodore's broad pennant originated in 1674 with an order directing captains officiating as commodores in command of squadrons to wear a large red distinguishing pennant.

In February 1702, the flag officers of the white squadron were given the use of the Union flag instead of their white flags. A few weeks later the Lord High Admiral's use of the Royal standard was discontinued forever, and the first known orders were issued concerning Admiral's boat flags. These were to resemble their command flags, but to be different in so far as there was to be one white ball for a Vice-admiral and two for a Rear-admiral, the two being arranged diagonally. In May of the same year, the ensigns and command flags of the white squadron were again ordered to be white, the boat flags being different in that there was one or two blue balls in the upper canton; the diagonal arrangement was abandoned, in the red and blue squadrons also, for the Admiral's boat flag.

As a compliment to the Royal Navy, after Trafalgar, the rank of 'Admiral of the Red' was introduced in November 1805. In the year following commodores were ordered to wear broad pennants of their squadronal colours. This arrangement was altered in 1824 by the introduction of two classes of commodore; the senior wearing a red broad pennant, the junior a broad pennant of blue.

In 1864, squadronal colours were abolished. The flags of the white squadron only were re-

1.34   Admiral (Red Squadron). Union Flag at the main.

1.36   Vice-admiral of the White. Union Flag at the fore; White Squadron Pennant at the mizzen.

1.35   Rear-admiral of the Blue. Union Flag at the mizzen; Blue Squadron Pennant at the fore.

1.37   Rear-admiral of the Blue. George Cross at the mizzen; Blue Squadron Pennant at the mizzen.

tained and commodores of the second class now wore their broad pennants at the fore, a red ball in the canton when in boats. The balls changed from blue to red in the Admiral's boat flags and, in the case of Rear-admirals, were rearranged in 1898 in their disposition with one red ball in the upper and one in the lower canton, next to the mast. As masts diminished in number with the development of steam, it became impossible to always keep flags at their appropriate mastheads; the balls, which were originally only intended for boat flags were now permanently recognized for all purposes and remain so today.

Today, distinguishing flags are provided for:
(a)   The Chief of the Defence Staff;

(b)   A lieutenant general at NDHQ;
(c)   A flag officer, such as:
The Commander, Maritime Command (Vice-admiral/lieutenant general).
The Commander, Maritime Forces Pacific (Rear-admiral/major general).
The Commander, Northern Region (Commodore/Brig. General).
(d)   A captain(N), commander or lieutenant commander;

Deportment
Distinguishing flags for officers other than those of 'flag rank' are flown only within the recognized limits of the command, such as the base area,

1.38 Vice-admiral of the Red. George Cross at the fore; Red Squadron Pennant at the main.

1.40 Rear-admiral (Blue) of England. Union Flag at the mizzen; Blue Squadron pennant at the mizzen; Blue Ensign at the ensign staff.

1.39 Vice-admiral (Red) of England. Union Flag at the fore; Red Squadron Pennant at the main; Red Ensign at the ensign staff.

1.41 Commodore of the Red. Broad pennant at the main; Red Squadron pennant at the main; Red Ensign at the ensign staff.

military college or station. They do not replace traditional regimental pennants or commissioning pennants, which continue to be flown according to customary usage.

The distinguishing flag designated for a given appointment is flown by an officer appointed to acting capacity, regardless of his actual rank.

The only distinguishing flags authorized to carry a badge are the distinguishing flags for:
(a) The Chief of the Defence Staff;
(b) A lieutenant general at NDHQ; and
(c) The commanders of the following commands:
     Maritime Command

Maritime Forces Pacific
Mobile Command
Air Command
Communications Command
Canadian Forces Europe
Canadian Forces Training System
Northern Region

The distinguishing flag for an entitled officer is hauled down immediately after he:
(a) Dies (Flag is half-masted);
(b) Transfers command to his successor;
(c) Proceeds on leave;
(d) Is confined to hospital; or

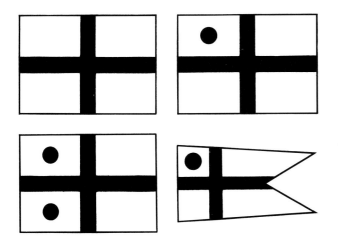

1.46   Commander, Northern Region distinguishing flag.

1.42   Distinguishing Pennants. Left to right: Admiral; Vice-admiral; Rear-admiral; Commodore.

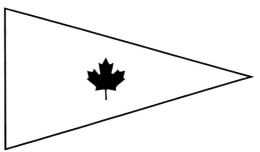

1.47   Captain (N), commander or lieutenant commander distinguishing flag.

1.43   Chief of the Defence Staff distinguishing flag.

(e) Proceeds on duty outside his area of jurisdiction.

These distinguishing flags are only flown in HMC ships when the officer concerned is acting in his official capacity.

The change of a flag officer's flag is arranged previously by message and is normally carried out at 0800.

Distinguishing flags are not flown:
(a) In more than one place at a time;
(b) In a ship in which the personal Canadian flag of the Sovereign or the Governor General of Canada's flag is displayed; or
(c) When command has been delegated to a subordinate for a period in excess of 48 hours.

1.44   Commander, Maritime Command distinguishing flag.

The Commissioning Pennant and Church Pennant

While no one knows the exact origin of the 'commissioning pennant' or the 'church pennant,' according to a paper prepared by the office of the naval historian in Ottawa (written in response to a query from the chaplain of the fleet), both originally shared a common function. The church pennant was originally a commission pennant, dating from the early eighteenth century when the fleet was divided into red, white and blue squadrons. The Admiral's flags, ensigns and squadron pennant were the colour of the squadron. As men were assigned to a ship for a particular commission, so the ships were commissioned

1.45   Commander, Maritime Forces Pacific distinguishing flag.

into a particular squadron. The pennant, showing their squadron colour, was the visible evidence of this. However, in a detached squadron operation under the command of a commodore who was not under the orders of a flag officer, the commodore's ship wore his red broad pennant and the Red Ensign while the private ships wore the Red Ensign and the common pennant. This had the St. George's Cross in the hoist, and a red, white and blue striped fly.

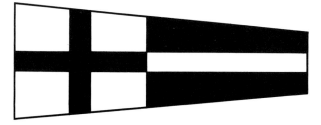

1.48   Church Pennant.

During the Napoleonic war the church pennant seems to have been worn by all private ships of the Royal Navy, but its use as a commission pennant ended in 1815 or 1816. Still, until the early 1950s the distinction between signal flags and other pieces was not clearly drawn. Between 1939 and 1945, for instance, the church pennant was involved in three signals — working the cable, man overboard and the recall for ship's boats.

Today the Church Pennant is hoisted in harbour at the peak if fitted and not occupied, or at the yardarm when ship's companies are holding divine service and are at prayers.

During divine service or prayers the Church Pennant is sometimes used to drape a podium or altar, but only as described above, and in dressing line construction. It is always hoisted and lowered with dignity.

Since squadron colours were abolished in 1864 and all ships flew the colours of the old white squadron, it is likely that the present Commissioning Pennant evolved from the white squadron commissioning pennant, just as the White Ensign descended from the original white squadron ensign. The Commissioning Pennant means the same today as it did then: that the ship serves as a member of the fleet through the commission of her captain, received from Her Majesty the Queen.

Another theory is that the commissioning pennant originated from the brash action of the Dutch Admiral Maarten Harperszoon Tromp, who, in a moment of impetuosity, hoisted a broom to the masthead of his flagship, indicating his intention to sweep the English from the sea. The rival English Admiral, not to be outdone, hoisted a horsewhip to his masthead, indicating

his intention to chastise the Dutchman. Since that time the narrow pennant, sometimes called a 'coachwhip,' purportedly symbolizes the original horsewhip, and as such is a distinctive mark of a warship. It is hoisted to the masthead whenever a warship is commissioned, and struck when the ship is paid off, hence the term 'commissioning pennant.' But since the term 'commissioning' meant that the Sovereign had ordered a ship to be made seaworthy and to sail with the fleet, and since that ship would be placed with a certain squadron for the duration of the Sovereign's need of her, the present pennant most likely developed from squadron pennants rather than the English whip and the Dutch broom.

Today the Commissioning Pennant is six feet (2 M.) in length and three inches (3 cm.) wide at the hoist, having a St. George's Cross on a white field at the hoist, and a white fly.

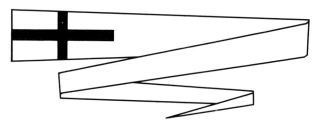

1.49   Commissioning Pennant.

Deportment
The Commissioning Pennant is worn by HMC ships in commission. It is displayed from a suitable halyard on the main mast or a small gaff. (It is also referred to in other regulations as a captain's pennant or masthead pennant.)

The Commissioning Pennant is broken in a ship upon commissioning at the same time as the hoisting of the ship's ensign, and it is worn throughout the ship's commission except when displaced by the personal flag of:
(a) The Sovereign;
(b) The Governor-General;
(c) The Chief of the Defence Staff;
(d) The Commander, or Deputy Commander of Maritime Command; and
(e) The broad pennant of a commodore commanding a formation afloat.
The Commissioning Pennant is displayed at the bow of a boat to denote:
(a) The presence of the commanding officer of a ship proceeding to or from his ship;
(b) The guard officer when acting in his official capacity; and
(c) Members of a court martial proceeding to or from the court.

The Squadron Command Flag

By 1964 the practice of painting the funnel to identify the ship of the squadron commander and division commander had been discontinued.

The Squadron Command Flag is not a distinguishing flag or a personal flag. It is used only for the purpose of indicating the location of the squadron commander, and does not displace personal or distinguishing flags.

Originally, the senior ship had been identified by a black band at the top of the funnel. This was replaced by the use of a Command Pennant, a swallow-tailed broad pennant with blue borders at the top and bottom, and the squadron number in the centre, also in blue.

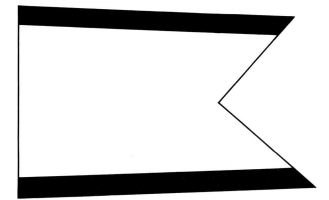

1.50   Command Pennant.

Deportment
The Squadron Command Flag is flown:
(a) In harbour, in the ship in which the Squadron Commander is embarked, at all times day and night; and
(b) At sea and when meeting or joining other warships. It may be hauled down when sufficient time has elapsed for visual identification.

The Squadron Command Flag must not:
(a) Displace the Commissioning Pennant;
(b) Be hoisted in a ship wearing a standard or other distinguishing flag or pennant; or
(c) Be displayed in the bows of a boat or on a vehicle.

Senior Canadian Officer Present Afloat (SCOPA) Pennant

In the "Catalogue of Pepysian Manuscripts" of 1675, mention is made of the problem of recognizing seniority among ships. Pepys writes to the comptroller of the Navy as follows:
"... I find that there hath been wanting to this day a clear determination how commanders are to behave themselves in reference to precedence, and giving command one to the other where they chance to fall in company..."

His specific question to the comptroller was:
"When several of His Majesty's ships happen to be together in any of His Majesty's ports or chambers, and neither of the Captains hath warrant from the Lord Admiral to command in chief there, shall the eldest captain or the captain of the ship of the highest rate set the watch and answer the salutes of any foreign or other ships that shall happen to come in there?"

The solution was that the senior officer of those present would be the individual identified for the purpose of salutes and honours.

Deportment
Today, when two or more of HMC ships are present in a port or roadstead, the senior Canadian ship hoists the starboard pennant at the starboard yard to indicate that the duties assigned to SCOPA are undertaken by that ship.

When in company with ships from other nations the starboard pennant is flown by the senior Canadian ship; however, the starboard pennant is not formally flown when SCOPA is wearing a flag or broad pennant unless it is required to avoid misunderstanding.

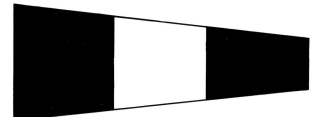

1.51   Starboard Pennant.

The senior Canadian officer present afloat is generally responsible for ensuring that established regulations, customs, and normal usages of the Service are observed by HMC ships in harbour at home and abroad. These include:
(a) Appearance of HMC ships and ship's boats;
(b) The proper observance of all ceremonial;
(c) Routines, insofar as changes or amendments are needed to meet ships' short term requirements; and
(d) Uniform observance of current orders and regulations with respect to ships' routines and the operation of equipment such as boats.

Queen's Harbour Master's Flag

The flag of the Queen's Harbour Master (QHM), through custom and common usage of the Commonwealth Navies, denotes the headquarters of the Queen's Harbour Master of HMC dockyards.

The QHM flag may be displayed continuously on a gaff or flagstaff outside or on the building housing the offices of the Queen's Harbour Master.

1.52   Queen's Harbour Master's flag.

Deportment
The Queen's Harbour Master flies his flag in the bow of the boat or vessel when executing his duty.

The QHM flag must not:
(a) Displace any distinguishing flag or pennant;
(b) Be accorded any salute or ceremonial; or
(c) Be displayed for any other purpose than denoting the presence of the Queen's Harbour Master or his deputy.

VI
The Origins of Naval Signalling

'Signum' was the military ensign of the Romans and orders were conveyed by raising and lowering it. Probably the earliest known signal was given by the Phoenicians as early as 400 B.C. when they raised the naval standard at their ships' sterns. The Greeks adopted this method from them, substituting a cruciform standard for the crescent and the globe. Mention is made by Thucydides of 'raising the semeion' in the Greek fleet, meaning that the officer in command raised the standard. This was usually the signal to begin action. The Romans used a vexillum (a square piece of plain coloured material, hung by the top edge from the cross piece at the head of a lance, and fringed at the bottom edge), for their signal for battle.

In 480 B.C., at the Battle of Salamis, the Greek Commander, Thermistocles, ordered an improvised flag, a red cloak, to be displayed; this signal ordered the outnumbered Greek ships to turn 90 degrees and ram the enemy ships instead of fighting alongside as was customary. This tactic resulted in the rout of Xeres' fleet and a halt to the threatened Persian invasion. Attention to the Admiral's signals was imperative, as shown by the story of the unfortunate Scylax who missed a signal and consequently was lashed to a port hole with his head outside and his body inside the vessel.

As early as three centuries before Christ, Polybius described two methods of conveying messages at sea, one devised by him and the other by Tacticus. These systems anticipated the underlying principles of later systems in that words could be spelled. Signal codes of the ancients are believed to have been elaborate; generally a flag was used, but shields were also displayed in certain preconcerted manners as at the battle of Marathon in 490 B.C.

The earliest known code of naval signals was drawn up in the ninth century A.D. by the Emperor Leo VI; it consisted of simply moving a banner to different positions or waving it. In his final paragraph to his seagoing generals he states:

"Let the exercise of these signals be practiced, so that all officers in command of ships under you may have certain knowledge of all such signals; of the reason why each is made, and when, and how, and may not fail; so that, well familiarized with the signals, they may readily understand them in time of emergency, and carry out the orders indicated."

In the middle ages flags, banners and lanterns were used to distinguish vessels belonging to various ports and squadrons, as marks of rank, to call a conference, and for reporting the enemy, etc. The invention of the cannon was an important addition to the signalling methods in use.

The first recorded use of the flag in English seas is recorded in the Bayeux Tapestry which shows a blue bordered white banner superimposed with a gold cross. It is thought this flag was used as a flag of command to denote the ship carrying William the Conqueror to England in 1066. The flag of command is also prominent in the Battle of Dover Straits in 1217 when Hubert de Brugh ended the threatened French invasion when he cut Eustace the Monk's banner from his ship.

The first tactical division into squadrons by means of flags took place in 1242 when leaders were distinguished by the flags of the districts from which they came. In Edward III's reign the true flag was first used as a means of conveying information or communicating orders. To call a conference the Admiral would hoist a flag of white, superimposed with a red cross. This flag is still used in the Royal Navy to denote the presence of an Admiral.

A new signal to call one or more particular ships was added in 1366. Other signals introduced were one to summon assistance; a manoeuvering signal and a recognition signal. Supplementary messages were conveyed by sail or lantern.

The orders for the Venetian Navy, drawn up by Moncenigo in 1720, laid down this system of signals and included a fine of 10 lira for every time the guard galley parted company with the Admiral. When at sea, the fleet gathered round the Admiral each evening to take his orders for the next day, and the captains were rowed across to the flagship. If the Admiral wished to call his captains together at any other time, the council banner was placed half way up the mast instead of on the after castle.

During Elizabeth I's reign instructions issued to Raleigh, Howard and Essex for their expedition against Cadiz in 1596 contain, among other signals, the following orders:

"It shall not be lawful for any second ship to follow chase unless the Admiral of the Squadron shall hang out two flags one above the other. If three ships are to give chase three flags are to be hung out. If it shall seem inconvenient the Admiral will halt the chase by hanging out the Flag of Council, the chase being misliked and that all give over and keep their course."

Boteler, a captain who served in the Cadiz expedition of 1625 and the Rochelle expedition of 1627, was the first to suggest using different coloured flags for signalling. The first attempt at a regular code is ascribed to Admiral Sir William Penn (1621 — 1670), but the credit usually goes to James II for he commanded the British Fleets as Duke of York. During the Third Dutch War (1673), he issued a new edition of the Commonwealth Code, and it appears that the code set out there was the first English one to appear in print. Previously signals had been included in the actual instructions; the appropriate flag being described in the text. The new edition included a coloured drawing of each flag, arranged in order with its appropriate meaning and position of hoist in parallel columns. The set comprised:

The Union flag
The Standard
Blue and White Ensign
The Dutch Flag
A red and yellow striped flag
A red, blue and white flag
A pendant
A red and white striped flag
A red and white diagonally striped flag

A white flag superimposed with a red cross

In some copies the last four are omitted but a yellow and white diagonally striped flag is mentioned in others as a signal for fireships.

An interesting addition to these flags took place in the Dutch Wars. It was the custom to hold divine service before a battle began. To indicate that ships were at prayers, a pendant incorporating the English and Dutch ensigns form and colours was hoisted. The pendant was known as the 'Church Pendant.' It is still used today, in its original form, to denote church services are being held.

In the English system the same flag was used in different positions to carry various messages.

The earliest 'instructions' (those of Blake, Deane and Monck) made use of only three flags and one pendant; the red flag being employed in three different positions. Twenty years later nine flags and one pendant met the requirements for signalling in the Duke of York's second and final revision to the Commonwealth code. There is a fine copy of this Royal code in the Admiralty Library in London. In this manuscript, probably made some time after the printed version, the colours are illustrated in the margin, and four additional flags are mentioned. Eighteen years later when Edward Russell took command of the Channel, reversing the verdict of Beachy Head, he added four flags of his own and discarded three of those which appear in the manuscript version of the 1673 code.

At the beginning of the Spanish Succession War (1703), Sir George Rooke revised Russell's instructions and his publication remained the standard authority for the next ninety years. (New orders were added from time to time in the form of 'Additional Instructions.') The National Maritime Museum has an interesting manuscript which may be the earliest English signal book in existence. It shows the flags hoisted in their correct positions on silhouettes of ships; the corresponding meaning is noted underneath. The date of the manuscript is not known, but it shows the signals used in 1711, including additional directional chasing signals introduced by Admiral Norris in 1710.

In 1714 Jonathan Greenwood privately issued the first printed signal book in pocket size. Its author states that "each signal is represented by a drawing of a ship flying the flag — or flags at the proper place, the purport being added underneath" — a method already in use in the French Navy. Although the instructions were regarded as confidential it appears that the signals were not, as the work is described as being "designed to supply the inferior officers who cannot have recourse to the full printed instructions."

The next signal book, also a private venture, was published by John Millan in 1748. In this edition the flags were set out along the top of the page with the relevant meaning below. The only new flags appearing were a white cross on a red ground; a blue and white horizontally striped flag; and a red and white horizontally striped flag.

The earliest representation of the 'chequered flag' is recorded in a signal manuscript dated 1758. It contains Hawke's autograph and is probably the one he used at the Battle of Quiberon. It also contains details of a blue flag with six white balls and a blue and white flag in five horizontal stripes. Later the white balls were replaced by a single white square in its centre. By Rodney's time this flag, known as the Blue Peter, was flown at the mainmast to recall ships' crews from ashore; it still does so today. The blue and white striped flag became Nelson's signal: 'prepare to anchor.'

By 1746 there were 16 flags in use to express 144 signals, by 1780 there were 50 flags — each hoisted in seven different locations providing for about 330 signals. Twenty-five years later at Trafalgar the signal book contained upwards of 400 signals.

As long as the signals were few and the flags of strongly contrasting designs, the old system was relatively simple, but when the number of signals increased and flags became similar, the system became complex. (It should be noted that the flags had to be distinguished in a dead calm as well as in a fair breeze, and against the sun where colours were not obvious.) In practice the colours were limited to red, blue, yellow, black and white. The best colour combinations were found to be: red and white; yellow and blue; blue and white; black and white; but with 50 odd flags other combinations had to be used.

The first formal attempt to regulate the flag system was made by Lord Howe in 1779 while he was Commander of the Channel Fleet. However the system of 'signals by numbers' which he outlined in his signal book published in 1776 was based on a method invented by Bourdonnais, a French officer, almost twenty years earlier. Bourdonnais simply assigned one flag to each number from 1 to 9, so that by combining the flags any desired signal could be produced. The numbers were arranged sequentially on a chequered chart with each side having as many squares as the number of colours to be used. The flag colours were indicated along the top and down the left hand side. For example, supposing three flags, red, white and blue were being used. They would be arranged as follows:

	Red	White	Blue
Red	1	4	7
White	2	5	8
Blue	3	6	9

The signal corresponding to 6 would be a white flag over a blue one.

Lord Howe's method of codification was to number each page of his signal book and to number each signal appearing on each page. In this way any particular signal could be conveniently referred to by quoting its number and the number of the page on which it appeared. He simplified the system by showing separately signals made by private ships and omitting any instructions, previously in use, which he considered obsolete. The first instruction in his book reads as follows:

"All the signals contained the General printed signals, which are likely to be needed on the present occasion, being provided for in this Signal Book; the signals (as appointed in the General printed book) will only be made either in conformity to the Practice of some senior officer present, or when in company for the time being with other ships not of the fleet under the Admiral's command and unprovided with these particular signals."

Lord Howe's system was probably continued by his successor Sir George Collier, whose personal copy of the *Howe Signal Book* is in the Holland Collection in London. The next two Commanders of the Fleet, John Byron and Marriot Arbuthnot, reverted to the old system of using additional instructions; those of Arbuthnot were particularly elaborate.

Lord Howe's work, however, was taken up by two keen signal reformers, Sir Charles Knowles and Captain Kempenfelt. In 1778 Knowles, while still a lieutenant, produced a book which included the "numerary square table" principle.

Kempenfelt, as first captain to three successive commanders-in-chief of the Channel fleet, was in a good position to improve on Howe's efforts. There is no doubt that he had access to Lord Howe's signal book and many of the instructions published by him are identical to those used by Howe.

The date of issue of the first "Kempenfelt Code to the Channel Fleet" cannot be determined exactly but the order book of HMS*Pluto* implies that the old system was still in effect when that ship left the fleet in November 1779. There is evidence, however, that it was issued before the death of Sir Charles Hardy, which occurred in May 1780.

Kempenfelt's code, although very similar to Howe's, included the following new features: the signals were numbered consecutively throughout the book; triangular flags were introduced as distinguishing flags for the squadrons; and complete compass and horary tables were included. Although Kempenfelt also used Bourdonnais's "numerary square table" he was not convinced that a numerary system provided the best solution to the problems of signalling. In a letter to Sir Charles Middleton on 17 October, 1779 he wrote:

"Signals printed out by numbers, and according to that method observed in these you (have) sent me, I have been long acquainted with. The numerary system involved the simultaneous use of three flags, whereas the older system called for only one at a time. This single flag was as often as not self-explanatory; whereas a three flag hoist assumed the faculty of distinguishing one flag from another; and this introduced a very real difficulty, hitherto unknown. In any case it would not be easy to detect the flag hoisted at the Mizzen topmasthead."

Kempfelt expressed his preference for a French two flag system. Nevertheless, he was referred to as being "one of the few officers that had taken up Lord Howe's plan of numeral signals."

When Howe became First Sea Lord (1783-1788) he issued a new signal book in which he abandoned the tabular method and reverted to the simple numerary code. The numbers he used for flags were later used at Trafalgar.

He introduced the following additional flags to those already in use:

White cross on a red ground: Affirmative
White with red border: Arrival
Union: To call officers
Blue and yellow chequered: Rendezvous
Red and white, yellow and blue and their inversions: Four quarters to compass
Blue and white striped: Preparative
White flag 1: Truce
             2: Open secret instructions
             3: To take effect at close of day

Under this system, Nelson's signal at Trafalgar, "prepare to anchor at close of day" would have required four flags: Preparative, No.6 (anchor as soon as convenient), No.3 (at close of day), white flag.

While the system of signalling was being developed the need for a more flexible verbal framework than the set instructions in use was becoming recognized. The first steps in this direction were taken by Sir Home Popham. The first edition of his code consisted of nearly 1,000 words taken from a dictionary. Popham realized that all the words required for a signal might not be included in his vocabulary and instructed that when a word required was not listed the word "most nearly synonymous" should be used. He also made provision for words to be spelled out.

In preparing for Nelson's famous signal, "England expects that every man will do his duty," the signalman, Pascoe, told the Admiral that "confides" was not in the vocabulary and suggested that "expects" be used instead (which it was), as this could be expressed by three flags while "confides" required 11 flags in eight hoists. He

agreed to spell "duty" out, probably realizing that the gist of the message had already suffered under the first substitution and to use "best" or "utmost" instead would have only added insult to injury.

In 1803 Popham issued an addendum consisting of nearly 1,000 phrases or sentences.

Once the words for a message had been chosen from the vocabulary and their corresponding number written down the signalman had to translate them into flags. The first flag denoted whether the signal hoisted was to be deciphered from the *Signal Book* or from the "Vocabulary Code" Popham designed his own telegraph flag to signify that, indeed, his Code was being used.

In 1816 Popham produced a revised and updated vocabulary which was later issued by the Admiralty as the *Official Vocabulary Signal Book*. Eleven years later the books were further revised and issued in three volumes. The first was known as the *General Signal Book* and contained revolutionary and battle signals; the second, words and general sentences for which alphabetical flags were used, and the third, night and fog signals.

Although signalling systems changed over the centuries, the general style of flag has remained remarkably consistant; most of the signal flags were still being used well into the twentieth century.

From 1857 until recently Royal Navy signalmen had to cope with two sets of alphabetical flags; those of the commercial or international code and those of the naval code. In 1901 both systems had 12 flags with the same design, but only the letter 'O' was common to both. Therefore a naval 'bunting tosser' had to remember that flags 'A,' 'B' and 'C' in the naval code were 'Y,' 'W' and 'Z' in the merchant code.

Between 1890 and 1910 flag signalling reached its peak in speed, accuracy and scope. The rank of signal boatswain was created in 1890; the first group of these experienced and valuable officers were appointed on 6 March of that year.

It was customary in the flag ship for a signal to be sent up with flags rolled in small bundles so it was impossible to see their composition until the signal was 'broken out' and its message sprung on the fleet. Although this was a striking and spectacular operation, it virtually disappeared during the last decade before World War I, with the advent of the electric morse lamp and wireless telegraphy.

Many amusing stories are told in the Service concerning flag signals. For example on one occasion King George VI, while on the bridge of HMS *Rodney*, overheard the flag lieutenant ordering the speed of the fleet to be changed to 6 knots. The signal for altering the speed was flag 'G' or in phonetics, flag 'George.' So the order to the flag deck was "Hoist George six." This was ignored by the King, but, when the order "Execute George six" was made (i.e. carry out the manoeuver) the King is said to have visibly winced.

VII
Ceremonial Anchorage

As is the case with most naval customs and traditions, the 'ceremonial anchorage' likely evolved from a particular battle function. In Admiral Lord Howe's fighting instructions of 1799, and those of Vice-admiral Nelson in 1805, there is specific reference to engaging the enemy by anchoring alongside him. They imply that all ships in the fleet would anchor and engage the enemy simultaneously.

The procedures mentioned in Admiral Lord Howe's Fighting Instructions vary only in terminology from the present day 'ceremonial anchorage'; his instructions were:

"When Signal 14 is made to prepare for battle and for anchoring, the ships are to have spring on their bower anchors, and the end of the sheet cable taken in at the stern port, with springs on the anchor to be prepared for anchoring without winding if they should go to the attack with the wind aft. The boats should be hoisted out and hawsers coiled in the launches, with the stream anchor ready to warp them into their stations, or to assist other ships which may be in want of assistance. Their spare yards and topmasts, if they cannot be left in charge of some vessel, should in moderated weather be lashed alongside, near the water, on the off side of the deck, from the enemy, whenever they are not wanted, if the ship should be fired at as they advance to the attack.[17]

The instructions of Lord Nelson on both the Glorious First of June, 1801, and the instructions for Trafalgar, 1805, were almost identical. Even as he was dying, Nelson was determined to anchor with the ships that had been taken at Trafalgar, and thus consolidate his victory.

Today a ceremonial anchorage can be carried out by a group of ships coming to a formation anchorage, or by a single ship on a special occasion. It is also a 'combat readiness' requirement.

Deportment
Prior to reaching "Ten cables to go," the following preparations are to be completed:
(a) Accommodation ladder to be rigged and turned outboard;

(b) Mediterranean ladder and boat's boom rigged;
(c) Boats turned out and manned ready for lowering;
(d) Ensigns and jackstaffs rigged;
(e) Brow area prepared for use; and
(f) Ship's bells and name boards fitted.
At ten cables: (If not already done by signal). The ensigns are shifted to the harbour position; and call signs and squadron commanders pennant are hoisted.
At five cables: Boats lowered to deck level.
At three cables: Hands fall out, stand by boats, booms and ladders.
At two cables: Boats and ladders lowered to the water line (clear of the water); and booms placed in the vertical position.
At one-half cable: Pins from the boat's disengaging gear are removed.
At letting go of the anchor: Boats are slipped and proceed to waiting positions on the quarters until the ship is finished with engines; the jack is hoisted; and the fitting of boats' booms and ladders is completed as quickly as possible.

For a ceremonial anchorage involving a group of ships, the senior officer conducts a 'countdown' of the distance to go, to ensure uniformity of action.

VIII
The Ship's Bell

The origin of bells is not known but in their various forms, made of a variety of materials, they have been used longer for making sound than any other device, with the exception, perhaps, of the drum.

Bells have been used for centuries in the Navies and merchant fleets of the world. The religious significance of the bell ashore was naturally carried on board ship and it was probably in the fifteenth century that the bell was positioned on the quarterdeck — that section of the ship which has always had special ceremonial significance.

One of the earliest mentions of the shipboard bell referred to the British ship *Grace Dieu* about 1485. Ten years later an inventory of the English ship *Regent* shows that she carried two 'wache bells.' They were probably not used widely up to the sixteenth century since extracts from fighting instructions of that time read:

"XXII. The watch shall be set every night by eight of the clock, either by trumpet or drum, and singing the Lord's Prayer, some of the Psalms of David, or clearing the glass."

"XXVII. In fogs (if any happen), when your ships are becalmed, you shall cause some noise to be made, by drum, by trumpet, by shooting off a musket or calliver now and then, or by some other means, that, hearing you to be near, everyone may take heed lest he fall foul of another."[18]

A seventeenth century English account places 'the great ship's bell' on the quarterdeck, where among other uses, it was the signal for sounding a broadside.

An order to the Dutch fleet as early as 1628 required that the ship's bell be rung three times before the commencement of divine services. It was also Dutch naval custom at this time to strike the bell before dinner and to use the bell's tone for beating time while the sailors were trimming sail.

The use of the bell for marking foul weather appears in sailing orders, dated June 20, 1675:

"8. If it prove foggy weather by night or day, we must ring our bells, and fyre a musket now and then."[19]

This practice gradually became a warning to other vessels in poor visibility and fog. In 1858, British Naval Regulations made it mandatory to do so and current maritime law requires ships to carry an efficient bell.

Before the chronometer was invented, time at sea was measured by the trickle of sand through a half-hour glass. One of the ship's boys had the duty of watching the glass and turning it when the sand had run out. When he turned the glass, he struck the bell as the signal that he had performed this vital function. It is likely that the practice of striking the bell once at the end of the first half hour of a four-hour watch, twice after the first hour, etc., until eight bells marked the end of the four-hour watch, evolved from this practice.

Despite changing customs and technology, the ship's bell remains one of the focal points of the ship. Apart from its everyday use of proclaiming the passage of time, the bell is still used as a fog signal and as a general alarm, at the captain's orders. When a church service is being held, the bell is sometimes used to summon the ship's company to worship. It is prized as one of the most valued pieces of the ship's original equipment and in many instances is all that remains of vessels which have preceded those now serving in the Canadian Navy.

A visitor to the Parliament Buildings, Queen's Park, Toronto, may notice that a ship's bell occupies an honoured place there; it is the bell of the cruiser, HMCS *Ontario*. On it are the names of children who were baptized onboard. Traditionally in Her Majesty's ships, children of members of the ship's company may be christened by a chaplain using the ship's bell inverted as a baptismal font. Afterwards the consecrated water is returned to the sea by the chaplain and the 'side' is piped during the ceremony. The child's name is then inscribed on the bell. In *Stadacona* Chapel, CFB Halifax, the permanently fitted baptismal font is the bell of HMCS *Uganda* bearing the date 1944, inscribed with the names of children baptized while the cruiser was in service.

Notes

1. "The Nelson Incident," *The Naval Review*, 34, No. 2, 1946, p.219.

2. Edward C. Russell, "The Origin of the Hand Salute," D/Hist File 1200 - 10, Vol. 7 (N/Hist), TD 3133, (1963).

3. Leland P.Lovette, LCDR (USN), "Naval Customs, Traditions and Usages," (United States, n.d., n.p.), pp. 26-29.

4. James, Duke of York, *Memoirs of English Affairs, Chiefly Naval (1660-1673), (London, n.p., 1792), pp. 81-82.

5. "*Notes on Gun Salutes*," *The Mariner's Mirror*, (St. Albans, Staples Printers, Aug. 1973), n. pag.

6. "Origin of the 21 Gun Salute," The Canadian Defence Military Defence Journal: *Defence Forces Review*, 23, No. 2, (Ottawa, n.p., 1956)

7. "An Unfortunate Birthday Salute," *The Mariner's Mirror*, (St. Albans, Staples Printers, n.d.), pp. 295-296.

8. "Gun Salutes," *Admiralty Manual of Seamanship*, Vol. I, (London, n.p., 1951), pp. 261-262.

9. "Duke of York's Instructions (Circa 1673)," Stowe MSS, 180, No. 155, (London, n.d.), pp. 86-87.

10. Alonso de Chaves, "Fighting Instructions," (n.p., 1530), pp. 12-13.

11. Lord Howe, "Fighting Instructions," (London, n.p., 1799), pp. 275-276.

12. Major C. Field, "Under Many Flags," The Army and Navy Illustrated, 11, (n.p., 1900), p.375.

13. Gresham Carr, ed., *Flags of the World*, (London, Frederick Warne and Co. Ltd., 1953), p.33.

14. Cecil King, "The King's Flags and Some Others," *The Mariner's Mirror*, (St. Albans, Staples Printers, May 1952), p.84.

15. Gresham Carr, ed., *Flags of the World*, (London, Frederick Warne and Co. Ltd., 1953), pp. 35-36.

16. Cecil King, "The King's Flags and Some Others," *The Mariner's Mirror*, (St. Albans, Staples Printers, May 1952), p.84.

17. Admiral Lord Howe, "Fighting Instructions (circa 1799)," (n.p.), pp. 277-278.

18. "Fighting Instructions, Clowes, Vol. I, (n.p.), n. pag.

19. Captain William Holden, "Fighting Instructions June 1675," Vol. II, (n.p.) p.226.

2 Naval Ceremonies

I
Colours, Halfmasting, and Sunset in HMC Ships

Colours

The modern practice for all ordinary occasions on HMC ships is to hoist the national colours in the morning and keep them up until sunset. But numerous references to hoisting or "heaving out" the colours indicate that in earlier days the custom was to only hoist at sea when there was some special reason for doing so. There was a routine for hoisting the flag in harbour in the time of Elizabeth I. The orders for Drake's fleet in 1589 and the "Brief Notes" of John Young around 1596 both contain statements to this effect. The hour at which the ceremony took place is not stated but those absent without leave at the time were deprived of their aftermeal.

At the end of the eighteenth century the practice was as follows:

> "At sunrise every ship in the fleet hoists her colours viz. the ensign and jack, unless it blows hard and the yards and topmasts are struck, in which case the colours are not hoisted but when some vessel is coming in or passing; at half past 7 o'clock the drums begin to beat and continue till 8, when the ship on board which the commander-in-Chief hoists his flag, fires a gun."[1]

It is not known when the hoisting of colours at sunrise was first introduced, but it was not before the seventeenth century. In 1844 the time was changed to 8 a.m. from 25 March to 20 September and 9 a.m. from 21 September to 24 March. If there was sufficient light for the ensign to be seen, it was hoisted earlier or later than these hours when the ship was coming to an anchor, getting under way, passing or meeting another ship, approaching a fort or town, etc.

It was certainly the custom in the early nineteenth century for the ratings hoisting the colours to doff their head-dress as a mark of respect, but this form of salute was subsequently dropped.

In the early part of the twentieth century the custom was partly revived but, since the procedure to be followed depended upon local orders it consequently varied from station to station. Queen's Regulations and Admiralty Instructions for the Royal Navy, printed in 1954, stated that "Men hoisting and lowering the colours are to remove their caps and place them by the foot of the ensign staff or mast before the ceremony."

Deportment

Presently, ships alongside in harbour or at anchor carry out the ceremony of 'colours':
(a) At 0800 daily;
(b) At 0800 daily where continuous daylight prevails;
(c) In accordance with local customs when in foreign ports; and
(d) Following the movements of the senior officer present.

Where 'colours' is not conducted at 0800, the orders for the striking of the ship's bell are to be amended accordingly.

The personnel required for the ceremony of 'colours' are as follows:
(a) The officer of the day/watch, (OOD)/(OOW)
(b) The quartermaster/corporal of the gangway;
(c) Bo's'n's mate;
(d) A man for the preparative pennant;
(e) A man for the jack; and
(f) A man for the ensign.

Personnel are mustered ten minutes prior to the ceremony to ensure that each is familiar with the procedures. The OOD ensures that they are in their proper positions before the preparative pennant is hoisted.

Five minutes before the ceremony of colours the senior officer present hoists the preparative pennant, and all ships follow suit. At 'colours' the 'prep' is dipped (lowered about four feet), and the man detailed to handle the ship's ensign salutes and reports "Eight o'clock, Sir." The OOD will respond "Make it so," and the bo's'n's mate of the

2.01 Positions to be manned for the ceremony of 'colours'. 1. Jack. 2. Prep. 3. Bell. 4. OOD/QM. 5. Ensign.

inboard ship of the nest strikes the appropriate number of bells. On completion of the striking of the bell, the OOD instructs the quartermaster to "Pipe the still." The bo's'n's mate pipes "Attention on the upper deck, face aft" on the upperdeck broadcast, and those detailed respectfully hoist the ship's ensign and jack.

When the 'prep' is hauled down, the man on the ensign salutes and reports "Carry on, Sir." The OOD then orders the carry on to be piped by the quartermaster, and the bo's'n's mate pipes "Carry on" on the broadcast. (Neither the 'still' or 'carry on' is piped by any ship before it is sounded by the senior ship present.)

2.02 Position of the ensign on completion of the ceremony of 'colours'.

Ships of destroyer size do not normally parade guards at 'colours.' However, if the occasion arises, the procedure is as follows:
(a) The guard is composed of: One Slt or Lt(N); One petty officer; Twenty-four LS and below maximum, or twelve LS and below minimum.
(b) The guard is assembled in a designated area with bayonets fixed, and are fallen in facing aft in two ranks athwartships.
(c) After assuming command, the guard commander draws his sword, then stands the guard at ease.

(d) Other personnel necessary for 'colours' are fallen in at their appropriate positions.
(e) At one minute to 'colours,' the guard is brought to attention, and their arms are shouldered.
(f) When the 'prep' is brought to the 'dip,' the inboard ship sounds the appropriate number of bells, the alert is sounded by a bugler, or the 'still' is piped, and the guard presents arms.
(g) When the 'carry on' is sounded, the guard shoulders arms, then orders arms, unfixes bayonets and is dismissed.[2]

Half-masting

Unless special instructions are received, all flags are half-masted on all HMC ships on the death of:
(a) The Sovereign;
(b) A member of the Royal Family related in the first degree to the sovereign (i.e., husband or wife, son or daughter, father or mother, brother or sister);
(c) The Governor General, and
(d) A federal cabinet minister.
Within a province, unless special instructions are received, all flags are half-masted on all HMC ships on the death of:
(a) The Lieutenant Governor, and
(b) The Provincial Premier.
The honours listed above are accorded from the day of death until sunset the day of the funeral.

The national flag, ensign, ship's ensign and jack, as appropriate, are flown at half-mast in all HMC ships upon hoisting until 1120 hours on 11 November (Remembrance Day). In addition, they are flown at half-mast when ordered by National Defense Headquarters or a command headquarters and during the funeral of a service member being held at a particular unit or in a ship.

HMC ships approaching or leaving port or an anchorage where any other ship of war has its colours at half-mast must, while within sight of that ship, half-mast their own colours.

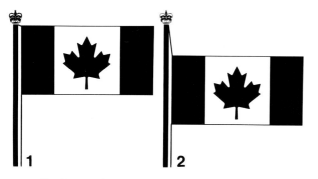

2.03   Position of the ensign when half-masted. 1. Close-up.
2. Half-masted.

Dress-ship occasions, when extraordinary circumstances require ships to half-mast their colours, are:

(a) Dressing lines are lowered;
(b) Ship's ensigns and jacks are half-masted, and mast-head flags are hauled down;
(c) Ships under way half-mast their ensigns and jacks, and haul down their masthead flags; and
(d) In foreign ports, local custom is adhered to.

Personal and distinguishing flags continue to be displayed whether underway or not on occasions when colours are half-masted.

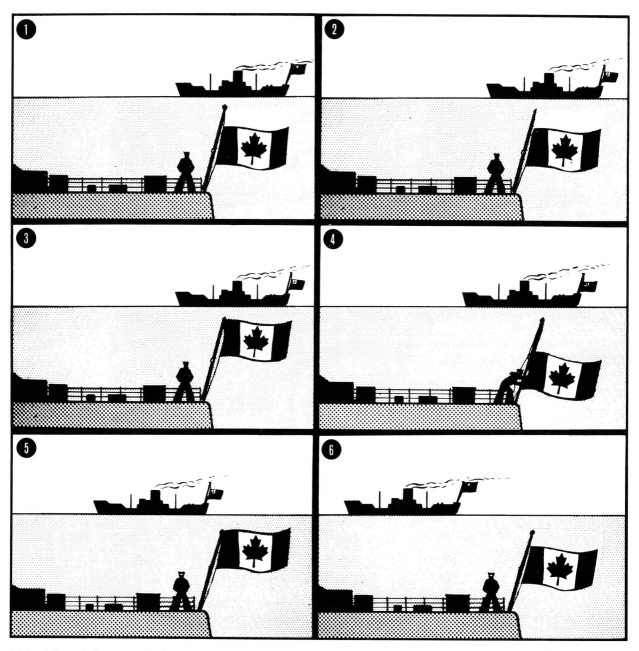

2.04   Acknowledgement of salutes from merchant vessels. 1. Ensign half-masted. 2. Passing ship dips. 3. Ship's ensign hoisted. 4. Ship's ensign dipped. 5. Ship's ensign re-hoisted. 6. Ship's ensign half-masted.

On occasions when the national flag is flown at half-mast, the ensign, if flown, is also half-masted, as is the jack.

The boat's ensign is worn at half-mast on all occasions and in any waters when:

(a) A body is being conveyed in a boat, and

(b) The ship's colours are at half-mast.

HMC ships whose colours are at half-mast acknowledges salutes by merchant vessels. The ship's ensign is hoisted close up, dipped, rehoisted close up, and then half-masted.[3]

Sunset

The shipboard ceremony of 'sunset' entails the lowering of the ship's ensign and jack.

HMC ships alongside in harbour, or at anchor, carry out the ceremony of 'sunset':

(a) At the calculated time of sunset;

(b) At 1700 daily where continuous daylight or darkness prevails; and

(c) In accordance with local custom when in foreign ports.

The personnel required for this ceremony are the same as those for 'colours,' with the exception of the duty electrician, whose job is to switch on aircraft warning lights and upper-deck lighting when the 'carry on' has been sounded.

The procedure is similar to the ceremony of 'colours,' except that no bells are sounded, flags are lowered instead of hoisted, and the appropriate lighting is provided upon completion.

II
Tattoo, Retreat and Sunset Ceremony

The 'tattoo, retreat and sunset' ceremony of the Canadian Navy is a composite of customs whose history and traditions go back several hundred years, although the complete ceremony as we know it is of fairly recent origin.

The climax of the ceremony is the lowering of the national flag or ensign, to the accompaniment of the orchestrated sunset call. This is a ceremonial version of a daily custom observed in all naval shore establishments and ships in harbour.

The form of the ceremony today remains esentially the same as that followed in the early 1600s. The band was added for effect.

Deportment

The band and two field guns march on towards the dais. The band counter-marches and the guns take up their positions. The band then returns to a position immediately ahead of the guard. The evening gun is then fired. This is the signal for the 'tattoo' to begin, and upon completion the trumpeters sound the first post.

Next comes the 'retreat.' The guard and band march past the dais and the salute is made to the reviewing officer. The guard and band carry out precision drill, fixing bayonets on the march, taking up the final position in the centre of the review ground for the proving of rifles.

Following the proving of rifles, the evening hymn is played. After the guard has fixed bayonets and shouldered arms, the band plays the orchestrated sunset, or retreat call. The ensign is slowly lowered. As the guard comes to the final movement of the present arms, a broadside is fired and the band plays "O Canada" and "God Save the Queen." On the last note of "God Save the Queen," the guard is ordered to shoulder arms and the final gun is fired to signify the end of the ceremony.

The guard is then ordered to form threes, the

2.05 Ottawa, 1 July, 1961. The band, saluting guns' crew and guard move onto the review ground.

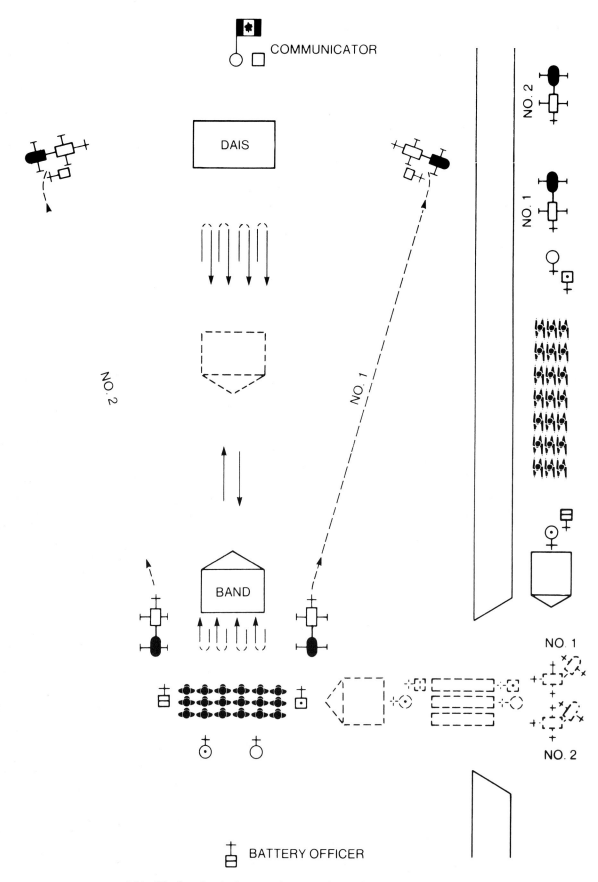

COMMUNICATOR

DAIS

NO. 2

BAND

NO. 1

NO. 2

NO. 1

NO. 2

BATTERY OFFICER

2.06   The band, saluting guns' crew and guard move toward the dais.

guns' crews limber up and form the order of march. The guard officer orders the 'quick march' and the units move off the review ground in that order.

The personnel requirements for this ceremony are:

Officers: One lieutenant(N) and one commissioned officer or one sub-lieutenant; one lieutenant(N) or sub-lieutenant bandmaster.

Battery officer (Saluting guns): One chief petty officer 2nd class or one petty officer 1st class.

Guides: Two petty officers 1st class.

Gun captains: Two petty officers 1st class or two petty officers 2nd class.

Guard: 48 men

Saluting guns crew: Maximum 32 per gun (with reverse drag ropes fitted); minumum 20 per gun; 5 men — firing guns' crews.

Band: As available — maximum of 50.

Communicator.

Phase One: The Ceremony

The band, saluting guns' crews, and guard march onto the review ground, moving toward the dais.

The band continues straight ahead and the guns' crews, just before reaching the mid-point of the area, wheel half right and half left.

On reaching their respective corners, the guns' crews take round (wheel the guns and limber in such a manner as to have the gun barrel pointing in the required direction) and mark time.

The band, having countermarched in front of the dais, signals crews to halt. This is done on the battery commander's signal to the bass drummer. The guns' crews halt and carry out the drill for loading. The band continues to march until it reaches the guard, then countermarches once more and halts. The guard, on reaching the centre walk, halts, turns into line and dresses. An order is given to "Halt," but dressing is done automatically.

2.07   Guns' crews have wheeled half left and right; band countermarches in front of the dais.

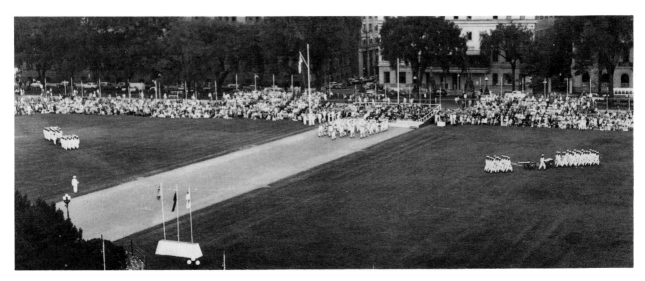

2.08   Band has countermarched. Guns' crews move to their respective areas of the review ground.

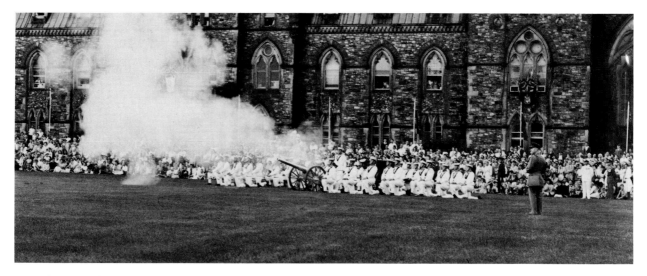

2.09   Firing of the evening gun.

The final movement of the "Band — halt" is the signal for one gun to fire the 'evening gun' (one shot).

Phase Two: The Tattoo

During the late seventeenth century the British troops of King William III were stationed in the Lowlands. As was the practice in those days, active operations ceased in the late autumn, with the troops of the rebel forces going into billets in the towns and villages in and around the battle fields. For these troops, the social centres of the towns were the inns and taverns, which the majority visited during the long evenings. To induce the soldiers to return to their billets at the end of the evening it was necessary to get them out of the inns. The best way was to have the innkeepers turn off their beer taps and stop selling spirits to the troops. The time for doing this was between 9:30 and 10 p.m. and at that time a drummer was sent marching through the streets beating a warning call for the revellers. The sound of the drums was also the signal for the innkeepers to close down. The old Dutch expression for this closure was "doe den tap toe" which freely translated into English is "shut off the taps." Although no one is quite sure of the origins of the word "tattoo," the consensus is that the Dutch phrase was shortened to "taptoe" by the British, and that by constant use the pronunciation of "taptoe" has changed to "tattoo."

The 'evening gun' begins the tattoo.

On the evening gun, the drum major and the drummers step off at the quick march, advance ten paces and then countermarch. They march back through the band, breaking into the slow march. When the drum major and drummers go completely through the band they countermarch once again and break into the quick march.

The countermarching of the band places the drummers behind the trumpeters who will play the first post to mark the end of the tattoo phase of the sunset ceremony.

After the drummers break into the quick march, the buglers step off, arriving in front of the drummers and one pace ahead of the drum major.

At a given signal, the drum major, drummers and buglers halt. The buglers incline inwards and play the 'first post.'

This is the end of the 'tattoo' phase, and the ceremony now moves on to the third phase, or the 'retreat.'

Phase Three: Retreat

Beating 'retreat' is one of the oldest ceremonies in either Canadian or British military tradition. The origin of the ceremony is obscure but it is believed to date back into the sixteenth century. The first reference to it appears in the military records of 1554.

Some historians, however, maintain that the ceremony began during the Crusades. At that time it was the custom to cease fighting at dusk and resume at dawn. The warriors were called back to the camp by a roll of the drums. When firearms were introduced into warfare, bugles were added to the signal, as the drums alone were confused with the gunfire.

The ceremony carried out today closely follows that of the sixteenth century. The towns and villages in those days were fortified with walls and moats, outside of which the inhabitants raised their crops and grazed their cattle and sheep. At sunset a call was sounded on the trumpet or bugle. This was the 'retreat call' which summoned the guard to be paraded for the night and also served as a warning to those outside the walls to return to the safety of the fortress. After darkness fell, the gates were closed to all. This

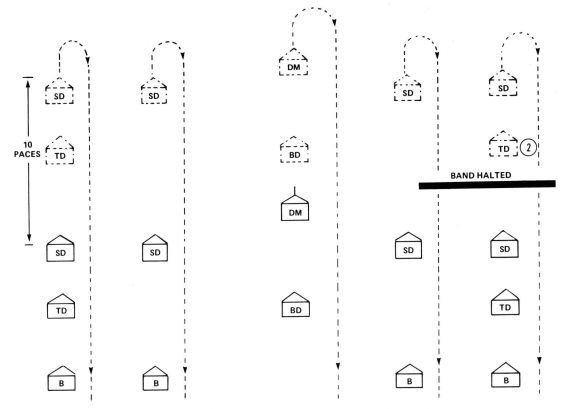

2.10   Band halts, snare and trap drummers countermarch.

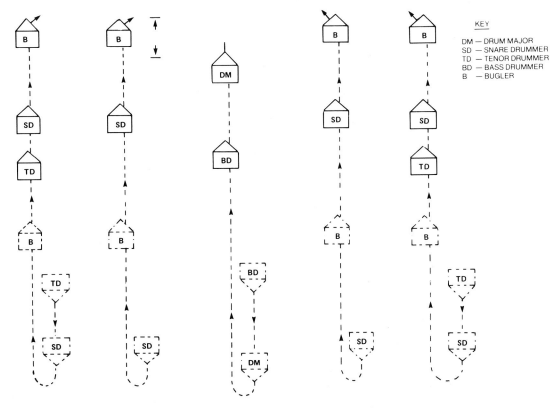

2.11   Buglers and drummers halted.

KEY

DM — DRUM MAJOR
SD — SNARE DRUMMER
TD — TENOR DRUMMER
BD — BASS DRUMMER
B   — BUGLER

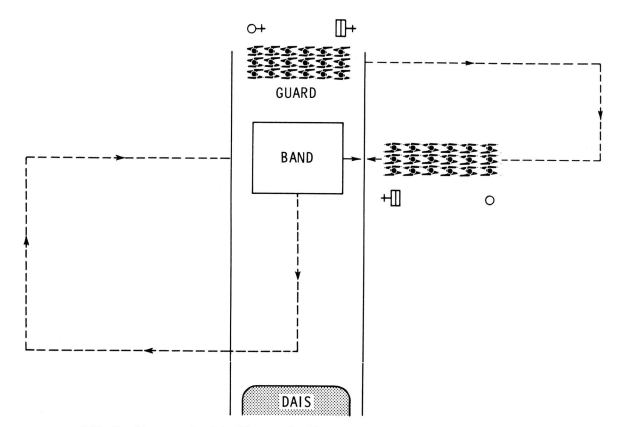

2.12 Band has completed the "first post", and steps off with the guard for the march past.

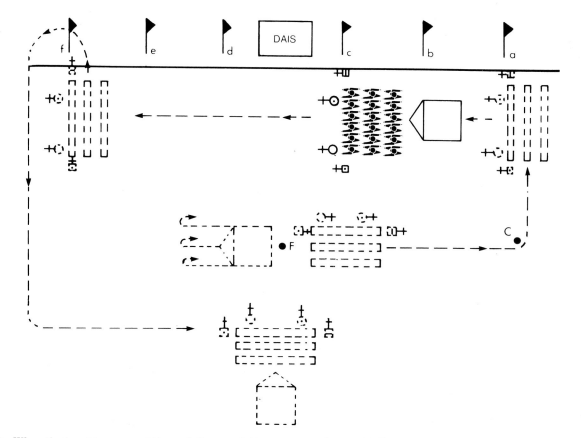

2.13 When the band has passed through the guard, it countermarches and follows the guard round for the march past.

2.14   Band moves to its position in the rear of the guard.

2.15   The march past as seen from the reviewing stand.

2.16   The march past as seen from No. 2 saluting gun.

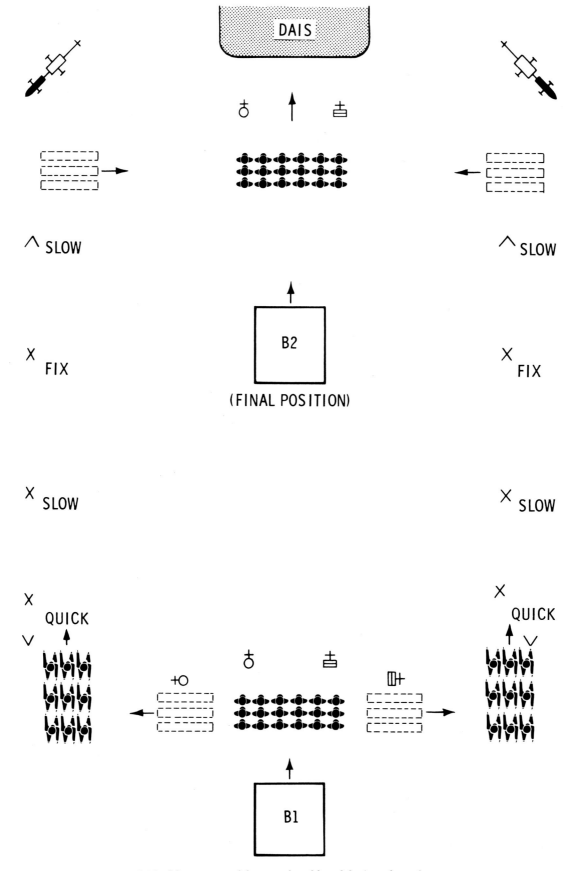

2.17 Movements of the guard and band during phase four.

2.18   Band and guard in position in front of the reviewing stand.

procedure was also followed in the early settlements of Canada, and anyone unfortunate enough to be left outside the walls after dark was in grave danger of being attacked by lurking Indians.

In today's ceremony, when the 'first post' is completed, the guard and band step off, and the buglers countermarch to take up their allocated positions in the rear of the drums.

The band makes a right wheel, marches to the edge of the reviewing ground and right wheels twice more. During this time, the guard has stepped off and wheeled right twice and opened the ranks sufficiently to allow the band to march through the ranks of the guard.

On completion of the march past, the guard marches down the left side of the parade site and then wheels left to take up position at the rear of the parade area, centred on the dais. The band marches past, then moves to a position in rear of the guard facing the dais.

Phase Four: Subsection Drill

The guard, having previously numbered in two equal sections, performs the drill as follows: (All movements are carried out to drum signals during this phase).

The snare drummer gives a roll on his drum, followed by a single beat on the bass drum. At this signal, half sections turn right and left, dwell a pause of two marching paces and step off at the quick march for a distance of 20 paces. Both sections then turn to face the dais and mark time for four paces. During the four mark-time paces, both sections form two deep and step off on the fifth beat, which is on the left foot. They advance toward the dais for six paces. The bass drummer then signals the sections to break into the slow march. They march at the slow for six paces and commence 'fix bayonets,' on the march. The

fixing of bayonets on the march takes a total of 16 paces. On completion of the 'fix,' the sections carry on for six further paces at the slow march, and at the signal from the bass, break into the quick march. They carry on at the quick for 16 paces, mark time for four paces, turn inwards, mark time for two paces, and step off towards each other. When both sections meet in the centre abreast the dais, they halt at a drum signal, dwell a pause of two marching paces, turn towards the dais, dwell a further pause of two marching paces and dress.

The band remains at the halt, playing until the sub-sections have stepped off at the quick march after fixing bayonets. They then step off to take up a position in rear of the guard.

Phase Five: Proving Rifles

The sub-section drill of the previous phase has now formed the guard into two ranks. For the proving of rifles, the guard officer separates the two ranks by ordering the 'open order.' After the guard is dressed to half arm intervals, the guard officer orders bayonets unfixed, volleys loaded and rifles presented.

The drummers give a roll on their drums, the battery officer fires No. 1 gun.

When the field gun fires, the right guard fires his rifle. The remainder of the guard fire in sequence, along the front rank to the left, then along the rear rank to the right.

This movement is carried out three times in sequence — load, present, drum roll, field gun, fire. On completion of the third 'ripple firing,' the guard officer orders the guard to unload, order their arms and stand at ease.

2.19   No. 1 gun fires.

2.20   The guard at the "present arms", preparing to prove rifles.

Phase Six: The Evening Hymn

The band now plays an appropriate hymn, e.g., "The Day Thou Gavest Lord Is Ended." On completion of the hymn, the guard officer orders the guard to fix bayonets.

Phase Seven: Sunset

The communicator reports to the guard officer at one minute before the time of sunset. At that time, the guard officer orders the guard to shoulder their rifles.

At the report "Sunset, Sir," the band begins to play the orchestrated sunset. At the seventh measure of music, the bass drummer makes an accentuated beat on his drum. This is the signal for the guard officer to order the guard to present arms.

On the last movement of the present, the battery officer fires one gun. The band completes playing the orchestrated sunset. This is followed by "O Canada" and "God Save The Queen," each separated by drum rolls.

Phase Eight: Moving Off

At the conclusion of "God Save The Queen," the guard officer orders the guard to shoulder their arms. On the last movement of the shoulder the battery officer fires one broadside. This marks the end of the ceremony. The officer of the guard orders the guard to return to the close order. When this is ordered, the guns' crews limber up and form the order of the march.

The guns' crews step out or step short as necessary to permit the exit of units in the order guard, band and guns' crews.

2.21 The guard at the "present arms" during the lowering of the flag.

2.22 The guard, band and guns' crews leave the reviewing ground.

2.23 The gun carriage and limber with a full gun's crew in the drag ropes.

III
Divisions and Evening Quarters

Divisions — The Ship's Company

Before 1100 A.D. warships were open rowing boats of about 50 tons, fitted with a mast on which was hoisted a square sail. Because they could carry only a limited number of men, those in charge were easily able to see to the well-being and security of each crew member. However, by the early part of the eighteenth century, ships carried six or seven hundred men who were divided into two watches without the officers being assigned any particular responsibility over them. This failure to supervise the men, except by the bo's'n's mates, made conditions of dirt, disease and misery inevitable.

From about the middle of the century, however, thoughtful commanders began to organise their ships' companies in divisions commanded by lieutenants. Vice-Admiral Thomas Smith, who commanded the squadron in the Downs in 1755, gave comprehensive orders on supervision to his captains, although he was not formally authorized to do so by the Admiralty.

His orders read as follows:

"By Thomas Smith Esquire Vice-Admiral of the White Squadron of his Majesty's Fleet and Commander in Chief of His Majesty's Ships and Vessels employed and to be employed in the Downs.

For the more effectual keeping clean the men belonging to His Majesty's Ship under your command which must greatly conduce to their health — you are hereby required and directed to observe the following instructions.

Divide the midshipmen and those acting as such into as many parties as you have lieutenants.

Put one of those parties under the direction of each of the lieutenants.

Divide the rest of your ship's company (carpenter's crew, gunner's crew, quartermasters, other inferior petty officers, boat's crews and boys, excepted) into as many parties as you have lieutenants, and put one of those parties under charge of each lieutenant.

Each lieutenant to take an account of the clothing and bedding of each man in his party, and report the same to you, keeping an account of the same himself.

Each lieutenant to subdivide his party of men into as many smaller parties as there are midshipmen allotted to him, giving an inventory to each midshipman of the clothes and bedding belonging to each man whom he has put into the said midshipman's party.

Let each midshipman's party consist as near as possible of proportional numbers of able seamen, ordinary and land-men, to the intent that if men are wanted to be detached on any service from the ship, the detachments may be made by one or more parties; by which means the men who are not seamen will sooner become so, and all will be kept in better order by being immediately under the eye and direction of the officer they are accustomed to; and for the same reason let the parties be divided, both for half watch and third watch, as near as possible.

Given under my hand onboard His Majesty's Ship *Oxford* in the Downs this 13th Novr., 1755."[4]

The divisional system became widespread in the American War (1775-1783). A scheme similar to Smith's was introduced by Lord Howe on taking command in North America at the beginning of the war. The pertinent portion read as follows:

Instructions and standing Orders for the General Government and Discipline of ships of War.

"Preamble:

Whereas an uniform system of discipline established in this squadron would be productive of many essential benefits; the subsequent regulations, prepared in that view, are to be conformed to, and continue in force till further order.

2nd

To form the ships' companies into divisions and sub-divisions.

The petty officers and seamen of the ships' companies are to be formed into two or three divisions, according to the complement and classes of the ships, each division to be under the inspection of a lieutenant and subdivided into squads, with a midshipman appointed to each, who are respectively to be responsible for the good order and discipline of the men entrusted to their care."[5]

In 1779, Admiral Richard Kempenfelt outlined the organization as it has more or less applied since then:

"The only way to keep large bodies of men in order is by dividing and subdividing them, with officers over each to inspect, regulate their conduct, to discipline and form them. Let the ship's company be divided into as many companies as there are lieutenants, except the First Lieutenant, whose care should extend over the whole. These companies to be subdivided and put under the charge of mates and midshipmen, and besides this, every twenty-five men to have a foreman to assist in the care of the men, as a sergeant or corporal in the Army."[6]

Of course, simply dividing the ship's company, under the supervision of lieutenants, was not enough to make the system work. Weekly inspections were introduced to ensure that all the men were properly dressed and that they were still in possession of all their issued kit. It was also necessasry for the commander of each party to be present during training, and whenever possible to take charge of the training himself. These points were specifically mentioned both in Vice-admiral Smith's and Lord Howe's orders.

Today, the ship's company is still divided into 'divisions.' This is done on the basis of the individual's trade, so that all bo's'ns are in the 'deck division,' all administrative and supply personnel are in the 'supply department'; and so on. The tradition of the weekly inspections is now carried on in the form of the mustering of the ship's company (a muster is referred to as 'divisions').

Ceremonial divisions in HMC ships today encompasses inspections by various dignitaries, an Admiral's (or his representative's) post work-up inspection, re-activation after refit, 'commissioning' or 'paying off,' or any other occasion where the commanding officer inspects his ship's company.

The procedure for these divisions varies slightly depending on circumstances, and whether or not divisions are being held on the ship itself, or on the jetty or in another building. On occasions when the ship's company is required to muster for the 'ceremony of divisions,' they will normally fall in on the quarterdeck in *DDE*'s and on the flight deck in *DDH*'s and *AOR*'s. Divisions fall in as follows:

(a) Combat dept. — Port side, facing inboard
(b) Combat systems eng. dept. — Port side, facing inboard
(c) Deck dept. — Port side, facing inboard
(d) Marine eng. dept. — Starboard side, facing inboard
(e) Logistics dept. — Starboard side, facing inboard
(f) Administration dept. — Starboard side, facing inboard

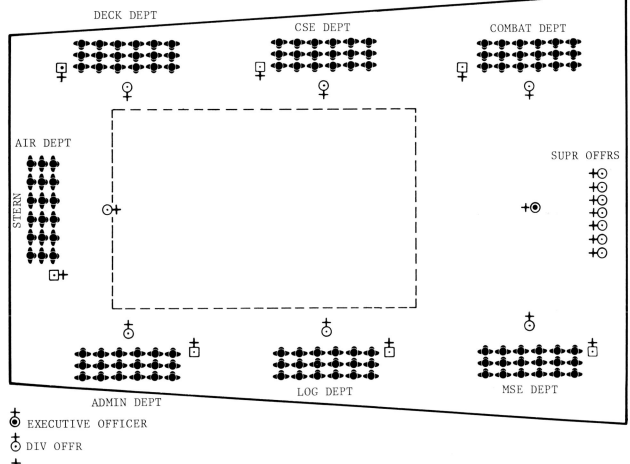

EXECUTIVE OFFICER

DIV OFFR

DEPT CO-ORD

2.24 A typical ship's company at divisions.

2.25 Ship's company of HMCS *Restigouche* at ceremonial divisions for their ship's re-activation after refit.

(g) Air dept. — Aft athwart ships, facing forward
(h) Supernumery officers — Forward, athwartships, facing aft

Men of the rank of petty officer second class (P2) and above fall in at the right flank of each department in the same number of ranks as the master seamen and below. In ships without an air department, the divisions are re-organized so as to form the three sides of a square on the quarterdeck.

When ceremonial divisions are piped, divisional petty officers fall in their divisions at designated locations. Each division falls in, in two or three ranks according to the space available, facing inboard. After falling in, each division is numbered, sized, open ordered and stood at ease.

When the division officer approaches the division, the petty officer comes to attention and orders the division to attention. Once he has taken command of the division, the divisional officer, accompanied by the divisional petty officer, inspects the division. When the inspection is completed, the divisional officer reports his division to the executive officer.

On the arrival of the commanding officer, the executive officer calls the ship's company to attention and reports the divisions to the commanding officer. Divisions are then inspected by the commanding officer/executive officer.

After the completion of the inspection, awards and presentations are made, and a prayer service may be conducted by either a chaplain, the commanding officer or a selected officer.

Following the prayer service, the executive officer reports to the commanding officer, and if the CO does not wish to address the ship's company, he will depart. When the commanding officer has departed, the executive officer dismisses the officers, then the chiefs and petty officers, and then finally the remainder of the ship's company.

The normal routine for ceremonial divisions is expanded somewhat for occasions such as the Admiral's inspection. This ceremonial inspection consists of inspection of a guard and the ship's company, rounds and an address to the ship's company. It is scheduled immediately following the ship's combat readiness inspection, at a date mutually convenient to the Admiral and the ship's programme.

Within HMC ships and naval establishments, it is not always possible to mount the size of guard required by ceremonial protocol. In these instances, a petty officer's guard is used. This guard consists of:
(a) A petty officer second class
(b) A master seaman or leading seamen
(c) Twelve able or ordinary seamen.

When the Admiral (or his representative) arrives, the guard presents arms and the band, if present, plays the musical salute. The petty officer reports to the inspecting officer that the guard is ready for inspection, and then accompanies the inspecting officer on the inspection. After inspecting the guard, the reviewing officer inspects the remainder of the ship's company. In the past, the divisional officer would not only state his own name and ship's duties, but also the rank, trade group and name of each man in his division.

When the inspecting officer has completed his inspection of the remainder of the ship's company, and when prayers are completed, presentations are made. The inspecting officer addresses the ship's company, and then departs to make rounds of the ship.

Rounds are conducted as for normal captain's rounds. All departments and parts of the ship are made ready with the appropriate personnel standing by.

2.26 Rear-admiral W. A. Hughes, CD, RCN, CF, conducts rounds during the Admiral's ceremonial inspection.

On completion of rounds, the Admiral returns to the captain's cabin to sign the ship's books.

Daily divisions are the same as the captain's ceremonial divisions except that the captain does not conduct an inspection.

Evening Quarters

'Evening quarters' have for many years been conducted in the same fashion as daily divisions. They used to be the exercise of all the ships 'divisions' at their action stations. The RN Fighting Instructions of 1530 through 1550 described 'evening quarters' thus:

"... about 5 o'clock the drummer beats to quarters. Every person in the ship, from the captain to the smallest boy in the ship, repairs to his station. The first division is quartered on the upper deck, i.e., to say on the quarter-deck and the forecastle, and is under the immediate command to the first lieutenant. The second division is quartered to the seven aftermost guns on the main deck, and the third division is quartered to the seven foremost guns on the same deck, and are under the inspection of the second and third lieutenants. The men of these divisions have to see all things ready and clear for action. There is a captain, a sponger and boarder, a fireman and a sail trimmer to each gun. The captain of the gun has to fight her, or fire her off; the sponger and boarder [one person] has to sponge the gun in action and to be ready to board the enemy's vessel; the fireman with his bucket is to attend in case of fire; the sail trimmers are to trim the sails when required. There are also pumpers and swabbers, who pump out the ship, or free her from water, in case of a leak springing in action. The powder men or boys are those who supply the guns with powder; there are also some on the lower deck who pass along the powder from the magazine up to the powder men on the upper deck.

Some of the marines are quartered to the great guns, the rest to the small arms, their lieutenant commanding them. The carpenter and two or three of his crew attend about the pumps and wings of the ship. The station of the gunner and his mates is in the magazines, to issue powder, etc. There are men stationed in the different tops to repair defects in the rigging, etc., as well as they can in time of action. A good and experienced quarter-master steers the ship; the mate of the ship conns. An old seaman is stationed to the relieving tackles down in the gunroom, to steer the ship in case the tiller ropes are shot away. The order how to steer in such cases is given him through a wooden tube which is fixed through the deck.

When exercising, the crew go regularly through all the manoeuvers as if actually engaging a foe, (except firing, of course). If they should be engaged in real battle, that exception would soon be cast to one side. After the drum has beat to quarters and everyone mustered thereat, and all the officers reported to the first lieutenant and he to the captain, the retreat is beat."[7]

'Evening quarters' as described here, including a simple divisional inspection, are no longer held in HMC ships.

IV
The Launching of a Ship

Throughout recorded history ship launchings have been accompanied by some sort of ceremony. Religion has played a large part in launching ceremonies; it seems that sailors long ago viewed a ship's launching very much like the baptism of a newborn child. The ceremony is also probably related to the superstition of appeasing the deities that ruled the weather.

There are three traditional ceremonies common to the building of ships. These are: keel laying; launching and naming (christening); and commissioning.

'Launching' and 'naming' ceremonies are

essentially the responsibility of the builders, since the ship has not yet been turned over to the Department of National Defence. The responsibility for commissioning ceremonies lies with National Defence Headquarters.

Keel Laying Ceremony

The 'keel-laying' ceremony is an informal affair arranged, for the most part, by the ship's builders. After invited guests have arrived, a representative of the yard gives a short address. A section of the keel is then lowered into place, and the sponsor declares the keel "well and truly laid."

While there is no presentation made to the builders or the sponsors today, there are recorded instances of added ceremony, including the presentation of mementoes.

A short article in the *Illustrated London News* describes the building of the *Meanee* line-of-battle ship at Bombay in 1848 and the attendant ceremonies:

> "The...ceremony of driving the silver nail into the keel was performed in November.... The ceremony consists of driving a silver nail with a silver hammer, with sundry invocations in the native tongue, calling for the blessing of the Almighty on the future ship. The head builder immediately afterwards covers the head of the nail with a wooden plug. The ceremony concludes by the Governor conferring a present of shawls upon the master builder and his two chief assistants."[8]

Other items such as silver hammers or 'plates' were given to the master shipwrights for building new ships.

Deportment

Today, when a keel is laid, an appropriate ceremony is arranged with the ship builder. The 'keel-laying' ceremony usually follows this procedure:

(a) The guests arrive at the ways;
(b) Representatives of the builder address the guests;
(c) A section of the keel is lowered into place;
(d) The sponsor declares the keel to be "well and truly laid"; and
(e) A blessing is then asked for the ship such as the following prayer used by Dep. Chaplain General C.H. MacLean in 1967:

> "They that go down to the sea in ships, that do business in great waters; these see the works of the Lord and His wonders in the deep.
>
> Oh! that men would praise the Lord for His goodness, and His wonderful works to the children of men.
>
> Brethren, we are met here today to lay the keel of a new ship. Seeing that in the course of her duties she may be set in many and great

dangers, let us unite our prayers and praises in seeking the blessing of Almighty God upon all who work to build her; that they may build faithfully and well and when she comes to sail upon the sea, she may sail safely and be a happy haven to all who sail in her.
>
> Prayer:
>
> Almighty God, the Sovereign Lord of all the Earth, Who art the wise Creator and Master Builder of all things; we praise Thee for the vision of men who design fine ships and the craftsmen who build them. Give them, we pray Thee, pride in their labours and integrity in their craft, so that when this ship shall stand complete in all her strength and beauty, those who sail in her may commit themselves to the dangers and perils of the deep with a sure confidence in those who have laboured well and with a certain trust in all Thy mercies, Who alone canst bring us to our desired havens: and this we pray for Christ's sake, Amen."[9]

Naming a Ship

With the possible exception of the mythical *Argo* of Jason, no records of actually naming a ship appear until about the third century A.D. Certain passages from Herodotus and Plutarch, and the Biblical reference to the ship in which Paul sailed from Melita as having the "sign of Castor and Pollux," have been interpreted as referring to names, but the interpretation seems unreliable. In the Homeric catalogue of the *Iliads*, ships are simply identified by the tribes who manned them. Even in Britain as late as the twelfth century, "the ship of John de Weymouth" or "the cog of Thomas de Dunewic" sufficed for identification. However, by the middle of the thirteenth century, the custom of naming became general, and unnamed British ships became the exceptions. The names were generally secular rather than religious.

Before World War II warships of Commonwealth Navies and, since then, several other Navies, were named after former ships of great achievement or after naval heroes. This has become traditional and has much practical value, for the following reasons:

(a) The ship's company learn of the deeds and sacrifices of predecessors and this stimulates pride in the service and 'espirit de corps'; and
(b) Artifacts belonging to a previous ship and the attendance at a commissioning ceremony by members of that ship's company or their descendants add prestige and dignity to the ship and the occasion.

In the Royal Navy, the origin of naming ships can be traced back as far as the early thirteenth century. During the Tudor period, however, the practice became common. HMS *Fortune,* for example, was the name given to a ship in 1512. There have been twenty-three other *Fortunes,* the latest becoming HMCS *Saskatchewan* in 1943. Other famous names include *Revenge, Swiftsure, Tiger, Vanguard, Victory,* and *Warspite.* HMS *Crescent* traces her name back to 1642, and there have been eleven or twelve with that name, the last becoming HMCS *Fraser* in 1937. HMCS *Decoy* traces its ancestry back to 1810, with five ships carrying on the name, the last becoming HMCS *Kootenay* in 1943.

As far as can be determined by the Directorate of History, there has never been an official policy for selecting names. During World War II, however, the Naval Board decided that destroyers were to be named after rivers and that other fighting ships were to be given place names. There were, of course, exceptions which include the tribal class destroyers, the armed yachts and motor craft. The actual selection of names was carried out at a lower level. The names selected were submitted to the Admiralty to avoid duplication, who submitted them to HM the King for approval.

In the case of the Canadian patrol frigate (CPF) and its succesors, the names to be perpetuated were to be the names of former HMC ships in the following order of merit:
(a) HMC frigates lost in action in World War II;
(b) HMC corvettes which were victorious in action and were subsequently lost in action in World War II; and
(c) HMC frigates and below which distinguished themselves in action and through long service in World War II.

A preliminary review of the history of the RCN in World War II, when the above criteria was being applied, shows the order of merit given:
(a) HMCS *Valleyfield* — This was the only Canadian frigate lost in World War II. She served from December 1943 until May 1944 when she was torpedoed off Newfoundland with the loss of 115 officers and men. In recognition of the sacrifice of so many officers and men, it has been proposed that her name be given to the first patrol frigate of the new class.

HMC corvettes which were victorious in action and subsequently lost in action were:
(a) HMCS *Regina* — Served from January 1943 until August 1944. She sank an Italian submarine in the Mediterranean in February 1943. Participated in 'D' Day operations and was torpedoed in the English Channel in August 1944. There were 66 survivors.
(b) HMCS *Alberni* — Served from January 1941 until August 1944, the longest time in action of any of the Canadian corvettes lost in World War II. She shared in the probable destruction of a U-boat, participated in the 'D' Day

operations during which she shot down a German bomber, and was subsequently torpedoed off the Isle of Wight with the loss of 59 officers and men.

Other frigates and corvettes which distinguished themselves in action and through long service were:
(a) HMCS *Swansea* — Served from October 1943 to September 1945. She sank one U-boat and shared in the sinking of two others. She was converted following World War II and was finally paid off in 1966.
(b) HMCS *Saint John* — Served from December 1943 to October 1945. She sank one U-boat and shared in the sinking of another.
(c) HMCS *Saint Catherines* — Served from July 1943 to November 1945. She shared in the sinking of one U-boat. She continued in service after World War II and was paid off in 1950.
(d) HMCS *Calgary* — Served from December 1941 to June 1945. She shared in the sinking of one U-boat and was attacked by glider bombs.
(e) HMCS *Ville de Quebec* — Served from May 1942 to July 1945. She sank one U-boat.
(f) HMCS *Port Arthur* — Served from May 1942 until July 1945. She sank one Italian submarine.

HMC corvettes which were sunk and then commemorated by a second ship of the same name were:
(a) HMCS *Charlottetown* — Served from December 1941 to September 1942 when she was torpedoed off Gaspé. There were 55 survivors. She was replaced by the frigate *Charlottetown* which served from April 1944 to September 1945.
(b) HMCS *Louisburg* — Served from July 1941 to February 1943 when she was sunk by a torpedo bomber off Gibralter. Thirty-eight officers and men were lost. She was replaced by the corvette *Louisburg* which served from December 1943 to June 1945.
(c) HMCS *Levis* — Served from November 1940 to September 1941 when she was torpedoed off Greenland. There were forty survivors. She was replaced by the frigate *Levis* which served from June 1944 to September 1945.

Taking into account the Canadian Naval practice of assigning the '300' series to frigates; secondary naming considerations; the merit of having an existing patron city or community; the value of an association with naval reserve divisions; and the fact that names *St. Catherines* and *Swansea* have been retired more recently then that of other ships, the following hull numbers and names are proposed for the first six ships:

Hull	Name	City/Community
330	HMCS *Valleyfield*	Valleyfield, Quebec
331	HMCS *Regina*	Regina, Saskatchewan
332	HMCS *Alberni*	Port Alberni, B.C.
333	HMCS *Saint John*	Saint John, N.B.
334	HMCS *Calgary*	Calgary, Alberta
335	HMCS *Ville de Quebec*	Quebec City, P.Q.

These names are considered to appropriately commemorate the sacrifices and deeds of the personnel who served in these ships.

It has been suggested also that the CPF and its successors be named after cities containing naval reserve divisions, as follows:

Division	Suggested Ship's Name
HMCS *Queen*	*Regina*
HMCS *Brunswicker*	*Saint John*
HMCS *Montcalm*	*Quebec*
HMCS *Tecumseh*	*Calgary*
HMCS *Chippawa*	*Winnipeg*
HMCS *Nonsuch*	*Edmonton*
HMCS *Donnacona*	*Montreal*
HMCS *Cabot*	*St. John's*
HMCS *Scotian*	*Halifax*
HMCS *Malahat*	*Victoria*
HMCS *Unicorn*	*Saskatoon*
HMCS *Griffin*	*Thunder Bay*
HMCS *Carleton*	*Ottawa*
HMCS *Cataraqui*	*Kingston*
HMCS *York*	*Toronto*
HMCS *Hunter*	*Windsor*
HMCS *Discovery*	*Vancouver*

The first four have already been discussed; the following information is provided with for the remainder:

(a) HMCS *Winnipeg* — An Algerine class minesweeper which served from July 1943 to January 1946. She served as a senior officer's ship in both Escort Group W6 and W5. She was paid off into the reserve in Esquimalt in 1945, but returned to the east coast in 1956, and in 1959 was transferred to the Belgian Navy.

(b) *Edmonton* — There was no Canadian warship of that name in World War II.

(c) HMCS *Montreal* — A frigate which served from November 1943 to October 1945. She joined Escort Group C-4 and was employed continuously on convoy duty until 1944. She then joined Escort Group 26 and in December 1944 rescued survivors of U-1209 wrecked on Wolf Rock southwest of Land's End.

(d) *St. John's* — There was no Canadian warship of that name in World War II. Newfoundland names were not commemorated in any of HMC ships since the province was not then part of Canada. Similarity to the name St. John suggests need for another name, possibly *Avalon*, in commemoration of the World

War II naval base in St. John's.

(e) HMCS *Halifax* — A corvette which served from November 1941 to July 1945. She was the first RCN corvette to be completed with a long fo'c'sle. Her service was spent both in escorting convoys from Aruba and Trinidad until in 1944 she joined Escort Group C-9. She was sold for conversion to a salvage vessel.

(f) *Victoria* — There was no Canadian warship of that name in World War II. HMCS *Victoriaville* was named after a town in Quebec. HMCS *Beaconhill* was considered to be the city of Victoria's ship. HMCS *Esquimalt*, a Bangor class minesweeper, was in service from October 1942 until April 1945 when she was torpedoed and sunk in the Halifax approaches with a loss of 39 officers and men — the last casualty of World War II. It has been proposed therefore, that the Victoria ship be HMCS *Esquimalt*, which coincides with the current location of HMCS *Malahat*.

(g) HMCS *Saskatoon* — A corvette which saw service from June 1941 to July 1945. She served as a member of Escort Groups W-8 and W-6. After paying off, she was sold for conversion to a whale-catcher.

(h) *Thunder Bay*/HMCS *Thunder* — A Bangor class minesweeper which saw service from October 1941 to October 1945. She participated in sweeping the assault lanes for 'D' Day, and the approaches to Cherbourg and Bordeaux. She also assisted in boarding a German trawler.

(i) HMCS *Ottawa* — The first destroyer of that name was torpedoed and sunk in September 1942 with a loss of 5 officers and 109 men. The second ship of that name shared in the sinking of three U-boats, and the third is still in commission.

(j) HMCS *Toronto* — She was a frigate which saw service between May 1944 and September 1945. She was employed principally in operations in the Halifax area.

(k) *Windsor* — There was no Canadian warship of that name in World War II.

(l) HMCS *Vancouver* — The first ship of that name was a pre-World War II destroyer paid off in 1936. The second ship of that name was a corvette which saw service from March 1942 to June 1945. She served on the west coast and was principally employed in escort work between Kodiak and Dutch Harbour.

Taking into account the preceding information, the hull numbers and names proposed for the six ships following those already named are:

Hull	Name	City/Community
336	HMCS *St. Catherines*	St. Catherines, Ont.
337	HMCS *Charlottetown*	Charlottetown, P.E.I.

338	HMCS *Esquimalt*	Victoria, B.C.
339	HMCS *Halifax*	Halifax, N.S.
340	HMCS *Avalon*	St. John's, Nfld.
341	HMCS *Winnipeg*	Winnipeg, Man.[10]

Regardless of the name, reference is always made to a ship as 'she.' The origin of this tradition is difficult to establish. Ships have not always been considered feminine since the prows of Phoenician and Egyptian ships were graced with male animals. The word ship is masculine in French, Italian, Spanish and Portuguese, and has no gender in the Teutonic tongues. During the seventeenth century, vessels were called 'men-of-war,' 'merchantmen,' 'India-men' and the like. An account of the Battle of Agincourt, written in 1426, includes the line "Every ship wayed his anker."[11]

Two well known authorities, though, should perhaps have the last word. Shakespeare, in Act III, Scene 3, of "The Winter's Tale" has a clown observe: "Now the ship boring the moon with her mainmast," and the Bible, in the description of Paul's journeys in Acts XXI, third verse reads: "and sailed into Syria, and landed at Tyre; for there the ship was to unload her burden."

Launching a Ship

The ceremony attendant on launching a ship is very ancient indeed, and has been modified by different civilizations at different times. A Babylonian account of the launching of the Ark, handed down from the year 21 B.C., mentions the sacrifices of two oxen. Icelandic sagas tell of a custom known as *Bluun Rod* or 'roller reddening.' It was the custom that victims were bound to the rollers over which the war-galley was run down to the sea, so that the stern was sprinkled with blood. There is also a parallel for this gruesome practice from the ancient world, for there are references to the Carthaginians launching ships over the dead bodies of Roman soldiers. Captain Cook found similar practices in the South Pacific Islands. In certain parts of India, ships are still launched over pumpkins filled with a mixture of tumeric and vermilion, which burst and splash the hull and spectators with the pigment. This is probably a vestige of the human sacrifice ceremony, whose purpose was to give the ship a symbolic living spirit.

Launching customs among the Greeks and Romans are difficult to establish because of their practice of beaching ships between voyages which make it impossible to distinguish between accounts of launching and those having to do with blessing the seamen and their venture on any particular voyage. It is almost certain, however, that the initial launching ceremony involved the setting up of an altar to one or more of the gods or goddesses and the installation of their images (or 'pupi' from which the word 'poop' is derived). This was followed by sprinkling the bow with red wine as the vessel was consigned to the keeping of the immortal sign it bore. The wine ceremony was probably a substitute for an ancient blood sacrifice.

During the Middle Ages, ships were launched in the Mediterranean with a joyous religious ceremony, parts of which probably derived from the Egyptians, and were used until recently in Greece and Russia where the rites of the Orthodox Church still prevailed. The ship was decked with streamers and garlands of flowers. A priest then went through the ship with a lighted torch anointing its various parts with sulphur and egg to 'purify it.' He then consecrated the vessel to some saint, after which the actual launching took place.

It is assumed that the British launching customs came from the Greco-Roman or the Norse, but it is certain that the Canadian customs came from the British. The present custom of bestowing a name at launching is of recent origin, considering the long history of ships and ship building.

The "Roll of Accounts" during the reign of Henry V shows that the Bishop of Bangor was paid five pounds for his expenses in going to Southampton in July 1418 to bless the great ship *Henri Grace à Dieu* which had been launched only a short time before. This was most likely a 'christening' or naming ceremony. Religious 'christenings' of the time did not use wine. Sir William Laird Clowes, in his carefully prepared history entitled "The Royal Navy," wrote: "There is no trace, in the fifteenth century of ship-baptism with wine." There was a trend during that century of choosing names with a religious significance.

The British warship *Sovereign* was relaunched in 1488 and renamed after extensive renovation. Henry VII was present and the ship was blessed by "a mitred prelate with attendant train of priests and choristers, crozier in hand, with candle, book, and bell, and holy water stoup." In countries which have remained Roman Catholic, similar ceremonies have continued.

In France during the eighteenth and nineteenth centuries, the ceremonies for merchant ship launchings closely resembled those for the christening of infants. A godfather carried a bouquet which he presented to the godmother. Both sponsors then pronounced the name of the vessel to be so named. The bow was then sprinkled with holy water and the service concluded with a benediction.

With the coming of the Reformation, in the reign of Henry VII, ceremonies in Britain became secularized and have remained so. A description of a typical launching was written by Phines

Pett, one of the greatest of English master shipwrights. The vessel was the *Prince Royal* and the launching date September 24, 1610:

"The noble Prince himself accompanied with the Lord High Admiral and the great Lords, were on the poop, where the standing great gilt cup was ready filled with wine to name the ship so soon as she had been afloat, according to ancient custom and ceremony performed at such times, and heaving the standing cup overboard...His Highness then standing upon the poop with a selected company only besides the trumpeters, with a great deal of expression of princely joy, and with the ceremony of drinking in the standing cup, threw all the wine forwards toward the halfdeck, and solemnly calling her by the name of the *Prince Royal*, the trumpets sounding the while, with many gracious words to me, gave me the standing cup into my hands." [12]

The practice of presenting a cup to the master shipwright had become fairly common by 1664. Samuel Pepys in his diary of October 26, 1664, described the launching of the *Royal Catherine* stating that, at his request, the King presented the cup to the master of the dockyard, Mr. Pett. It appears that Pepys bought the cup on behalf of the Admiralty and expected certain favours from Pett in return.

The changes in practice during the seventeenth century have a modern echo. At the beginning, the builders supplied the goblet and after it was thrown overboard, some hardy swimmer recovered it and usually tried to sell it back to the builder. In an effort to avoid the expense of buying back the cup or having another one made, some wise builder rigged a net around the stern of the ship to catch it. Public sentiment was so strongly aroused that the King ordered the practice stopped. The builders then protested and Charles II ordered the Crown to provide the cup.

Between 1610 and 1664 the custom of the sponsor riding the ship down the ways ceased, probably due to the possible danger to the eminent personage. Later the christening took place after the vessel was safely afloat. This was the custom in 1943 when certain lend-lease ships built in the United States for the Royal Navy were christened immediately before the commissioning ceremony.

In the interest of economy the standing silver cup was discontinued in 1690, and a bottle was substituted as the container. It was applied in the modern manner by breaking it over the bow, but the contents were usually red wine or sherry. The first record of British men-of-war christened this way was in a 1780 newspaper which described the launching of HMS *Magnanime* at Deptford.

Christenings were invariably performed by a male member of the Royal Family or by a dock-yard commissioner until, in 1811, George IV, then Prince Regent, introduced the first lady sponsor. However, the lady's aim was so bad that she hit and injured a spectator, who subsequently sued for damages! The Admiralty then directed that in future the bottle be secured to the stern of the ship by a lanyard, a method in use today.

Another interesting point is the varying reference to the 'bow' and the 'stern' in accounts of the launching ceremony. The practice of building ships with the 'bow' down seems to have been typical in the Low Countries from the Middle Ages to the late nineteenth century. Paintings in 1544 and 1606 clearly show vessels being built this way. The title page of Cornelis van Yk's book on Dutch shipbuilding (1697) shows four vessels with bow entering the water first. A contemporary of van Yk's, Nicolass Witsen, wrote in the 1690 edition of his "Aeloude en Hedendaaghsche Scheeps-bouw en Bestier," while pointing out the oddities of English ship-building practice, that the English built their ships with the stempost pointed toward the land. The reason for this difference in practice, Witsen suggested, was that the English used docks which were dug out and had doors. When the vessel was finished, the doors were opened and the water flowed in, presumably at high tide, floating the ship. Records of such docks in Holland and Zeeland are very rare before 1800. The kind of excavation needed for such a dock, especially for larger ships, was not possible at most building sites since the land was often already below sea-level, and it would be difficult to prevent water flowing into the dock. The practice was not limited to the Low Countries, either. Baugen in the late eighteenth century shows a merchant ship under construction with the bow facing the water. The location is unquestionably the Mediterranean. It was only after the introduction of the screw propeller that it became necessary for ships to be launched stern first. This procedure seemed necessary to avoid undue stress on the foot of the propeller frame in the last second before the weight of the hull became water-borne.

Today when the sponsor smashes the champagne bottle on a new ship's hull, she is performing a duty deeply set in the traditions and superstitions of the sea. Arrangements for the launching ceremony (or the first floating) and naming ceremony are made between National Defence Headquarters and the ship's builder. The name of the lady selected to perform the ceremony is approvd by NDHQ, and the nominee is not informed of her selection until approval from NDHQ is received. Prior to the ceremony, preparations for launching are completed by the builder.

2.27 Dockyard workers prepare HMCS *Saskatchewan* for launching.

2.28 The launching ceremony begins.

Deportment

The ceremony is usually conducted as follows:

(a) Guests assemble upon the platform.

(b) The "Maple Leaf" is played by the band, followed by one verse of "Eternal Father Strong to Save"

(c) There is an address by the ship's builder, and other appropriate guests (usually not more than three).

(d) The officiating clergy then blesses the ship. The following ceremony for the blessing of a ship at launching was set out by the Deputy Chaplain General(P) in 1967:[13]

When called upon to bless the ship, the chaplain shall say:

Brethren, seeing that in the course of our duty we are set in the midst of many and great dangers, and that we cannot be faithful to the high trust placed in us without the help of Almighty God, let us unite our prayers in seeking His blessing upon this ship and all who shall serve in her, that there may never be lacking men well qualified to offer in her their work to Thy greater glory and for the well-being of our nation and Commonwealth.

Then the people shall sing together the Hymn "Lead Us, Heavenly Father, Lead Us":

Lead us, heavenly father, lead us
O'er the world's tempestuous sea;
Guard us, guide us, keep us, feed us,
For we have no help but thee;
Yet possessing every blessing
If our God our Father be.

Saviour! breathe forgiveness o'er us,
All our weakness thou dost know,
Thou didst tread this earth before us,
Thou didst feel its keenest woe;
Lone and dreary, faint and weary,
Through the desert thou didst go.

Spirit of our God, descending
Fill our hearts with heavenly joy,
Love with every passion blending,
Pleasure that can never cloy:
Thus provided, pardoned, guided,
Nothing can our peace destroy!

The chaplain then reads: Psalm 107 Verses 23-32, 43:

23. They that go down to the sea in ships; and occupy their business in great waters;

24. These men see the works of the Lord: and his wonders in the deep.

25. For at His word the stormy wind ariseth: which lifteth up the waves thereof.

26. They are carried up to the heaven and down again to the deep: Their souls melteth away because of the trouble.

27. They reel to and fro, and stagger like a drunken man: and are at their wits' end.

28. So when they cry unto the Lord in their trouble: He delivereth them out of their distress.

29. For he maketh the storm to cease; so that the waves thereof are still.

30. Then they are glad, because they are at rest: and so He bringeth them unto the haven where they would be.

31. O that men would therefore praise the Lord for his goodness: and declare the wonders that he doeth for the children of men!

43. Whoso is wise will ponder these things: and they shall understand the loving-kindness of the Lord.

The Prayer:

Almighty God, who hath given men skill to devise and construct all manner of works: we praise Thee for the men who have laboured with brain and hand to build this ship and have brought her to this stage of completion. Grant Thy blessing upon their leaders, we pray; and to those who now shall carry on their good work give like skill and devotion in their tasks, so that when this ship shall finally be completed and sail upon the great waters, it may be a tribute to wise master builders and a safe, sure haven for those who sail in her; and this we pray through Jesus Christ our Lord.

The Lord's Prayer then follows. The Hymn "Fight the Good Fight" is then sung:

Fight the good fight with all thy might,
Christ is thy strength and Christ thy right,
Lay hold on life, and it shall be,
Thy joy and crown eternally.
    Run the straight race through God's good grace,
    Lift up thine eyes, and seek his face;
    Life with its way before us lies,
    Christ is the path, and Christ the prize.
        Cast care aside, upon thy Guide,
        Lean, and His mercy shall provide;
        Lean, and thy trusting soul shall prove
        Christ is its life, and Christ its love.
            Faint not nor fear, His arms are near,
            He changeth not, and thou are dear;
            Only believe, and thou shalt see
            That Christ is all in all to thee.

Benediction:

The Lord bless this ship. May He grant good success and protection upon all who labour in her, and may the blessing of Almighty God, the Father, Son and Holy Ghost be upon us, now and always. Amen.[13]

(e) The sponsor then breaks a bottle of champagne over the superstructure of the ship and says:

"I name thee HMCS (name), God Bless this ship and all who sail in her."

(f) As the ship starts down the ways, the ship builder calls for "Three cheers for Her Majesty's Canadian ship."

(g) The band then plays "God Save the Queen"

2.29 Mrs. H. S. Rayner, wife of VADM Rayner, CNS, names HMCS *Saskatchewan*.

2.30 The key slip is knocked away . . .

2.31 . . . and *Saskatchewan* is off down the slips.

followed by "O Canada."

Once construction is completed, the ship is commissioned with a ceremony arranged by the comanding officer designate, NDHQ and the ship's builder. NDHQ confirms and publishes:

(a) The name of the guest of honour;

(b) The names of the officiating clergymen;

(c) The approved programme; and

(d) The official guest list.

The ship's company falls in on the jetty and the guests assemble awaiting the arrival of the

2.32   HMCS *Saskatchewan's* ship's company await the guest of honour during her commissioning on 16 February, 1963.

official party.

The bugler sounds the 'alert' when the official party arrives, and appropriate honours are paid to the guest of honour. The guest of honour then inspects the guard and band, if appropriate. Once the guest of honour is seated, the 'carry on' is sounded.

The senior representatives of the Department of National Defence, the ship's builder and the guest of honour then give short addresses. Once the addresses are completed, the official acceptance documents are signed. When the ship has been officially accepted, the commissioning service is conducted, as follows:

The Exhortation
Brethren, seeing that in the course of our duty, we are set in the midst of many and great dangers, and that we cannot be faithful to the high trust placed in us without the help of Almighty God, let us unite our prayers and praises in seeking God's blessing upon this ship and all who serve in her, that she may safely sail under God's good providence and protection.
Hymn (Tune — Melita)
    O Father, King of Earth and Sea,
    We dedicate this ship to Thee,
    In faith we send her on her way,
    In faith to Thee we humbly pray,
    O hear from Heaven our sailor's cry,
    And watch and guard her from on high.
        And when at length her course is run,
        Her work for home and country done;

Of all the souls that in her sailed,
Let not one life in Thee have failed;
But hear from heaven our sailor's cry,
And grant eternal life on high.

Psalm 107, VV 23-32, 43 are read responsively.

Captain: I call upon you to pray for God's blessing on this ship. May God the Father bless her.
    Ship's company: Bless our ship.
    Captain: May Jesus Christ bless her.
    Ship's company: Bless our ship
    Captain: May the Holy Spirit bless her.
    Ship's company: Bless our ship.
    Captain: What do ye fear seeing that God the Father is with you?
    Ship's company: We fear nothing.
    Captain: What do ye fear seeing that God the Holy Spirit is with you?
    Ship's company: We fear nothing.
    Captain: Our help is in the name of the Lord.
    Ship's company: Who hath made heaven and earth.
    Captain: The Lord be with you.
    Ship's company: And with Thy Spirit. Amen.
    Let us Pray
    O Eternal Lord God, who alone spreadest out the heavens and rulest the raging of the sea; who has compassed the waters with bounds until day and night come to an end; be pleased to receive into Thy Almighty and most gracious protection the persons of us Thy servants, and the fleet in which we serve. Preserve us from the dangers of

the sea and from the violence of the enemy; that we may be a safeguard unto our most gracious Sovereign Lady, Queen Elizabeth, and her Dominions, and a security for such as pass on the seas upon their lawful occasions; that the inhabitants of our Commonwealth may in peace and quietness serve Thee our God; and that we may return in safety to enjoy the blessings of the land, with the fruits of our labours; and with a thankful remembrance of Thy mercies to praise and glorify Thy Holy Name; through Jesus Christ our Lord. Amen.

Almighty and Eternal God, the strength and support of those who put their confidence in you, be pleased, we beseech you, to bless this ship which is being commissioned today; guard and protect her from all danger and from all adversity; protect her against the visible and invisible snares of the enemy that she may defend the paths of justice and overcome, with your help, the powers of the enemy. Pour into this ship, the officer who commands her, and all her officers and men the richness of your blessing, guidance, and protection. May they ever be inspired by your holy law. May they grasp with their minds, cherish in their hearts, and carry out in their actions the teaching that leads to the safe haven of eternal life; through Christ our Lord. Amen.

Our father, who art in heaven, hallowed be Thy Name; Thy kingdom come; Thy will be done on earth as it is in heaven. Give us this day our daily bread; and forgive us our trespasses as we forgive those who trespass against us; and lead us not into temptation, but deliver us from evil. For thine is the kingdom, the power and the glory, for ever and ever.

The Blessing
Go forth into the world in peace; be of good courage; hold fast to that which is good; render unto no man evil for evil; strengthen the faint hearted; support the weak; love the Brotherhood; fear God; honour the Queen.
And the blessing of God Almighty, the Father, the Son, and the Holy Ghost be upon you, and remain with you always. Amen

Once the religious portion of the ceremony is over, the captain gives a short address, and then orders the ship to be commissioned. The bugler sounds the 'alert' followed by "O Canada," at which time The National flag of Canada (the ship's ensign) and the naval jack are hoisted, and the commissioning pennant (masthead pennant) is broken.
Appropriate presentations are made, and then the commanding officer orders the ship manned. As the band plays "Heart of Oak," the ship's company marches on board. Divisions are

2.33   Chief and petty officers man HMCS *Saskatchewan*.

2.34   The ship's captain, Commander M. W. Mayo, RCN, is piped aboard the newly commissioned *Saskatchewan*.

formed so that the junior members of the ship's company are the first on board. They are then followed by the chief and petty officers, with the Chief ERA and the cox'n the last men to board. Finally the wardroom members march onboard.
When the ship's company has manned the ship, the captain then exercises his traditional prerogative and is piped aboard. He then greets all the guests who will attend the reception to follow.

V
The King's and Queen's Colours

The consecration of regimental 'colours' is an ancient ceremony. One of the earliest recorded ceremonies of a regular consecration of 'colours' was to the 85th Foot in 1760. The first mention of the use of the 'drum altar' at colour presentation appears in the 1808 records of the 76th Foot, when 'colours' were placed on drums.

Practice evidently varied widely at that time. In some cases the colours were laid on a table in the field; in others, the ceremony was carried out in a church, the colours being laid on the altar. In 1830 the principal chaplain to the English forces suggested an official form of regulation for the consecration ceremony, but no official regulation can be found concerning the presentation of colours until 1867. These state that the drums were to be piled in the centre of the field, with the new colours placed against them. The Queen's colour was to be on the right. After the consecration they were to be handed to whomever was to present them to the unit. This ceremony continued practically unchanged in various editions of ceremonial regulations.

While Army units have had colours or their equivalent throughout recorded history, and ships have always worn identifying flags or ensigns, the RCN did not receive special colours until after HM King George V had approved their use.

In 1924, HM the King approved the use, by the Royal Navy, of colours corresponding to the King's colours as carried by military forces. Admiralty Fleet Order 1057/24 gave details of the approval, description, distribution and attendant regulations. The distribution, as originally approved, was to be: one to each home port and one to each of the Atlantic fleet, Mediterranean station, East Indies station, Africa station, and North America and West Indies station commands.

Application was made in 1924 for the RCN to use colours under the same conditions as those approved for the RN, the colours to be kept at the RCN barracks at Halifax and Esquimalt. In 1925 the Governor General was informed that the King had approved the use of a service colour by the RCN of the identical design and under similar conditions to that approved for the RN.

The purchase of two colours for the RCN having been approved as a charge against the 1926 — 1927 estimates, an order was placed through Admiralty in December, 1926. The two sets of colours were received in Canada through naval stores sometime during 1927. There is correspondence on file beginning December, 1927, about how and when the Pacific Command colour would be presented. There is also a reference on file that as of 10 July, 1928, the King's colour for Halifax was "now in the custody of the naval store officer."

In August 1928 direction was given that the King's colour should be taken on charge by the senior naval officer Halifax from the naval store officer Halifax. Arrangements to have the colour presented were never completed. So far as records

2.35   King George VI and Queen Elizabeth arrive at Beacon Hill Park for the presentation of colours to the RCN in May, 1939.

2.36   King George VI presents his colours to the 'colour officer'.

indicate, neither in the Atlantic nor Pacific command were King George V colours presented by anyone. They were, however, taken into use and paraded in accordance with custom and the orders of the times. They were laid up in 1937 after King George V's death.

In October 1936, two replacement colours bearing the cypher of HM King George VI were ordered through Admiralty. The new colours were to be sent direct from the Royal naval stores depot, Deptford to the naval stores officer Halifax and Esquimalt. By letter dated 26 May, 1937, the commander RCN barracks, Halifax advised that the colours of King George V had been replaced

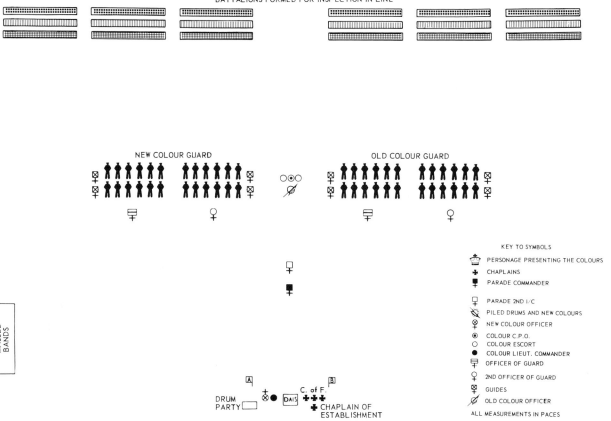

2.37 Formation of the parade.

by the new colours and requested instructions as to retention of the superseded colours. Naval HQ approved that the superseded colours be placed in St. Mark's Garrison Church, Halifax. New King's colours were received in Canada in 1937, one each for the Atlantic and Pacific commands.

During the Royal tour of 1939, HM King George VI formally presented his colour to the Royal Canadian Navy at a ceremony in Victoria, B.C. on 30 May.

This ceremony was considered to include the consecration and presentation of the colour for the East Coast Command as well.

Her Majesty, Queen Elizabeth, presented her colours to the Royal Canadian Navy on 1 August, 1959, in Halifax, Nova Scotia. The following paragraphs describe the ceremony during which the 'old colour' was replaced with the new one.

When colours are presented to a command which has not previously held them, the procedure is similar, but only one Royal guard and one colour party are paraded: those parts of the ceremony performed by the 'old guard' and the 'old colour party' are omitted; the Royal guard occupies the positions shown for the left division of the new guard and the right division of the 'old guard.'

The parade included the following units:

Units	Officers	Chief and Petty Officers	Leading Seamen and below
2 Royal guards	2 Lieutenant commanders	8 Petty officers	192
	2 commissioned officers		
2 Colour parties	1 Lieutenant commander	2 Chief petty officers	
	2 Lieutenants		
Massed Bands	As available		
Drum party		2 Petty officers	8
Armed or unarmed companies	There were, and should normally be, at least four armed or un-armed companies on parade.		

2.38   HM Queen Elizabeth arrives at the parade ground in Halifax for the presentation of new colours to the RCN, August, 1959.

Formation of the Parade

The armed or unarmed companies marched on first and formed for inspection in line. The new Queen's 'colour party,' with the colours cased and carried by the 'colour chief petty officer,' marched on and took up its post on the left of the dais.

When the remainder of the parade was formed, the new colour guard was marched on, turned into line and formed in two ranks.

The old colours, escorted by the 'old colour guard,' were then marched on with the band. The parade was called to 'attention' by the parade second-in-command. When in position, the old guard officer ordered the 'colour party' to take post, and they marched into position between the old and new guards. The old guard officer formed his guard into two ranks in open order and dressed them.

Sequence of Events

When the parade had been formed, it was reported to the parade commander by the parade second-in-command.

The parade commander then ordered:

"Show the King's colour."

At this order, the colour officer came to attention, sloped the colour, took one pace forward and turned left. He then paraded the colour along the frontage of the guards, turning about on reaching either flank. He was then ordered to "Take post" by the parade commander.

Shortly after the completion of the showing of the old colour, the Flag Officer Atlantic Coast, Rear-Admiral H.F. Pullen, OBE, CD, and his guests arrived at the dais. At 3:00 p.m., Her Majesty the Queen arrived at the parade accompanied by His Royal Highness Prince Philip, Duke of Edinburgh. Her Majesty was received by the Flag Officer Atlantic Coast and conducted to the dais, where the honoured guests were presented to Her Majesty.

The Royal standard was broken at the flagstaff, the parade gave the Royal salute and the massed bands played "God Save the Queen." The Parade Commander, Captain W.M. Landymore, OBE, CD, reported the parade to Her Majesty who, accompanied by the Flag Officer Atlantic Coast, inspected the Royal Guard.

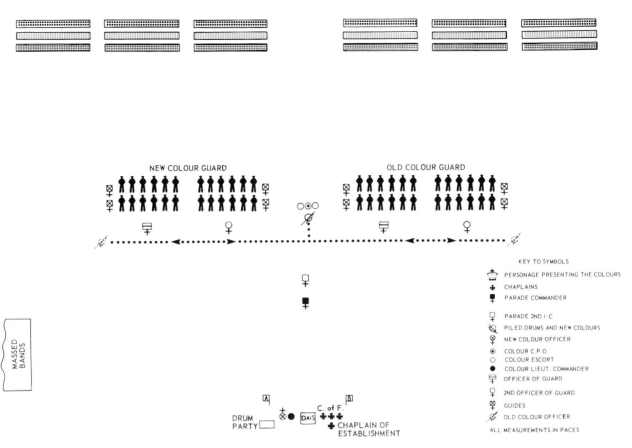

NEW COLOURS CASED

NEW COLOUR GUARD   OLD COLOUR GUARD

KEY TO SYMBOLS

PERSONAGE PRESENTING THE COLOURS
CHAPLAINS
PARADE COMMANDER

PARADE 2ND I/C
PILED DRUMS AND NEW COLOURS
NEW COLOUR OFFICER
COLOUR C.P.O.
COLOUR ESCORT
COLOUR LIEUT. COMMANDER
OFFICER OF GUARD
2ND OFFICER OF GUARD
GUIDES
OLD COLOUR OFFICER

ALL MEASUREMENTS IN PACES

MASSED BANDS

DRUM PARTY   DAIS   C. of F.
                                  CHAPLAIN OF
                                  ESTABLISHMENT

2.39   The parade gives the Royal Salute and the massed bands play "God Save the Queen".

2.40   The parade awaiting the arrival of the Queen and the firing of the Royal Salute.

2.41 HM Queen Elizabeth inspects the guards.

2.42 The old King's colour is trooped by the old colour party.

On completion of the inspection, Her Majesty returned to the dais and the massed bands and 'old king's colours' trooped. The bands marched across the frontage of the parade at the slow march, counter-marching and returning at the quick march and forming in their original positions.

The 'old king's colour' then trooped at the order of the parade commander. The 'colour party' marched at the slow from its position in the centre of the guards, wheeled left when ten paces clear, and marched across the frontages of the old

guard, the companies on parade and the new guard.

The 'colour' finally halted in a central position between the guards. The parade presented arms before the colour was first marched out, returning to the shoulder when it wheeled left. Unit commanders saluted the colour as it crossed their front.

When the 'old colours' had been trooped, the parade commander ordered it marched off the parade. The 'old colours' marched off at the slow to the tune of "Auld Lang Syne." The parade gave the 'general salute' and presented arms.

The parade remained at the 'present' until the colour disappeared from view. The 'old colour' was marched to a convenient place where it could be cased.

The parade then prepared for the consecration of the 'new colours.' The drum party piled drums in front of the dais, between the dais and the guards.

Once the drums were piled, the flanks of the companies on parade marched round to form three sides of a square.

The chaplain of the fleet and the other chaplains took their positions in rear of the piled drums, facing the dais. The parade commander took post on the right side of the drums, with the 'colour lieutenant-commander' on the opposite side.

The parade commander then ordered the 'new colour' to be marched on. The 'new colour' (cased) moved into position from the rear of the companies. The colour was uncased by the 'colour lieutenant-commander' and placed upon the drums.

When Her Majesty the Queen was conducted to a position near the drums, caps were removed by order of the parade commander, and the Flag Officer Atlantic Coast then invited the Commander Chaplain(P) to consecrate the Queen's colour and the Command Chaplain(RC) to address the parade. The service was as follows:

Flag Officer Atlantic:

Reverend Sir, on behalf of the Royal Canadian Navy, I ask you to bid God's blessing on this colour.

Command Chaplain(P) replied:

We are ready so to do.

We are met together before God to ask His blessing upon this colour, the solemn symbol of our loyalty to our Queen and Country. May it never be unfurled save in the cause of justice, righteousness and truth.

The Lord be with you.

All: And with thy Spirit.

Command Chaplain(P):

Let us pray.

Almighty and everlasting God, we are taught by Thy Holy Word that the hearts of kings are in Thy rule and governance, and that

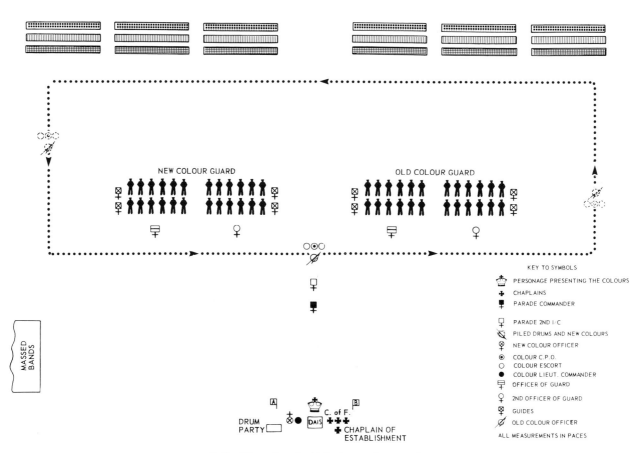

2.43   The colour halts between the guards.

KEY TO SYMBOLS

♔ PERSONAGE PRESENTING THE COLOURS
✚ CHAPLAINS
♙ PARADE COMMANDER
♙ PARADE 2ND I/C
⚡ PILED DRUMS AND NEW COLOURS
⚥ NEW COLOUR OFFICER
◉ COLOUR C.P.O.
○ COLOUR ESCORT
● COLOUR LIEUT. COMMANDER
♙ OFFICER OF GUARD
♀ 2ND OFFICER OF GUARD
⚥ GUIDES
∅ OLD COLOUR OFFICER

ALL MEASUREMENTS IN PACES

DRUM PARTY
C. of F.
DAIS
✚ CHAPLAIN OF ESTABLISHMENT

Thou dost dispose and turn them as it seemeth best to Thy godly wisdom. We humbly beseech Thee so to dispose and govern the heart of Elizabeth, Thy servant, our Queen and Governor, that in all her thoughts, words and works, she may ever seek Thy honour and glory, and study to preserve Thy people committed to her charge in wealth, peace and godliness. Grant this, O Merciful Father, for thy Son's sake, Jesus Christ our Lord, Amen.

O Lord our God, who from Thy throne beholdest all the kingdoms of the earth, have regard unto our land, that it may continue a place and a people to serve Thee to the end of time. Guide the governing of this great Commonwealth, here and in the far corners of the world, and grant that all who live beneath our flag may be so mindful of that threefold Cross, that they may work for the good of others, according to the example of Him who died in the service of men, Thy Son, our Saviour, Jesus Christ. Amen.

Laying his hand upon the colour the Command Chaplain(P) said:

In the faith of Jesus Christ and to the Glory of God, we consecrate this colour, in the name of the Father, and of the Son, and of the Holy Ghost.

May it ever be to us a sign of our duty to our Queen and country.

Amen.

All:

Our Father, who art in heaven, hallowed be thy Name. Thy Kingdom come, Thy will be done, in earth as it is in heaven. Give us this day our daily bread. And forgive us our trespasses, as we forgive them that trespass against us. And lead us not into temptation; but deliver us from evil; for Thine is the Kingdom, the power and the glory, for ever and ever. Amen.

All spectators were then invited to join in the singing of the hymn: "Eternal Father Strong to Save"

Eternal Father, Strong to save
Whose arm hath bound the restless wave,
Who bidd'st the mighty ocean deep;
Its own appointed limits keep:
O hear us when we cry to Thee
For those in peril on the sea.

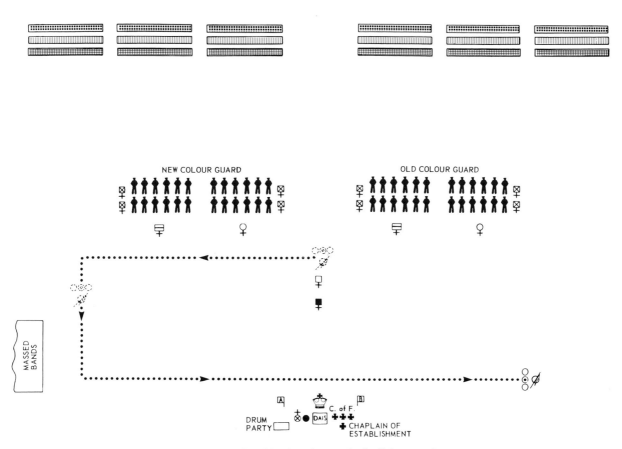

2.44　The old colour is marched off the parade.

O Trinity of love and power
Our brethren's shield in danger's hour;
From rock and tempest, fire and foe,
Protect them wheresoe'er they go:
Thus evermore shall rise to Thee
Glad hymns of praise from land and sea.
The Blessing:
The Lord bless you, and keep you;
The Lord make his face to shine upon you,
And be gracious unto you;
The Lord lift up the light of his countenance
upon you,
And give you peace. Amen.

After the consecration service was complete, and the parade replaced caps, the colour was handed by the 'colour lieutenant-commander' to Her Majesty. Her Majesty then presented the colour to the new 'colour officer,' who received it on bended knee.

With the exception of certain drill movements, the ceremony or presentation and consecration in 1979 was the same as the one previously described.

The ceremony on June 27 began with the arrival of Her Majesty Queen Elizabeth the Queen Mother. Her personal standard was broken at the masthead, and Her Majesty was received by the Commander, Maritime Command, Vice-Admiral A.L. Collier, who conducted Her Majesty to the dais where the honoured guests were presented. The parade then gave a Royal salute and the band played the national anthem.

Her Majesty, attended by the Commander, Maritime Command and the Parade Commander, Captain(N) F.W. Crickard, inspected the Royal guards. Her Majesty then returned to the dais, and the band trooped. The 'old colour' was then trooped, and marched off the parade.

The drums were piled and the 'new colour,' cased, was brought forward to be uncased and placed upon the drums. Admiral Collier then conducted Her Majesty to the drum altar and invited the Chaplains-General of the Canadian Forces to consecrate the colours.

The 'colour lieutenant-commander' handed the colour to Her Majesty to present to the 'colour officer.' Her Majesty then returned to the dais where she addressed the parade. Admiral Collier replied to Her Majesty, after which the parade gave three cheers for Her Majesty.

The parade saluted the colour, and as the

national anthem was played, the colour was escorted to its position between the two Royal guards. At that time there was a fly past of Maritime aircraft.

On completion of the flypast, the guards and band marched past Her Majesty, reformed, advanced in review order and gave a Royal salute.

Her Majesty then left the dais, and drove past the escort battalion before departing from the parade.

Approximately 700 officers, men and women were on parade for the occasion, with many more providing the necessary support. They represented the whole of the Command since the Fleet School in Halifax provided the 'old guard' and the 'old colour party,' while the 'new guard and colour party' were taken from West Coast ships and units. The escort battalion of four companies was provided by Halifax-based ships and units. The east and west coast bands were massed and augmented by naval reservists.

2.45   The old Queen's colour is draped on the drum altar for the consecration service.

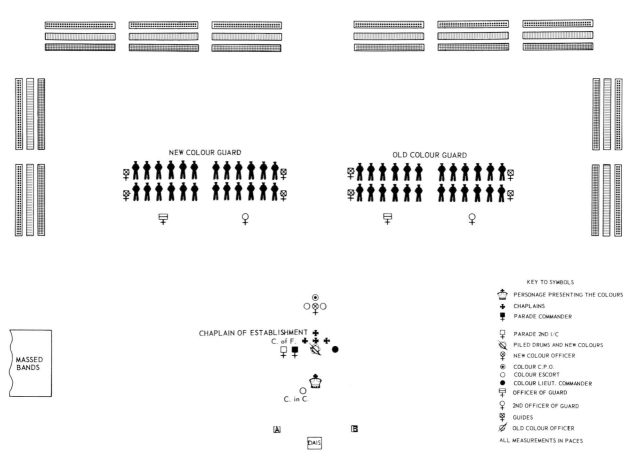

2.46   The parade after the new colours have been marched on.

2.47 HM Queen Elizabeth presents the Queen's colours to the new colour officer.

2.48 The Royal guards and colour party march past.

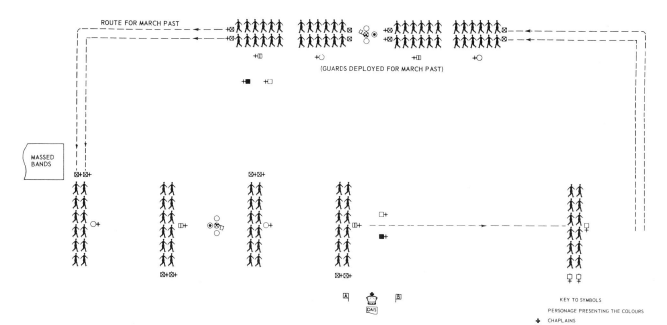

ROUTE FOR MARCH PAST

(GUARDS DEPLOYED FOR MARCH PAST)

MASSED BANDS

KEY TO SYMBOLS

PERSONAGE PRESENTING THE COLOURS

✚ CHAPLAINS
♟ PARADE COMMANDER

♛ PARADE 2ND I/C
⚘ PILED DRUMS AND NEW COLOURS
♀ NEW COLOUR OFFICER
⊙ COLOUR C.P.O.
○ COLOUR ESCORT
● COLOUR LIEUT. COMMANDER
⊟ OFFICER OF GUARD

♀ 2ND OFFICER OF GUARD
⊠ GUIDES
⚲ OLD COLOUR OFFICER

ALL MEASUREMENTS IN PACES

2.49   The march past.

2.50   The old Queen's colour is trooped, then marched off the parade.

2.51   The new Queen's colour is draped over the drum altar for the consecration service.

2.52   The Queen Mother presents the new Queen's colour to the colour officer.

2.53 The new Queen's colour presented in Halifax in 1979.

VI
Fleet Reviews

The famous fleet anchorage at Spithead has been the scene of many naval reviews. Perhaps it owes its pre-eminence to Henry VIII who selected Portsmouth as a Royal Dockyard in June, 1495, and thus linked Portsmouth and the Royal Navy from the birth of naval history. It is in these historic waters that the Royal and Commonwealth Navies have assembled to honour the Sovereign.

In 1773, King George III set out from Kew, in the Royal coach with scarlet outriders, for the first Royal review. On his arrival he was saluted by a "triple discharge of cannon," and proceeded to the dockyard where admirals and captains were assembled, each with his barge, to escort the King to Spithead. They had dressed their crews in fancy colours, each to his own taste, as there was then no uniform for seamen. They themselves were in the full dress designed for them by George II in 1748.

The ships being reviewed were those that had fought the French in the Seven Years War; they later fought them across the Atlantic in the War of American Independence. They were led by the 90-gun *Barfleur*, later to make history under Cuthbert Collingwood on the "Glorious First of June."

The second fleet review took place in 1814 to celebrate the Treaty of Paris, and to show the Allied Sovereigns "the tremendous naval arma-

ments which has swept from the ocean the fleets of France and Spain and secured to Britain the domain of the sea." Fifteen ships and 31 frigates were present, all of them veterans of the Napoleonic Wars.

In 1842 the young Queen Victoria and Prince Albert held a "Grand Naval Review." They inspected the *St. Vincent*, and also the new three decker, HMS *Queen*. The Queen on this occasion endeared herself to her sailors by drinking a mess basin of grog!

In 1845, when the Queen inspected the experimental squadron, she used the new *Victoria and Albert*, first of the two paddlers, and the Board of Admiralty attended in their steam yacht, *Black Eagle*. This was the last time that a Royal review consisted only of sailing ships, and nearly the last time that the Queen could watch the *Trafalgar*'s men run aloft and set the sails "with feline agility and astonishing celerity."

The Crimean War provided occasions for two reviews, one before and one after. The first, in 1853, included for the first time screw ships of the line, and the second, in 1856 was the first for the ironclad ships, four 1,500-ton floating batteries, whose presence marked the end of the wooden ships which still lay in the anchorage. Over 100 gunboats were present, "puffing about like locomotive engines with wisps of white steam trailing from their funnels," as one observer described them.

In 1867 a review was held for the Sultan of Turkey. For the first time every ship flew the White Ensign, for the old red, white and blue squadrons were no more. The five-masted *Minotaur* with her powerful broadside, and the graceful 14-knot sisters, *Warrior* and *Black Prince*, both of them turreted ships, were new designs.

Four more reviews were held at Spithead before the turn of the century. All of them, in their own way, were milestones in naval history, illustrating the changing pattern of new weapons development.

Reviews in the next century began to reflect a new trend as Germany steadily evolved as a naval power. The building race was on and battleships slid down the ways in ever increasing numbers. At the famous Review in 1914, with the fleet already lying under the shadow of war, no fewer than 59 battleships were anchored at Spithead, a tremendous spectacle of power.

In 1924, King George V came to Spithead to review his fleet, as he did eleven years later, in 1935, for his Silver Jubilee. Both reviews reflected the changing opinions on naval warfare, by displaying the unwieldy bulk of the aircraft carriers.

In 1937, when the fleet assembled again for a coronation review, five carriers were present, revealing of the way in which aircraft were beginning to dominate naval thought. In 1953, after another war had been fought, the largest assemblage of fighting ships ever seen assembled at Spithead for a naval review.

The British Columbia Centenary Naval Review held in July 1958, marking the 100th birthday of that province, was the first naval review held in Canadian waters. On that occasion 32 ships took up the review anchorages in Royal Roads in four lanes. Her Royal Highness Princess Margaret, in HMCS *Crescent*, officiated as the reviewing officer.

The first occasion in Canada's history in which a reigning British Monarch reviewed Canada's Navy took place on 26 June 1959. This review was held in Lake St. Louis near Montreal following the official opening of the St. Lawrence Seaway. The Queen accompanied by HRH Prince Philip in the Royal Yacht *Britannia*, with the President of the United States and the Prime Minister of Canada on board, sailed down the line of 16 naval vessels of the RCN and the USN.

A second review was also held that year in August, in Halifax, when Her Majesty the Queen reviewed the ships and submarines of the RCN which were anchored in the harbour.

Other RCN fleet reviews have been held in Halifax and Victoria during the 1967 centennial celebrations, and in Victoria for the Captain Cook bicentennial celebrations.

2.54   The fleet in position for the review conducted by HM Queen Elizabeth in August, 1959.

2.55   The fleet dressed over all in preparation for the arrival of HM Queen Elizabeth.

VII
Paying Off

The chief performer in paying off the ship was the ship's cook, who at one time had the status of warrant officer. *The Naval Chronicle* of 1815 reports:

"According to an established form in the Navy, when a ship is paid off, no officer must quit the port, or consider himself discharged, until the pennant is struck, which can be done only by the cook, as the last officer, at sunset; and should he be absent no other person can perform the office, however desirous the officers may be of taking their departure, and although there may not be a single seaman or marine on board. A curious instance of this took place on the *Caledonia's* being paid off. When the time arrived for hauling down the pennant, no cook could be found, from which cause the officers were under the necessity of waiting a day or two until he made his appearance."[14]

When the ship finally reached the end of her commission, she would usually return to 'reserve' and all the members of the company would be paid as they went ashore. Hence the term "paying off."

Today, HMC ships are paid off into one of three categories:

Major refit or conversion; reserve; or disposal.

The 'paying off' pennant dates from the nineteenth century when cleaning rags in a decommissioning ship were apparently knotted together and hoisted as a sign that they would no longer be used. Custom dictated that the pennant's length would be equal to the length of the ship for a normal commission. For an extended commission, the pennant's length would also be extended. The length was determined by actual length of the commission (in months) divided by the scheduled commission (in months). This figure was then added, as a fraction of the ship's length, to the length of the commissioning pennant.

In HMC ships today, the 'paying off' pennants are a uniform length of 380 feet, regardless of the period of commission.

VIII
Change of Command

The ceremony attendant at a change of command will vary depending on the seniority of the individuals involved and the circumstances surrounding the time of the change.

When the change of command involves a squadron commander or the commander of a command, the flag of the outgoing commander is hoisted at the starboard yard and the flag of the incoming commander is hoisted at the port yard during the ceremony of 'colours' on the day of the change.

A gun salute, as appropriate, is fired upon the arrival of the incoming commander who is met by an appropriate guard, band and divisions representative of the units under his command.

The presiding officer (if any), normally the senior formation commander, accompanied by the incoming commander, inspects the parade and then takes the salute as the parade marches past.

Following the march past, the parade re-forms on the inspection line. When the change of command involves the command commander, the Queen's colour may be paraded. In such a case, the 'colour party' will position itself so that the 'colour bearers' can present the colours to the outgoing commander. He will in turn, Queen's colour first, present them to the presiding officer, signifying the return of his command to his superior officer. The presiding officer will, in turn, present the colours to the incoming commander, signifying the trust he has placed in the incoming officer. The incoming commander will then present the colours to the 'colour-bearers.'

When the 'colour party' has taken its place in the parade, the change of command certificates are signed, under the supervision of the presiding officer.

The presiding officer and the outgoing commander then address the parade. The incoming commander may also address the parade. Once completed, the presiding officer and the out-going commander will take their places on the dais, and the parade will march past, then advance and give the general salute.

As previously noted, this procedure is changed depending upon circumstances and the seniority of individuals involved. For commanding officers of HMC ships, divisions are usually held on the quarterdeck or on the jetty adjacent to the ship, so there is no room for marching. The ceremony attendant upon a change of command also varies according to the seniority of the individuals involved. It may be possible that only the approp-

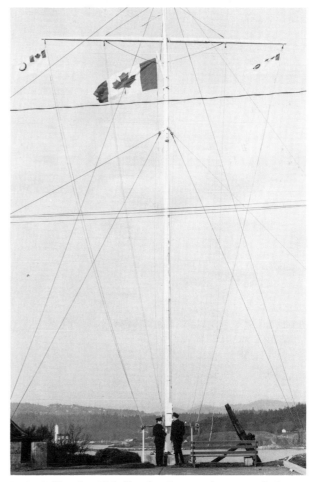

2.56 (5 March, 1982). For the change of command of Maritime Forces Pacific, Admiral Hughes' flag is at the starboard yard and Admiral Edwards' is at the port yard.

2.57 (5 March, 1982). Rear-admiral G. L. Edwards, CMM, CD, is met by the guard and band prior to the change of command.

riate guards are paraded.

Additional ceremonies may be introduced, such as sail or fly pasts. These may be conducted either before or after the ceremony, or during the

2.58 (5 March, 1982). The incoming and outgoing commanders of Maritime Forces Pacific sign the change of command certificates.

2.59 Sail past during change of command.

2.60 (5 March, 1982). The outgoing commander of Maritime Forces Pacific is driven past shore establishments of the command, Esquimalt.

signing of the change of command certificates.

Once the parades have been completed, there remains the ceremony of rowing the commander or commanding officer ashore in the ship's boat.

The first recorded incident involving this

2.61 (5 March, 1982). Rear-admiral W. A. Hughes, CD, RCN, CF, prepares to depart for his ceremonial 'rowing ashore'.

2.62 The admiral's barge manned by the captains and commanding officers of the Pacific Command.

ceremony appears to be in the year 957. It appears that King Edgar held such dominion over the seas adjacent to England, that when he held his court at Chester, he:

> "...caused the Kings of Scotland, Cumberland, Isle of Man, and five petty Kings of Britain, to row him in a barge, which he steered himself from Chester, along the River Dee, to the Abbey of St. John the Baptist, where they bound themselves to defend his rights by land and sea."[15]

When an officer commanding one of HMC ships, squadrons or commands relinquishes command to his successor, he is to be pulled ashore in the ship's whaler, even if the ship is alongside in harbour.

En route from a parade square or office, shore establishments may be reviewed from an open vehicle, prior to the ceremonial rowing ashore.

The accommodation ladder is rigged, and the whaler brought alongside the lower platform.

The crew is composed of the ship's officers, with the executive officer acting as the cox'n, and the department heads in the oarsman's positions. The crew for a squadron commander or command commander is composed of the captains under his command.

As the officer approaches the quarterdeck of the ship, the OOD/OOW orders the 'ceremonial side party' to sound the 'still,' bringing the ship's company to attention. As the officer steps onto the upper platform, the 'side' is piped, and it is piped again when the boat leaves the lower platform of the accomodation ladder.

The cox'n then steers the boat so as to pass down the manned side of the ship. The 'carry on' is sounded when the boat passes clear of either the stern or the bow of the ship. A squadron commander may be taken past the ships of the squadron, and a commander, past all the ships present. Those to be reviewed will have the side manned and be prepared to cheer ship.

IX
Religious Services

Baptisms

Baptisms conducted on board HMC ships fall into two categories. The baptism, conducted on request for children of members of the ship's company, is described here. The second form of baptism, called 'crossing the line ceremony,' is dealt with in Section XI.

The baptism of children on board ship is conducted in the wardroom. The ship's bell is mounted in a special holder which has been draped in the naval jack; the bell can then be used as a font for the baptism.

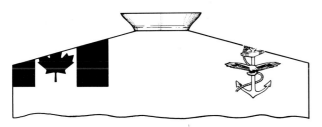

2.63 Ship's bell draped in the Naval Jack.

After the ceremony, the chaplain pours the water into the sea from a position on the quarterdeck or boatdeck. The 'side' is piped by the quartermaster and the OOD salutes as the water is poured overboard.

The child's name and the date of the service are later engraved on the bell. When the cerem-

ony is over, the guests return to the wardroom where an appropriate officer proposes a toast to the child on behalf of the ship. The family and guests then attend a small reception, again customarily held in the wardroom.

Detailed procedures for the service are discussed with the officiating chaplain. The church pennant is hoisted during the ceremony.

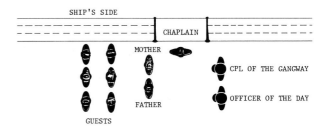

2.64 Position of attendants at a baptism ceremony.

Weddings

It has always been a naval custom for officers to ask for permission to marry. This request is made in the form of a letter to their commanding officer.

The officer must also have approval to be married in uniform. The appropriate uniform may be either ceremonial dress with medals and with or without swords, or the usual uniform of jacket and tie. The wearing of 'mess dress' is not correct at a wedding ceremony, although it can be used for the reception.

Naval officers may be designated to form an arch of swords (sword cutting edge facing upward) through which the bride and groom pass upon leaving the church.

2.65 Arch of swords through which the bride and groom pass after a marriage ceremony.

When a member of a ship's crew is married in the port in which the ship is lying, a garland of evergreens is hoisted at the masthead on the day of the ceremony.

Burial at Sea

A funeral at sea is one of the most impressive of shipboard ceremonies. In the early days, the sailmaker was called upon to sew the canvas shroud in which the body would be consigned to the deep. At the last stitch in the lap of the shroud over the face, the needle was thrust through the nose of the deceased to prevent the body from slipping out of the canvas. Today, since ships can make land quickly, burials at sea are seldom necessary, but on occasions when it is unavoidable the time-honoured tradition is carried out with great solemnity.

It is the custom for the ship's surgeon to report a death to the officer-of-the-watch, who in turn reports to the captain. The event is then entered in the log with the exact position of the ship at the time of death.

The hour when the ceremony takes place depends to some extent on the geographical position of the ship at the time. The body (sewn in the canvas shroud) is placed on a grating and covered with the national flag. Usually, if there is no chaplain present, the captain takes the service. The ritual ends with the ancient words:

"We therefore commit this body to the deep to be turned into corruption, looking for the resurrection of the body when the sea shall give up her dead and the life of the world to come...."

At the phrase "commit this body to the deep," two seamen tilt the inboard end of the grating which rested on the ship's rail. They hold the flag so that the body slips from under it into the sea.

All officers and men not on duty attend the funeral of a shipmate. If the ship is in harbour and the burial takes place on shore, all who can be spared from duties on board go ashore to pay their last respects.

In the funeral procession, the carrying of reversed arms is an acknowledgement that such weapons are wrongfully used by mankind. Three volleys are fired over the open grave as a reminder of the Holy Trinity. The object is to scare away evil spirits of imaginary devils, since according to an old superstition at such times men's emotions are so intense that their hearts stand ajar, making it easy for evil spirits to slip in. It is still a common belief today that devils are afraid of noise and in some European monasteries it is customary to let off crackers at sunset to scare the devils out of the sacred place, after which the door is promptly shut on them.

The "last post" played on the bugles at the end of the funeral is always a sad and moving sound. It is said to be the 'Nunc Dimitis' of servicemen; the last bugle call to one who has left all earthly things.

The national flag is always laid over the corpse at the funeral as a reminder that the individual died in the service of his country, and the country is paying a last tribute to him.

The naval gun carriage is used in state and some military funerals. The equipment consists of a field gun carriage, limber, two drag ropes, and two reverse drag ropes. The gun carriage is fitted with a funeral board which has straps for securing the casket.

The gun crew consists of one junior officer or petty officer, and 32 master leading seamen. In a state funeral, four drag ropes and four reverse ropes are fitted, and 28 additional men are required.

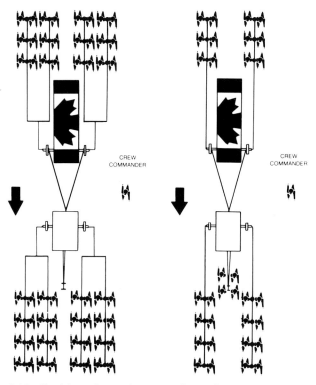

2.66   Position of attendants at a funeral ceremony.

Today, it is more common to scatter the ashes of a deceased person then to bury him at sea. The general ceremony, however, remains the same. The guard and bearer party are formed up on the jetty, facing inward, when the gun carriage or hearse arrives at the ship's side.

As the gun carriage or hearse approaches, the guard presents arms and remains at the present as the casket is removed. After shouldering arms, the guard follows the bearer party on board. As the casket is brought on board, the ceremonial side party pipes the 'still.'

Whenever possible, the casket is positioned

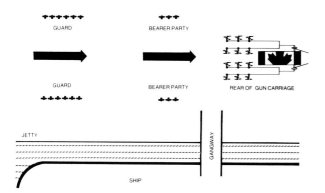

2.67 Arrival at jetty prior to putting to sea.

onboard so that it is fore and aft, with the foot of the casket forward.

The guard is formed in two ranks at the head of the casket in an athwartship position. The guard rests on arms reversed until the mourners are onboard.

During the passage to sea, four men from the guard are detailed as the vigil. They are positioned at each corner of the casket, facing outwards obliquely, resting on their arms reversed.

Prior to the ship's arrival at the burial position, the vigil is dismissed and the casket moved to the launching ramp by the bearer party. The decorations are removed from the casket before it is placed on the launching ramp. When the casket is in position, the bearer party remains on either side of the casket, maintaining their grip on the handles.

The guard is formed up, fore and aft, facing outboard, in two ranks, resting on their arms reversed. The guard commander is in the rear and the ceremonial side party is on the right of the guard. At the commencement of the service, all military personnel, except the guard and the ceremonial side party, remove head-dress.

Upon completion of the service, the chaplain takes one pace back, and this is the signal for the guard commander to give the cautionary word of command, pausing briefly to allow personnel to replace head-dress, then ordering the guard to "present arms." The guard presents arms from the position of resting on arms reversed. On the last movement of the present, the bearer party commits the body to the sea, and all others not under command salute.

Simultaneously, the ceremonial side party pipes "Last Post" and, after a ten second delay, "Reveille." Following "Reveille," three volleys, if used, are fired, the guard shoulders arms, and is dismissed. Floral tributes are dropped in the sea on completion of the service.

Laying Up of Colours

The King's and Queen's colours have always held a special place in naval traditions. While in use, they are under the protection of the command. When a new colour is presented, the task of safekeeping the colours is transferred from the command to a suitable church. They are deposited as a token of gratitude to Almighty God, for his providential care of a unit in the discharge of its duty; to provide a memorial to the men who served under the colours, and to furnish an inspiration for patriotic service and sacrifice to all who may see them.

There are only two proper positions for colours and flags permanently deposited in churches. If they are intended for use in future services in the church, they are to be stored in stands in perfectly upright positions, except when they are being carried. The staff of flags or colours permanently deposited for safekeeping should project in a horizontal position from the wall, the whole colour or flag hanging down without a crease.

Colours or flags should not be draped over pulpits, altars, tables or any other article of furniture for decoration. The only exceptions to this rule are when colours are laid on the altar during the service of 'depositing colours,' or at a military service for the consecration of colours, when they rest on the drum altar.

When colours are hung in churches, they are always on the side of honour. Whether the colours are hung in the chancel below the communion rail, or (as in some cases), in the nave, the Queen's colours are on the right hand side of the congregation as they face the front or altar. On the other hand, when colours are hung in the sanctuary above the communion rail, the position is reversed. In churches without a chancel, or where the sanctuary is not clearly defined, the Queen's colours are normally on the wall to the left of the congregation as they face the altar or pulpit.

On arrival at the church, the 'colour party' remains at the back of the church, or in the vestibule, with the 'colour lieutenant-commander.' Personnel from the Command enter the church and take the pews allotted for them, with the commander in the innermost seat of the forward, right-hand pew. On conclusion of the normal service, the colour party forms up in the vestibule. The 'colour lieutenant-commander' then knocks three times on the church door with the hilt of his sword.

The attending chaplains, on hearing the knock, proceed to the door and open it. The 'colour lieutenant-commander' then says:

"Sir, I have been commanded by (name of commander), Commander of Maritime Com-

2.68 Colour commander knocks on the church door during the 'laying of colours' ceremony.

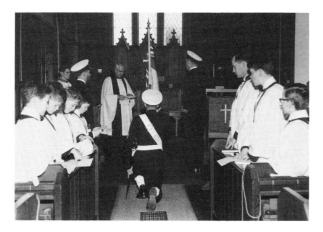

2.69 Colour officer presents old colours to be deposited for safekeeping.

mand, to inform the authorities of this church, that he has repaired here today with the old colours of the command, and desires that they be deposited herein."

The senior chaplain then says:

"Sir, every facility will be afforded the Commander of Maritime Command in executing his most laudable purpose."

The 'colour lieutenant-commander' then returns his sword to its scabbard, and led by the chaplains, march in slow time to the chancel steps. The senior officer joins the party there.

The chaplains halt, turn about and face the 'colour party,' and the congregation stands.

Addressing the chaplain, the senior officer says:

"On behalf of the officers and men of Maritime Command, I have the honour to inform you that these are the colours of the Command, and to request that they be deposited here for safekeeping as a token of their gratitude to Almighty God, by whom alone victory is secured; for His providential care and gracious benediction granted them in the discharge of duty. In so acting, they also desire to provide a memorial to the men of all ranks who served under these colours, and to afford an inspiration for patriotic service and sacrifice to all who may worship here for all time to come."

The chaplain answers:

"In the faith of Jesus Christ, we accept these colours for the glory of God, and in memory of those who were faithful, many of them unto death, in the sacred cause of Queen and country, and in confidence of the inspiration they will afford to all who may behold them; in the Name of the Father, and of the Son, and of the Holy Ghost, Amen."

The 'colour lieutenant-commander' then turns about and receives the colour from the 'colour officer,' turns about and presents it to the chaplain. The 'colour party' presents arms, and the officers salute. The band plays "God Save the Queen."

The chaplains and officers turn about, the chaplains moving to the altar, the officers moving to their seats in the front pews.

The NCO's of the 'colour party' move to a side aisle or to the vestry.

The appropriate service is then conducted by the chaplains, and may be modified to suit locations other than a church.

On completion of the blessing and while the people are still kneeling, "sunset" is sounded. The National anthem concludes the service.

X
The Naval Gun — Afloat and Ashore

The first gun is said to have been brought on board a ship called *Christopher of the Tower* in 1406. It is possible that this date is late by half a century, but even so it took a long time for the gun to establish itself as a ship weapon. Although, like all other ship weapons of that day, it was designed to kill men, it had to compete with other old and well-tried rivals such as arrows and darts. It won in the end, but only after it had been greatly improved. Then there was a sudden demand for it which led to the necessity of finding sites on board to house a large number of 'pieces.' This in turn led to a great increase in the size of the 'castles.' This process was already far advanced by the end of the fifteenth century.

The only places to house the guns in large numbers were the castles. Traditionally all serious fighting took place from these vantage points, and in fighting which consisted almost exclusively of 'boarding and entering,' the principal role of the gun was to repel the invader. The alternative, later implemented, was to place them in the hull of the ship, and to fire upon the enemy through port-holes in her side. The invention of the port-hole took place about 1500.

When guns were first introduced, naval ships were still for the most part contracted for by the Crown and provided by the merchant fleet. Consequently, their expansion (which was necessary to receive the new weapons) required construction of a temporary nature. In most cases, such as that of the *Mary of the Tower*, this meant that she would first be fitted with temporary 'castles,' then furnished from the King's arsenal with the fighting weapons of the day, the fighting men would come on board and she would be considered ready to go to sea to do the King's business. When the task was completed, she would return to the Tower, the fighting men would leave, the King's weapons would be returned to his stores, the 'castles' would be removed, and she would return to take up her ordinary trading activities. This system made merchantmen and naval ships nearly indistinguishable.

When Henry VIII succeeded his father, he introduced major reforms in the naval system. He built a fighting fleet and gave it the new weapon which made sea warfare, as it is now known, possible. The King took great personal interest in the fleet, and for a time was extremely interested in artillery. His shipwrights were instructed to produce a fighting ship, with a weapon capable of battering other ships to the death. This was a revolutionary idea, since it combined the 'ship-killer' and 'great gun.'

Although the exact date of the arrival of the great guns is not known, the ship in whose sides the first gun-ports were cut to receive them (the first broadside ship) is said to have been the *Mary Rose* in 1513.

Once they had made their appearance, it was up to the ship's crews to make the most of them. This meant, as it does today, that constant practice of gun drill was essential to ensure success. In "Exercise of the Small Arms and Great Guns for the Seamen on Board His Majesty's Ships," printed in 1765, the practice of exercising the ship's crew in the firing and reloading of the great guns was related as follows:

"Exercise, in the Royal Navy, is the preparatory practice of managing the guns and small arms in order to make the ship's crew perfectly skilled therein, so as to direct its execution successfully in the time of battle. The exercise of the great guns was, till lately, very complicated and abounding with superfluities, in our

Navy as well as others."[16]

The exercise manual of 1765 was filled with these "superfluities" and the drill to fire the gun took forty different orders. However by 1802 they apparently were reduced to fourteen, no doubt making it easier to control the guns during a battle.

It was the rule to fire the guns once a day to ensure proficiency. The crew went to evening quarters to ensure that the entire crew was kept practiced at going to their action stations. This seemed like the perfect opportunity to fire the guns, and was thus adopted as the common practice.

"Upon beat-to-arms (everybody having immediately repaired to their quarters) the midshipman commanding a number of guns is to see that they are not without any necessary article, as (at every gun) a sponge, powder horn with its priming wires, and a sufficient quantity of powder, crow, hand-spike, bed, quion, train-tackle, etc., sending without delay for a supply of anything that may be missing; and for the greater certainty of not overlooking any deficiency, he is to give strict orders to each captain under him to make the like examination at his respective gun, and to take care that every requisite is in a serviceable condition, which he is to report accordingly."[17]

Here in slightly more detail, is the exercise procedure that was laid out in the exercise manual of 1765:

Words of Command	Observations
1. Take heed.	A precautionary word of command.
2. Silence.	
3. Cast off the tackles and breechings.	Figure 2.70 shows the gun secured for sea by the use of its tackles and breeching. In order to move the gun either in or out, it was necessary to allow all the tackles and breeching to run freely.
4. Seize the breeching.	The breeching was used to check the recoil of the gun when it was fired. It was necessary to 'seize' the knots of this rope so that it would stand up to this extra strain without coming undone.
5. Take out the tampion.	The tampion was used to prevent foreign material from entering the gun barrel.
6. Take off the apron.	
7. Unstop the touch hole.	With the tampion in the muzzel and the touch hole stopped, the gun was water-tight. The guns were always shotted, and these precautions kept the shot or powder from decaying.

8. Handle the priming wire.
9. Prick the cartridge.

This was done so that the priming powder and the powder in the cartridge could come into contact. The powder horn was used to hold the priming powder.

10. Handle the powder horn.

11. Prime.

Priming powder was poured into the priming vent through the touch hole.

12. Bruise the priming.
13. Secure the powder horn.
14. Take hold of the apron.
15. Cover the vent.

This would prevent any unexpected sparks from setting off the powder prematurely.

16. Handle crows and handspikes.

These were used to assist the train-tackles in running out the gun.

17. Point the gun to the object.

This was easy to do, since the very short range of the cannon meant that the gun was very close to the target.

18. Lay down crows and handspikes.
19. Take off the apron.
20. Take your match, and blow it.

Matches were strips of loosely twisted rope which had been dipped in nitrate. They would burn for an hour, but needed to be blown on to get them hot enough to touch off the powder.

21. Fire.

The match would be set to the touch hole, set off the priming and then the cartridge.

22. Stop the touch hole.

This was done to prevent excessive smoke from escaping from the touch hole back into the gun deck. Once the gun had been fired, it was necessary to clean it and reload.

23. Handle the spongestaff.

24. Sponge the gun.
25. Handle the cartridge.
26. Put it into the gun.

The cartridge was pushed as far into the gun as the loader could reach, the lower end first and the cartridge seam downwards. The wad was packing which compressed the powder cartridge into its chamber in the gun, and also prevented damage to the cartridge from the rammer.

27. Wad to your cartridge.

28. Handle the rammer.
29. Ram home the wad and cartridge.
30. Unstop the touch hole.

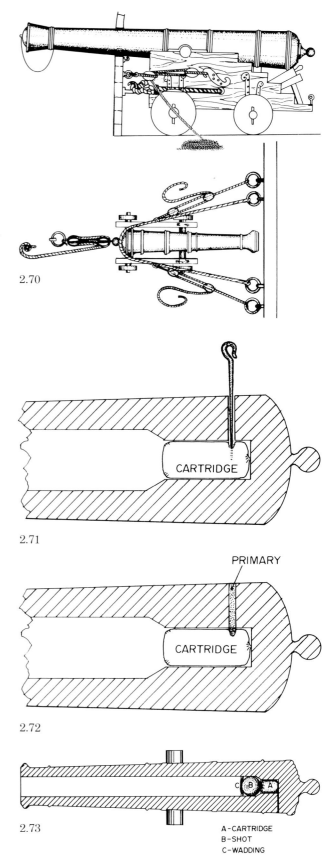

2.70

2.71

PRIMARY

CARTRIDGE

2.72

2.73

A - CARTRIDGE
B - SHOT
C - WADDING

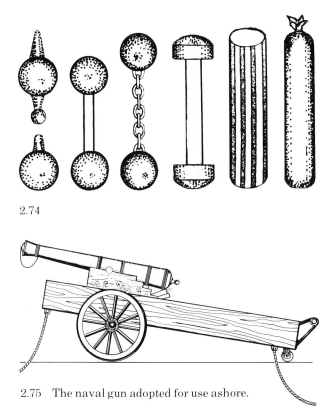

2.74

2.75   The naval gun adopted for use ashore.

31. Handle the priming wire.	
32. Try if the cartridge be home.	Gentle probing with the priming wire would show if the powder cartridge was properly packed into the gun.
33. Draw the rammer.	The rammer was removed when the cartridge was properly home.
34. Shot the gun.	Figure 2.74 shows the various forms of shot that were available for use in the great guns.
35. Wad the shot.	
36. Ram home wad and shot.	
37. Draw the rammer.	
38. Stop the touch hole.	This was done because the gun was now shotted, and even if not primed, there could be sufficient un-burned powder left in the touch hole to ignite the cartridge.
39. Lay on the apron.	From here, the gun could either be run out and fired again, or the tackles could be used to secure it in its 'sea' position.

When the great guns were first introduced, it was the Navy that had to deal with military problems wherever they occurred, so some method of using their considerable fire-power ashore had to be found.

A historical account of the capture of Quebec reports that sailors of Admiral Saunder's command dragged a gun up to the heights of Abraham "...which was most useful."

The next striking example of the Navy using their mountings for land service occurred during the Indian Mutiny. Captain Peel of the *Shannon* landed six of his 3-ton eight-inch guns, and with his landing party took an active part in the capture of Lucknow. They won the admiration of the Army because of how they moved their guns, especially when they persuaded several elephants to extricate the cannon from the mangrove swamps.

Although the 12-pounder breech loader was adopted for ship service in 1882, it was not until the outbreak of the Boer War that the naval field gun emerged as a potent weapon of war. In South Africa it was clearly demonstrated that the heavy long-range guns could be made mobile even in difficult country, and the credit fell to the Navy in originating this idea that later had such immense military significance. The original land mountings developed consisted of a log of wood, about fourteen feet long and one foot square. This formed the trail, which was mounted on an axletree with a pair of ordinary cape wagon wheels. The ship carriage, bolted down and secured, was placed upon it, but in a way that allowed it to be detached, for subsequent return to the ship.

Other mountings were developed later that allowed greater elevation; they were fitted with iron wheels and telescopic sights. Early in the campaign the Naval Brigade, composed of seamen, stokers and Royal marines, fought with distinction as infantry at the head of the British column. Later, they were mainly occupied in serving the guns. At Paardeburg they covered twenty-seven miles in twenty-two hours and brought the seige artillery (4.7-inch guns and 12 pounders) to within a mile of the enemy defences. After the Boer surrender they pressed on to the next objective. As on all similar occasions, direct fire was employed, usually at fairly short ranges, the officer of quarters spotting from a position nearby, where he had mounted his telescope on a tripod. The guns were frequently protected by earthworks and sandbags, because the Boer counter-battery and sniping was frequently effective.

Keeping the mountings mobile tapped the great energy and resource of the armourers and their mates; the appalling road conditions broke up wheels and timber alike. Repairs had to be made in wind and dust not to mention enemy sniping. While advancing to attack Pretoria, the weight of the 4.7 in. guns was too much for the bridge over the Klip River, and it collapsed. One of the mounting wheels broke, and the gun sank into mud. It took sixty-four oxen and several hundred men to finally extricate and repair it.

In the final phase of the campaign the Naval Brigade proved their worth in the defence and relief of Ladysmith. During the Boer seige which coincided with the Prince of Wales' birthday, all the naval weapons joined in firing a shotted Royal Salute of 21 rounds into enemy lines. The Boers' retaliated on Christmas Day by filling a six-inch shell with plum pudding, painting "Merry Christmas" on it, and firing it into the British camp, where it killed the last remaining pig.

The moral effect of bringing such heavy weapons into unexpected places was of immense value to the army. They gave their guns nicknames like 'Josephine' and 'Bloody Mary,' and managed to keep up a ship routine of 'colours' and 'up spirits' in all weather and conditions. Beseiging Ladysmith, a Boer wrote to his sister:

> "It is very dangerous to attack the town. Near the walls are two naval guns from which we receive very heavy fire. I think there will be much blood spilt before they surrender, as Mr. Englishman and his damn sailors fight hard."[18]

Today, the handling of the naval field gun, both in competition and for display purposes, is witness to the obstacles which faced the sailor/ field gunners. This usually takes the form of an obstacle race between two teams, and for the most part, the most intense competition is found between teams from the East and West Coast Commands of Maritime Forces.

The obstacle course consists of a five-foot high wall and a 30-foot chasm. The gun's crew must dis-assemble the gun and limber, then move the pieces over the five-foot high wall. The pieces must then be carried across the 30-foot chasm, and be reassembled, gun first, by the crew.

Once the gun and limber have been re-assembled, they must be loaded and fired, dis-assembled, returned via the chasm and the five-foot wall to the starting line, re-assembled and fired. The team to accomplish this first wins the competition. The 'naval gun run' is a strong reminder of what the Navy can do!

XI
Crossing the Line

This custom is so old that its origin cannot accurately be traced. From accounts of early voyages made by the Vikings, the ceremony was carried out on crossing certain parallels. From early accounts it had a religious basis, and is sometimes referred to as the 'sailor's baptism.' The Phoenicians, when they passed through the Pillars of Hercules, today known as the Straits of Gibralter, on their way to Cornwall to trade with the ancient Britons, performed ceremonies to propitiate the god of the seas. It is highly probable that human sacrifice played a part in these rites.

As knowledge of the world increased, and curious navigators thrust the bows of their ships farther and farther across the unknown waters, the same religious rite was observed at important geographical points: the Tropic of Cancer; the Equator, and later the Tropic of Capricorn. In the seventeenth century these ceremonies were generally designed to determine whether the individual was capable of withstanding the rigours of a life at sea, and were of the roughest sort.

The ceremonies that are carried out today have lost the religious significance and with the exception of some horse-play and a good sousing, can hardly be called rough. They are really an initiation to sea life. There are ceremonies for crossing the Equator, the Arctic Circle, the Antarctic Circle and the International Date Line. There are also ceremonies conducted on sighting the Grand Banks of Newfoundland and upon entering the Canadian 'Pays d'en Haut.'

Crossing the Line: The Equator

One week before the ship is due to cross the Equator, the cox'n and executive officer ascertain which members of the ship's company, (known as "shellbacks") have previously been initiated into 'King Neptune's Court.' The oldest and most dignified 'Son of Neptune' is selected to serve as "Neptunus Rex" at the ceremony. In addition, a number of uninitiated members of the crew (known as "tadpoles") are noted to be served with the Royal summons to appear before the court.

HMCS _____ on entering
Domain of Neptunus Rex
Notice and listen ye landlubber
I order and command you to appear before me and my court on _____ to be initiated in the mysteries of my special royal domain. If you fail to appear you shall be given as food for sharks, whales, sea turtles, pollywogs, salt water frogs, and all living things of the sea, who will devour you, head, body, and soul as a warning to land-lubbers entering my domain without warrant.

You are charged with the following offences (e.g., excessive sea sickness, foreign Port Melancholy)

Therefore, appear and obey or suffer the penalty
Davey Jones
Royal Scribe to His Majesty

The following is the cast of characters required for a "Crossing the Line Ceremony": (Their numbers will vary with the size of the crew.)

King Neptune
Oldest and most 'dignified' senior son of Neptune.

Queen Aphrodite
A good looking young seaman suitably attired in seaweed and rope netting.

Royal herald
A senior MARS officer as king of the sub-lieutenants.

Royal scribe
"Davey Jones"; the cox'n or ship's writer.

Mermaid
Customarily an unwashed chief stoker naked from the waist up.

Royal doctors and barbers
Charged with the treatment and appearance of all those summoned before Neptune.

Bears
The King's personal guard, charged with carrying out the punishments ordered by court.

Police
Actually secret police charged with ferreting out novices not previously summoned and reporting their presence to the court. The subsequent arrest of these greenhorns is also the duty of the police.

Royal bugler
A bo's'n.

Royal baby
Normally the fattest sailor aboard dressed in a diaper.

Act I Scene I:
(The Bridge) As if by mistake the whole scene is enacted over the main broadcast.
Time:
Around 1900 the night before crossing the line.

O.O.W.:
(Over main broadcast) Object bearing right ahead Sir. Looks like some sort of fish. *(short pause)* Appears to be surfacing Sir.

Captain:
Very good. That will be King Neptune's herald. We are closing the Equator rapidly. First lieutenant pipe clear lower decks to the forecastle, pipe deck officer muster the honour guard. Officer-of-the-watch, stand by to .... *(Captain is interrupted by the lookout.)*

Lookout:
Green one zero, Sir, a light, near.

Captain:
Very good, alter course towards it, Officer-of-the-watch.
(The ship will close the alleged light for about five minutes with no further patter in order to allow the ship's company to assemble on the forecastle.)

Scene II:
(Both herald and the captain speak through loud hailers - the captain on the bridge and the herald on the forecastle.

Herald:
(From behind the fog spray) Ship ahoy!

Captain:
(Ship's name)

Herald:
I've heard your ship's around,
Now tell me, whither bound.

Captain:
We're sailing to (port), a city of style,
We've steamed for many a mile,
Now I've got a lot to do,
So tell me, who are you?

Herald:
I am the herald of the court,
Of his oceanic majesty;
King Neptune ordered me aboard
And I'll commit no travesty.

Captain:
For you I'll stop my ship.
Come forth, and no more lip.
(Herald accompanied by Davey Jones the Royal scribe, a mermaid, 6 bears and a bugler, advance through the spray whilst the bugler sounds the alert.)
Look sharp then sire, if you please
By what right have you to challenge us on the high seas?

Herald:
By the custom of powers invested right
In King Neptune and Queen Amphritite
Who sent us to your mighty ship
To check and see if you are fit
We cannot take you across our line.
(Herald draws his sword, and the bears growl, mermaid titters....)

Captain:
It is of course without disdain
That I will accept your word,
We're crossing into your domain
So sheath that mighty sword.
(Sword of course, is a ridiculous looking affair).

Herald:
King Neptune will be glad I'm sure
To have you cross his border.
If you're a shellback let us hope
Your papers are in order.

Captain:
I've always been a tadpole
And will have to pay the price,
For some of my men
Won't care to be very nice.
For if you think some are not hard,
Have Davey Jones inspect my guard.

Herald:
I'll do your will
So sound the still. *(To piping party)*

(Piping party complies, and as he does so Davey Jones steps through the spray. Meanwhile, the guard has been marched to the front, and Davey Jones inspects it with a lot of slapstick ...e.g., points out haircuts with a dead fish he carries under his arm like a telescope.)

Davey Jones:
A frowstier guard I've never seen,
They look like hell and smell unclean.
(Bears commence shouting "unclean, unclean" at the top of their lungs.)

Herald:
Keep silence in the bears.
(Then addressing the crew)
Before this mighty ship of war
Had slipped from her home port
A spy of mine had come aboard
Her complement to sort.
He's scanned the names of every one...
Come forward now, your work is done.
(Royal scribe makes his appearance carrying a large book.)

Royal scribe:
The nominal list I've closely scanned
To learn by whom this ship is manned:
Two hundred persons more or less
Who by their conscience must confess
They have not joined our Royal mess.
They must be made to taste the salt
Of my Monarch's Royal main,
And choke upon our pills and soap
Where they can cross again.
(Bears once more start shouting "unclean, unclean")

Herald:
Later, oh, come what may
His Majesty will hold sway.
And by the ancient laws laid down
By custom will ordain
That all you tadpoles, young and old
Be initiated in our name.

Royal scribe:
All hail, King Neptune!

The day the ship crosses the Equator, a canvas bath of suitable size is rigged. Above one side of the bath, a ducking stool and the two royal thrones are rigged. To commence the ceremony, the Royal bugler/piping party sounds 'clear lower deck' and orders all of the ship's company to the vicinity of the bath - dress of the day to be bathing suits. When all are assembled, the Royal court makes their stately procession from the Royal robing room to the bath. The members of the court go to excessive extremes in designing their costumes. While great latitude in costumes is customary, Neptunus Rex must have a bushy grey or black beard, crown and trident. Upon the arrival of the 'Royal Family,' the personal flag of King Neptune ("The Jolly Roger") is broken, and attention is sounded by the bugler/piping party.

Act II Scene I
The Quarterdeck: Lower deck will be cleared to the quarterdeck and King Neptunes court will assemble in the weapons workshop. Bears and police having cleared a path in a traditional fashion, the court itself arrives.

Herald:
(On entrance) Hear Ye! Hear Ye! Make way for his most glorious oceanic majesty Neptune Rex ruler of all who sail upon the sea upon their lawful occasion hear ye! hear ye!
(On arrival of Neptune and Queen Aphrodite)
All hail King Neptune!

Bears and Police:
All hail King Neptune!

Captain:
On humblest duty, Sire, I bring to you the ocean's King
All here on board submit today to your most just and dreadful sway.

Neptune:
Good afternoon (Ship's name) at the start I must say
I have waited months for this glorious day
I am honoured indeed, that you now cross my path
And hope and believe you'll receive a nice bath.
My barbers are good, and of course renowned
Their razors as sharp as have ever been ground,
Their lather you'll like — and as for their pills,
They are better than Beecham's and cure every ill.

Captain:
Ere you punish our crimes with terrible fork,
I present for your favour my crew to your court.

Neptune:
From my courtly herald I've heard it told
That they're some in the crew so brave and bold
As to warrant my favour....there may be some missed, so Herald, bring forward my honour list.

Herald:
Captain!
For thoughtful understanding, their failing in Bajan Isles, the faces of your crew are still wreathed in smiles,
Your lash-ups place (ship's name) lowest on the punishment chart. Please accept the Royal Order of the Soft Heart.

Neptune:
Awarded the Royal Order of the Soft Heart.
I also command you, as King of the Sea,
To pay tribute while still on your knees,
This token to be an extra beer all around,
Or I'll take your ship and run her aground.

Herald:
Supply officer!
To you with your soulful cry, "Obligated!"
Which keep the crew forever frustrated

We present this order - as old as they come;
And for seven days you'll issue rum.
Give him the Order of the Scalp.
Neptune:
Awarded the Order of the Scalp!
Herald:
PO Cook!
The chief in the galley sweats and cooks,
And stands abuse and ugly looks,
He keeps the grub so warm for noon,
He's surely entitled to this spoon.
Neptune:
Awarded the Order of the Greasy Spoon!
Herald:
Fin Po!
Summon here, the pay P.O.
So that some honour we may bestow.
Neptune:
We find it in our Royal heart,
Because you came off leave,
This ship's company financially to reprieve,
To grant you thus with ink and quill
The Order of the Banished Bill.
Herald:
Chaplain!
Here is a shellback of great extension
Has crossed many times without any mention.
I hereby decree that the Chaplain, either
Protestant or Roman Catholic,
Be awarded this Order, Old Dog of the Sea.
Neptune:
Awarded the Order of Old Dog of the Sea.
Squadron Cdr,
For steaming your Squadron from Halifax/
Esquimalt Port.
Thus giving us the pleasure of holding this court.
You have driven this Squadron a distance not
small,
To Culebra, St. Thomas, Barbados and all.
I hope that you sure will never disdain,
This knightly Order of Propeller and Chain.
Royal scribe:
Captain!
It has been often written
That many a girl you've smitten
Canadian, Hawaiian, and Japanese
American, French and Cantonese,
Your stamina I shall announce,
Shows plenty of bounce for each ounce.
Neptune:
To permit my watch to vanish
How do you say "do you" in Spanish
If these magic words you do not know
I award you....the works.
Herald:
Cox'n!
It has been represented to me
That one of my barbers shouts and screams in
cockney
You order this crew to buck-up often

In a voice to sweeten and soften
It also has been said of you
That you specialize in mermaids, age twenty-two.
Neptune:
For these crimes so varied and heinous
We give you the Order of the "Big Penis."
Royal scribe:
Sick Bay Tiffy!
For causing discomfort, pain and harm
By jabbing your shipmates with glee in the arm
And because by count these victims are legion
To him a jab in the nether region.
(Two Bears approach from behind with an exaggerated hypo).
Neptune:
Carry out the sentence

At this point, in regal and flowery language, His Majesty King Neptune I (by the grace of mythology lord of the waters, sovereign of all oceans, governor and lord high admiral of the bath — to give his traditional titles) will address the novices as to their impending fate, warning them that none shall be overlooked, and that all "shall be initiated into the mystic-rites of the freedom of the seas, according to the ancient customs of our watery kingdom."

The Royal scribe will then call each candidate forward, and they will be presented individually to King Neptune by the Royal Herald. However, each novice must first be prepared by the Royal Physicians and Barbers. The treatment consists of an enormous pill or potion obviously not toxic but certainly laxative. The chiefs and petty officers, with the assistance of the sickbay tiffy, are charged with the preparation of this medicine. In addition, the Royal Physicians may use unlikely medical tools to complete a physical examination of each novice to ensure that they are up to the ordeal they face. The Royal Barbers now step in and lather the faces of the novices with something other than shaving cream. This will then be removed with a large wooden straight razor.

Not deemed sufficiently worthy, the novice is presented before King Neptune, and the charges against him are read out by the Royal Herald. After due consideration is given to each case by the Royal Family, King Neptune pronounces the appropriate sentence, and charges the bears to carry out punishment forthwith. From time to time, should the police report that some novices are hiding, the King may interrupt the proceedings to make public announcement of the offence, and order his police to arrest the offenders and bring them before him.

Herald:
AB Man!
For filling a urinal up, to the top

With grit from the deck and with string from a mop.
For carelessly causing such utter disgrace
To him twice around with a pie in the face.
(Bears gently push two paper pie plates filled with lather into face)

Royal scribe:
OS Bloggins!
For smiling when things just couldn't be tougher
And keeping a grin when they did get rougher
We bestow on you now so you don't have to suffer
The most Royal Order of "Baby Buffer."

Neptune:
(Allow him to walk away from the pool after the presentation of large shiny medal...then grabbed by Police and...)
But wait! lest you go for a dunk in the pool
You will make a small thing of King Neptune's rule
So in order to qualify here with the rest
I decree that you now must proceed with the test.

Royal scribe:
P2 Salt!
Neptune:
While eating my dinner beneath the blue sea
A set of false teeth dropped straight into my tea.
They were marked on the gums with the name "Andy Gale"
So to you here's a set from the mouth of a whale.
(Will make up a large cardboard set for presentation by King).

Neptune:
I was missing my own so your teeth I did try
But they jumped from my head when my wife they did spy.
With loud clacking they bit her square on the left breast
And then — no, I'd better not tell you the rest
I really did think it was all quite a riot
Tell me, just what is your regular diet
But for training your teeth to behave such a way
Dunk him well so he'll always remember this day.

Royal scribe:
C.P.O. Stoker!
Neptune:
Bring forth the stoker with tongue bilingual
Big of heart but shy on inches linual
For tutoring fishes with their French
We bestow on you the order of the Wrench

Royal scribe:
Lt. Weapons!
Neptune:
Man of noise and smoke and powder
Your bloody guns get louder and louder
For messing the oceans with your lead
Forthwith you'll be known as Two Gun Fred

Royal scribe:
AB. Scran!

Neptune:
For polluting slightly our fair domains
With crap you flush from your laundry drains
No amount of pleas our favour will recover
May you sweat forever with Pusser's Scrubber

Herald:
LS. Bluenoser!
This polywog creature of stature bold
Committed a crime that leaves us cold
A dastardly deed he tried to do
To start a revolt against a shellback true
And used his Highness's name in vain
I trust this court spare him no pain
For this crime he'll have to pay
I suggest duty 'sig' the rest of the day

Judge:
A dastardly deed this revolt you planned
And from this court you should be banned
But as a shellback you wish to become
Repent, this deed which you have done
So dunk him twice my worthy bears
To cleanse his soul of such affairs.

When crossing the International Dateline, novices are summoned to appear before the court of the grand dragon. At all 'crossing the line' ceremonies, special certificates and individual cards are issued to all members of the ship's company to commemorate the occasion.

An interesting variation of the ceremony is the one performed on sighting the Banks of Newfoundland, and on entering the Canadian inland waterways.

English vessels coming to the Grand Banks of Newfoundland held Neptune's Court according to proceedings carried out on board the *Thomas* in 1816 (described by Edgar K. Thompson in the *Mariner's Mirror*, August 1966, p. 232). An account dated sixty years earlier shows how the same tradition was developing among French mariners, and came to be performed far up the St. Lawrence River, and in the very heart of North America.

In April 1756 the French warship *La Sauvage* was part of a fleet that sailed from Brest, evaded Admiral Hawke's blockade, and steered for Canada with reinforcements and supplies for the forces there. Ensigne-de-vaisseau Louis-Guillaume de Parscau du Plessis recorded in his journal the ceremony of baptism that was held when the ship reached the Banks of Newfoundland. The custom was an old one, he wrote, and its principal purpose was to separate first-timers and passengers from some of their money. The same tradition was followed in many other areas of the sea, and anyone who had been baptized was exempt from having it done again. *La Sauvage* was a new ship, and so not only were some of the people on board to be initiated, but during the ceremony the ship herself had to be ransomed by the captain to keep her figurehead from being dirtied or mutilated by "King Neptune."

The ceremony was presided over by "His Serenity, the Old Man of the Grand Bank," who of course demanded his customary rights. The captain assented, and down from the top came Neptune with an oddly outfitted court. "He was hideous," wrote du Plessis, "and decked out in the most grotesque manner. He seemed all burdened down with age and was trembling in every part of his body." The stunts began. Each person on board who had never been to the Grand Banks before had their hand tied to a rope passed through a block overhead. As he was forced to swear various oaths, a sailor pulled the line to raise his hand in solemn declaration at all the proper moments. The initiate had to promise to exact a similar ceremony from others on later voyages.

While this inquisition was going on, the members of the court were standing around the tub with buckets of water poised, ready to baptize the novice at the slightest nod from King Neptune, who would agree to belay this punishment in return for cash: not gold, pearl or mother of pearl, but "coins...what we call small change." On this occasion, however, the captain forbade that anyone who could not pay should actually be doused with water, because of the cold weather. Bonhomme Grand Banc's men had to be content to polish the faces of these recalcitrants with lampblack. Du Plessis further observed that when the ship got into port, the sailors who had exacted ransom from newcomers lived it up with their loot, buying "wine and good cheer." Presumably these marine deities delighted in intoxication and debauchery!

Over the years this ceremony for sailors making a novel passage was carried into the interior of Canada. In the same year that du Plessis' voyage was made in *La Sauvage*, a similar initiation was being made on the St. Lawrence River a few miles below Fort Frontenac (Kingston, Ontario), well over a thousand miles from blue water. This was "Pointe au Baptême," so called because "of a baptism that was carried out there, as they do on the Grand Banks." The rationale for performing the ceremony at this site was that it was above the long and laborious stretch of rapids in the upper St. Lawrence River.

Later, the ceremony of playful homage and extortion shifted farther west to mark other milestones in Canadian development. In the 1780s it was being performed another thousand miles along the waterway, on the land dividing north-west Lake Superior. At this site one finally left the magnificent St. Lawrence system and entered the watershed of Hudson's Bay (Rupertsland).

Many of the 'voyageur canadiens' who kept up the tradition while paddling the interminable waters of the great northwest, had probably never seen tidewater, not to mention the sea, yet all the ceremonies marked the solemn rite attendant upon entering a new ocean of endeavour, as well as a sign of growing up and, by means of these cheerful indignities, becoming a man among men. The court of King Neptune has over the years seen a myriad of changes, but the one constant that remains is its good natured initiation for those who aspire to join the men of the sea.

XII
Christmas and New Year's Days

Christmas Day

Christmas Day is one of the few times that the discipline of the Navy is relaxed, and all members of the ship's company can mix freely. There is an air of gaiety in the ship, and the only official routine on that day is divine service. The same traditions and customs observed today have been carried on for centuries. Henry Teonge wrote in 1675:

"At four in the morning our trumpeters all doe flatt their trumpetts, and begin at our captain's cabin, and thence to all the officer's and gentlemen's cabins, playing a levite at each cabine doore, and bidding good morrow, wishing a Merry Christmas. After they go to their station, viz., on the poope, and sound three levites in honour of the morning. At 10 wee goe to prayers and sermon: text, Zacc.ix.9. Our captaine had all his officers and gentlemen to dinner with him, where wee had excellent food fayre; a ribb of beife, plumb puddings, minct pyes, etc., and plenty of good wines of severall sorts; drank healths to the King, to our wives and friends, and ended the day with much civill myrth."[19]

It was also the custom then when the ship's company was piped to 'dinner,' the captain and officers went the 'rounds.' At every mess the party had good fare pressed on them - cigars, cigarettes, a piece of plum duff, an orange - and all must be accepted in the spirit in which it was offered. A curious part of the proceedings was that the smallest ship's boy, dressed in officer's uniform, would call on the wardroom, where he would be toasted with all ceremony by all officers.

Regardless of the ship's location, a large bunch

of evergreens must be placed at the masthead (or some other conspicuous place) at dawn on Christmas morning. Messes are decorated with evergreen and coloured streamers and whatever other decorations the men can procure. This is easy in port, but at sea some consideration of the coming event serves to remind all to stow some material away for the event.

While the decoration of the ship has a high priority, it is the festivities and the food that make the Christmas celebration something to be remembered.

Today, the Christmas celebration is held before Christmas, since most HMC ships are in home port for the holidays.

There are no strict guidelines for the decoration of a ship, and ingenuity is the key to adorning the upper deck. Traditionally, the trucks and yardarms are decorated with sprigs of holly and the ship's backbone lighting is often rigged and switched on at sunset.

At 1100 hours on the day selected to hold the ship's Christmas dinner, the cox'n escorts the youngest member of the ship's company to the commanding officer's cabin. There, the commanding officer formally turns over command by exchanging tunics with the young seaman. The new commanding officer, escorted by the former commanding officer, may elect to conduct rounds of the entire ship, or the wardroom, chiefs' and petty officers' mess and the main cafeteria. He may also direct the president of the mess to authorize a round on the mess.

In accordance with custom, the wardroom officers also trade in their tunics for the Christmas meal. In this case, however, they trade them for aprons and chef's hats. Reporting to the chief cook, they are charged with serving the Christmas dinner to the remainder of the ship's company and their dependants in home port.

The young commanding officer, fatigued by his day in command, is most likely to declare a 'pipe-down' once the dinner is finished.

New Year's Day

At exactly midnight on 31 December, the youngest member of the ship's company (officer or man), sounds sixteen bells on the ship's bell. The first eight bells signify the passing of the old year, and the next eight bells herald the beginning of the new year. This is carried out by each ship, and is usually accompanied by the whistles and sirens of the ships nearby.

A new tradition for New Year's Day celebrations is developing in HMC ships in home port. More and more families are gathering for a New Year's Day dinner in the mess decks, where ordinarily sailors take their meals without the companionship of their wives and children. This

creates a pleasant and congenial atmosphere that lasts in the memories of the men long into the new year.

On both Christmas and New Year's Day the division between officer and man is relaxed, and an opportunity is afforded for each to understand and appreciate the other as ordinary men in spite of the stern discipline which is essential to naval objectives.

Notes

1. William Spavens, *The Seaman's Narrative*, (Chatham, n.p., 1796), p.127.

2. *Manual of Ceremonial - HMC Ships*, (Halifax, Maritime Command, 1981), pp. 3-27 to 3-29.

3. Ibid., pp. 3-29 to 3-32.

4. "The Divisional System in the Eighteenth Century," ed., Hodgeson and Hughes (1936), *Naval Review*, Vol. 18, (England, n. pub., 1930), pp. 644-645.

5. Lord Howe, "Instructions and Standing Orders," (England, n.p., n.d.), pp.87-88.

6. C.A. Piggot, "A brief History of the Divisional System," *The Naval Review*, No. 4, Vol. 60, (England, n.p., 1972), p.311.

7. Julian S. Corbett, ed., "Fighting Instructions 1530-1816," Naval Records Society, (England, n.p., 1905), pp.252-253.

8. Michael Bouquet, "Launching and Commissioning Customs," *The Mariner's Mirror*, No. 3, Vol.61, (St. Albans, Staples Printers Ltd., 1975) p.95.

9. C.H. MacLean, "Prayer For Keel-laying," D/Hist File, (Ceremonies, Customs and Traditions), (Ottawa, 1967).

10. The information contained in this section is taken from a memorandum written by the Chief of Maritime Doctrine and Operations (CMDO), File 11900 - CPF - 910 (CMDO), dated 3 March 1981. Exceptions are the historical data on HMCS *Winnipeg*, HMCS *Montreal*, HMCS *Halifax*, HMCS *Saskatoon*, and HMCS *Toronto*. This material was contained in: Ken Macpherson and John Burgess, *The Ships of Canada's Naval Forces 1910-1981*, (Toronto, Collins Publishers, 1981), pp. 134, 49, 92, 84, and 63 respectively.

11. Bernard Peyton Jr., "Why a Ship is a 'SHE'," *The Crowsnest*, No. 8, Vol. 5, (Ottawa, Queen's Printer, 1953), p.10.

12. "There'll Always be a Launching," *The Compass*, (n.p., Feb. 1959), pp.26-30.

13. C.H. Maclean, Deputy Chaplain General, RCN, "A Ceremony for Blessing a Ship at the Launching," Memorandum P 5111 - 5 - 13(CG(P)), (Ottawa, 1967), n.pag.

14. "The Ship's Cook, A Great Officer," *The Naval Chronicle*, Vol. 33, (England, n.p., 1815), p.377.

15. Isaac Schomberg, Esq., *Naval Chronology or An Historical Summary of Naval and Maritime Events from the time of the Romans to the Peace Treaty of 1802, With An Appendix, In five Volumes*, Vol. 1, (London, C. Roworth of Hudson's Court, 1802) p.5.

16. Kenneth Fenwick, "Early Gun Drill," *The Mariner's Mirror*, (St. Albans, Staples Printers Ltd., Feb. 1953), pp. 65-67.

17. Ibid.

18. Ibid.

19. Henry Teonge, "Christmas at Sea," *Clowes Diary*, Vol. 2, (n.p., 1678), p.225.

3 Miscellaneous Naval Customs

I
The Bo's'n's 'Call' and Its Use

Although it is known that the ancient Greek Navy used flutes to set the time for rowers, early English records make no reference to the 'call' prior to 1500 A.D. There is unfortunately no mention of flute, pipe or whistle in Torr's *Ancient Ships*, but the theory that the instrument known as a "bo's'n's call or whistle" developed from the "Pipes of Pan" is not unlikely.

Joinville, (who accompanied St. Louis on the crusade in 1248) while writing the life of the Saint, indicated that the whistle was used to command the crossbowmen to come on deck, and that the command was to be obeyed.

A work called *Norman Antiquities* refers to a picture of the eighth or ninth century in which a man on the deck of a ship is said to be blowing a whistle; however, this is questionable. A manuscript in the Vatican library shows that orders of M. Piero Monzenigo, Captain-general of the Venetian Galleys (1420) refer to the 'Comité' and the 'sous-Comités' using whistles to give the rowers the signal for each stroke of the oars.

About this time, the whistle came to be used as a badge of rank as well as an instrument of command. A fifteenth century manuscript in the Bibliothèque de l'Arsenal shows Philothetes, Admiral of the Argonauts, wearing a whistle of gold held by a golden chain. The manuscript also shows a statue of Philip de Chabot, Lord of Brion, Admiral of France and Brittany (1532) with a whistle hung round his neck by a cord.

Several examples of the Admiral's whistle are found in England. The earliest is in the church at Castle Hedingham in Essex, where a stone shield bearing the Arms of John De Vere, Earl of Oxford (Admiral of England 1485), shows one about fourteen inches in length. Pepys, collecting information for a history of the Royal Navy, found only three instances of the Lord High Admiral's whistle which appear to have been used for giving commands as well as a mark of honour.

The following appeared in Boteler's "Dialogues" of 1643:

"Captain: The particular duty of the cockson is to have an eie and care of the barge of shalope and of all the implements thereunto belonginge; and so to be ready with his bote company or gang of men to mann these botes upon all occasions and whensoever either the captaine of any p'son of fashion is to use the Bote, he is to have itt trimmed with her cushions and carpett, p'vided for itt by the Captaine, and himselfe is in p'son to bee ready to steere her out of her sterne. And with his silver whistle to cheare up and direct his gang of rowers and to keep them together when they are to waite. And this is the lowest officer in a shippe that is admitted to weare a whistle.

Admiral: How many be the officers in a shippe that carry whistles?

Captain: There are three: the Master, the Boatswaine and the Cockson, for though the Captaine may doe the same at his pleasure, yet it is neither usual nor with any necessity."[1]

Monson also makes reference to a master's whistle:

"As the master commands the tacking of the ship, the hoisting or striking of the yard, the taking in or putting forth the sails, upon winding of the master's whistle the bo's'n takes it with his, and sets the sailors with courage to do their work, every one of them knowing by the whistle what they are to do.[2]

The following lines, taken from "The Straights Voyage" or "St. David's Poem," written by John Balthorpe around 1671, contain what might be the first instance of the whistle being referred to as a 'call.' Balthorpe was a clerk on board the St. David, which was Sir John Harman's flagship in the Mediterranean from May 1669, to April 1671:

"Samuel Hatfield is our Bo's'n's name,
He's man enough, I'll say the same.
With silver call on deck he stands,
Winds it, 'make haste aloft more hands,
Come on, my lads, look to your gear,

Be sure that we have all things clear."[3]

Two final quotations in which whistles are mentioned are taken from the writings of Boteler. The first, incidentally, lays to rest the popular, but erroneous idea that 'piping the side' originated because captains after visiting ashore had to be hoisted on board:

"Speaking of two ships meeting at sea and hailing each other, if they prove to be friends, the hailing is renewed with whistles and trumpets."[4]

"Dialogue V: Such ceremonies as are usual and proper for the entertainment either of the Prince himself, or of his High Admiral or any of his Generals.

Notice being given of the intention of any of these to visit ships, etc., and to be received publicly with Ceremonies... The ship's barge is to be sent to fetch the visitor having the cockson with his whistle in the stern... Upon the more near approach of the barge, the noise of trumpets are to sound, and so to hold on until the barge come within less than musket shot, and what time the trumpets are to cease and all such as carry whistles are to whistle a welcome three severall times."[5]

A whistle closely resembling the one in Figure 3.01, but dating back to 1720, is the oldest one known to be in existence.

Figure 3.02 shows the various forms that the whistle or call has taken through the years.

The following quotation is an account of the manner in which a bo's'n's whistle or call should be used.

"If the whistle is blown into with moderate force a certain note dependent on the make of the instrument will be obtained. If, however, it be blown into with greater force and the air which would escape is throttled by the fingers, a note almost an octave higher will be sounded. By moderating the throttling, that is, by not closing the fingers completely over the side of the 'buoy,' any note between these may be obtained. An expert bo's'n's mate can probably produce eight notes by using hand and mouth. By gradually closing the fingers over it, it is possible to run from one note into the other, giving an effect somewhat similar to that obtained by sliding a finger down a string of a fiddle.

The hand should contain the side of the 'buoy' close against the ball of the thumb. The tip of the thumb should be resting on the shackle or rather beyond it. The first finger should grasp the whistle to the ball of the thumb by resting on the middle of the side of the 'keel.'

When throttled, the hand should be clenched, bringing the middle finger to the outer side of the 'buoy,' and the third and

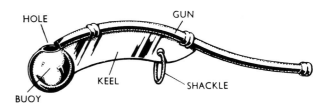

3.01 The bo's'n's whistle or "call", 1982.

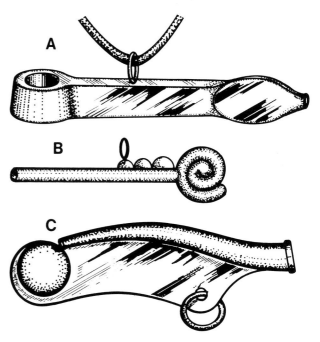

3.02 The bo's'n's call or whistle. A. 1562; B. 1630; C. 1700.

fourth fingers close against it, taking care not to touch any part of the edge of the hole in the 'buoy' as this would stop the sound altogether. When open the second, third and fourth fingers should be lifted together. When running a note up, as mentioned above, the second, third and fourth fingers are slowly closed (or opened). Tuning can be carried out by scraping the wind edge of the hole, and when properly tuned up a whistle should sound if held with its mouth to a gentle breeze."[6]

It should be understood that the 'expression' gives the method or 'touch' with which many calls are carried out. For example, in the call 'walk back,' the speed of the undulations indicated to the hands the speed of 'walking back' that was required of them. Similarly, the 'belay' sharply piped indicated a 'catch a turn,' not 'take your time and belay and coil down.'

Pipes on the Bo's'n's Call

(a) Figures indicate 'time' of the pipe in seconds.
(b) Line I indicates the 'open or 'normal' note of the call.
(c) Line II indicates the higher or 'throttled' note of the call.
(d) Lines shown thus ——— indicate a plain true note.
(e) Lines shown thus 〰 indicate a 'warble.'
(f) Lines shown thus ᜫᜫᜫ indicate a 'trill.'
(g) The slope of the line and the time in seconds speed of ascent or descent of a note.
(h) Pipes still in use are indicated by an asterisk.

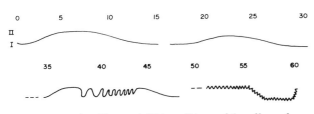

*3.03 'Dinner' or 'Supper'. This call is used for all meals other than those of watchkeepers, for which pipe Figure 3.24 is used. This pipe could be played by a chorus of bo's'n's mates.

3.04 'Sweepers'. This pipe follows the pipe "Clear up decks." It calls all upper deck and lower deck sweepers to their work.

*3.05 'The side'; also 'away galley' or 'Admiral's barge'. This call is a purely naval salute, and is used for the Sovereign and other members of the Royal Family when in uniform, naval flag officers, all officers commanding HMC ships and squadrons, and the guard officer when flying his pennant.

*3.06 'Still'. This call is used to call the hands to attention either as a mark of respect or for any other purpose, and is also used for stopping all work in order to prevent an accident.

*3.07 'Carry on'.

3.08 'Heave round the capstan'. Each note of this call is played as a separate and distinct note.

*3.09 'Call bo's'n's mate'. This call is to be repeated by all bo's'ns when they converge on the desired position.

*3.10 'Light to', or 'let go'.

*3.11 'High enough', or 'avast heaving' or 'hoisting'.

*3.12 'Belay', or 'catch a turn'.

*3.13 'Haul taut'.

3.14 'Haul or hoist' (standing hauls).

*3.15 'Veer', 'walk back', or 'ease'. The rate of 'walking back' is indicated by the rate of the undulations in the call, and the call continues for as long as 'walking back' is desired.

3.16 'Veer and haul'. First, 'walk back' (Fig. 3.15), then 'heave round the capstan' (Fig. 3.08) would have been sounded.

3.17 'Haul and veer'. First 'heave round the capstan' (Fig. 3.08), then 'walk back' (Fig. 3.15) would be sounded.

II/I 0 1 2 3 4 5 6 7 8 9 10 11 12

3.18 'Reelers' or 'sounding party'. Calls the hands for streaming or hauling in the patent log, and is also used for the sounding party, the duties of the latter having to be specified by a pipe following the call. When used in connection with the patent log, the call is followed by the pipe "Lay aft the reelers."

II/I 0 1 2 3 4 5 6 7 8 9 10 11 12 13

*3.19 'Lash up and stow', 'call the watch'; any long pipe which is not an immediate order. In this case, the 'pipe' is prefaced with 'd'ye hear there'. When used for 'calling the watch,' this call is followed by the pipe "Call—l—l—the port watch" (or part of the hands required) and signifies that those hands "called" are the hands required for duty. It is also used to bring some matter to the notice of the ship's company when "The word is being passed," and the pipe should always be prefaced on these occasions by the words "D'ye hear there" to indicate that the matter is for general information, for example "D'ye hear there the last mail will close at noon today" or "D'ye hear there ... The attention of the hands is drawn to the mess deck notice board," etc., etc.

II 0 1 2 3 4 5 6 7 8 9 10 11 12 13 14   Sharp Finish

*3.20 'Pipe down'. The meaning of this call is "Hands turn in" in which case no pipe follows the call, or "Everyone down from aloft." In this case the call is followed by the pipe "Lay down from aloft." It is also used when lowering the gantline for retrieving washclothes, night clothing, scrubbed hammocks, etc. Another meaning is "Hands will not be required until further orders." If used in this sense, however, it is usual to "Call the watch" (see Fig. 3.19) prior to "Piping down." The meaning will be apparent by either the time of day or the operation in progress.

II/I 0 1 2 3 4 5 6 7

3.21 'Mast head men or top men way aloft'.

II/I 0 1 2 3 4 5 6 7

3.22 'Lay out'.

II/I 0 1 2 3 4 5

*3.23 'Hoist away', 'stay away', 'walk or run with it', 'haul away'.

II/I 0 1 2 3 4

*3.24 'Away' boat except the galley or Admiral's barge. Also used when clearing up decks, in which case it is followed by 'c-l-e-a-r up decks', which is in turn followed by Fig. 3.04 call. This call should be followed by the drawn out pipe "Awa—a—a—y first cutter's crew" (or whichever boat's crew is desired). It is also used before short orders for which no special call is assigned, for instance, "Boys fall in," "Afternoon watchmen to dinner," etc.

It is the crew which is called away, and not the boat itself.

II
Grog and the Splicing of the Mainbrace

A mighty bowl on deck he drew,
And filled it to the brink;
Such drank the Burford's gallant crew,
And such the Gods shall drink.
The sacred robe which Vernon wore
Was drenched within the same;
And hence his virtues guard our shore,
And *grog* derives its name.[7]

Grog in the Making

For a long time now "Grog aboard and a girl ashore" have been all the solace that 'Jack Tar' asked for. "Blest with a smiling can of grog" he laughed dangers to scorn and forgot his toils, and has even been known to drink the health of his natural enemy, the 'purser.' He has even considered a taste for grog as an essential qualification in a sailor's wife:

"A butcher can provide her prog,
Three threads to drink, a tailor;
What's that to biscuit and to grog
Procured her by her sailor?[8]

Whatever may have been the dangers and toils of the week, on Saturday night "the ample can adorned the board," and the toast of "Sweethearts and wives" was duly honoured.

For many years Jack Tar drank beer in lieu of spirits, and plenty of it, since the allowance was a gallon per man per day. This is, however, not as excessive as it looks, considering that it took the place not only of spirits, but of cocoa, tea and even to a great extent of water, since facilities for storing water were extremely limited. Wine often substituted for beer especially when wine-laden ships were captured.

There were two types of beer supplied. One was a strong ale, issued in iron-bound casks for foreign service, and the other of milder brew for the home station. Both, apparently, were hopelessly bad.

For some time the supply was entrusted to contractors, but in spite of the most rigid rules, the quality got worse. Then port was tried, but apparently without success, and 1800 out of the 3000 butts purchased were resold to the brewers. As a last resort government breweries were established.

It was extremely important to provide beer that kept its quality, since ships kept at sea for much longer periods than now; fresh provisions were scarce, scurvy raged, and a good sound beer was an excellent anti-scorbutic. Although Government breweries improved the quality, the supply of good beer for sea-going purposes did not improve. Corruption was rife and the master brewers grew rich while ships' companies perished for want of proper nourishment. Gradually, wine mixed with water and spirits, (at first brandy, then whiskey and subsequently rum) were introduced as an alternative ration, but the ships were only supplied with beer while in port and for the first few days at sea.

The following excerpts from an "Admiralty Minutes Book" show how whiskey was introduced into the fleet, and how it gradually gave way to rum.

"24 March 1743. The College of Physicians having given their opinion that the best English spirits distilled from malt (of equal strength with French brandy) may be safely used as a part of sea victualling, and the Board having under their consideration whether it may not be best for His Majesty's Service, as well as more agreeable to the seaman and more conducive to their health, to have half the present allowance of beer supplied in such English spirits, especially in ships at home or cruising on this side of the Mediterranean...

15 October 1743. According to the reports of the Captains who have used them the spirits are of benefit to the health of seamen.

31 December 1743. A storeroom is to be built in each of His Majesty's Ships for the malt spirits furnished for the use of the seaman... the said spirits are to be sent on board in puncheons, hogsheads and quarter casks, and that proper care be taken in issuing and starting the same.

16 January 1745. The Board have taken into consideration the frequent sickness onboard several of His Majesty's Ships, and also the manner of issuing the beer and spiritous liquors to the seamen; and thinking it will be more agreeable to the seamen in general, and more conducive to their health, if, instead of spending solely upon the beer and brandy (spirits) afterwards, they should be allowed a

portion of each every day.... (Orders to be given accordingly)." [9]

Brewing finally stopped in 1831 and rum became the only beverage.

The first allowance, half a pint a day, was issued in two servings, but so much quarrelling and insubordination took place at the evening serving that Admiral Vernon (known as the "Old Grog") instituted the practice of diluting it with water. This practice earned for the mixture the name it still bears. The Admiral's uncomplimentary nickname stemmed from the peculiar boat cloak, made of coarse material called 'grogram,' which he wore while walking the decks of his flagship.

Admiral Vernon probably never dreamed that he was starting a tradition, as he was violently opposed to strong drink and its ill effects on the morals of his men. He would have preferred to prohibit its use entirely, but agreed to try the weaker mixture, hoping it would serve as a preventive measure against the fevers that had decimated many previous expeditions to the Caribbean.

In the late 1730s, after a distinguished carrer in the Navy, Admiral Vernon entered politics and, as a member of the British Parliament, demanded more energetic military measures against Spain. Repeatedly assailing the government for its failure to face Spain's challenge in the New World, he finally declared that he could capture Porto Bello, the mighty Spanish stronghold in Panama, with a squadron of only six ships. The Government promptly called his bluff, gave him the six ships, and sent him off to live up to his word.

"Old Grog" surprised everybody, including the Spaniards. Porto Bello was caught unprepared for the attack and surrendered on the second day of fighting. When the news reached London, Vernon was the hero of the day, and remained so for years to come. But to the sailors of his small squadron, "Old Grog" was either a hero or a cheat, depending upon whether a man liked his rum neat or diluted with water. For it was after the capture of Porto Bello that "Old Grog" introduced watered rum to the men who were long used to a pint a day of straight spirits. Flushed with victory and mellowed by the rum, the sailors of the flagship, HMS*Burford*, raised their cups in a toast to "Old Grog," and the name stuck to the new drink.

Grog soon caught on throughout the Royal Navy and before long its provision became not only a tradition, but a statute of law.

The traditional daily ceremony for the issue of grog began with the sounding of 'up spirits' on the bo's'n's call at six bells in the forenoon (1100 hours). On this signal, the officer-of-the-day, the master-at-arms, the supply petty officer, and the butcher assembled at the door of the spirit room. The master-at-arms unlocked the two heavy padlocks, and the party filed into the dimly lighted room among the casks, stowed "bung up and bilge free." The butcher would then tap a barrel, insert a siphon pump into the bung hole, and carefully draw off the day's total ration for the ship's company. Neat tots were then issued for the petty officers, and the remainder was transferred to a small cask, called a "barrico" (pronounced "breaker"). The barrico was then padlocked and carried from the spirit room to the big oaken rum tub, with its shining hoops of brass and its inscription, "The Queen - God Bless Her." Here, the barrico was left in the care of a sentry.

Five minutes before 'hands to dinner' was piped at noon, the 'rum call' was sounded on the bugle, and each mess sent its messman to the rum tub with a jug (or 'fanny') to draw the ration for his mess. Again, under the watchful eye of the officer-of-the-day, a rigid ceremony was performed. The requisite volume of water was carefully measured out and, after having been tasted by the petty-officer-of-the-day to ensure that it was not salt, was poured into the rum tub. The barrico was then unlocked and the rum emptied into the tub. The supply petty officer, or 'jimmy bungs' (the time-honoured name for that individual who dished out the rum), took his place opposite the master-at-arms and awaited the arrival of the messmen. The exact amount of grog necessary for the ship, some fifty gallons for a large vessel, was then carefully measured out.

Assuming the messman from No.6 mess was the first to arrive he would call out: "Number 6 mess." The steward would check the mess' ledger for the number of men in "6" mess, then order the appropriate amount of grog. The steward would reply, "Half out of six." 'Jimmy Bungs' would take six pints of grog, then draw one-half back to the tub. This left five and one-half pints, (eleven half-pints for the mess of eleven men) which would then be poured into the mess 'fanny.' The procedure would be repeated for all the messes in the ship. Any residue left in the rum tub was poured down the scuppers while the officer-of-the-day looked on.

The amount of the rum ration, as well as the ratio of rum to water in the mixture, was steadily reduced over the years. Even so, diluted as it was, during the evening serving drunkenness became the rule rather than the exception, and accidents and offences steadily increased.

Even the prevalent use of corporal punishment failed to check the abuse. Lord Nelson and his flag captain, Hardy, though ordinarily humane and generous, were compelled to use the utmost rigour against offenders, and many instances of corporal punishment for drunkenness are re-corded as having taken place on board *Victory* between August 1, 1803, and October 31, 1804.

If each man had taken his share there would probably not have been a problem, but after the introduction of tea many men began to refuse their evening ration, which went to the cook of the day. There are instances on record of a particular cook getting the grog of 32 men. A bo's'n's mate, giving evidence before a committee in 1850, on being asked what the cook did with the rum replied, "he sat down between him and another one (his mate) and drank it."

Moreover, it was common practice to make payments in rum for small services, such as making up clothes, etc., so any man so inclined had plenty of opportunities to satisfy his appetite.

Less severe punishment was also handed out. Sir Charles Napier, serving in HMS *Powerful* gave two or three dozen lashes for a first offence, and four dozen lashes for the second.

One officer, it is reported, in an attempt to reform a smart hand but an incorrigible drunkard hired a cell as soon as he reached harbour and kept the man imprisoned until his leave was over. On being released, the astonished Tar asked if the treatment would be repeated every time the ship entered a port. He was assured that this would be the case and, after considering his predicament for a few days, he requested that his grog be stopped.

The procedure of 'drinking at the tub' was also tried. Instead of the cooks of messes being served the grog for the lower deck, the mess basins of the whole ship's company were arranged in rows by the tub, and each cook got the allowance for his mess and divided it into the basins. Then each man picked up his basin, drank his grog, and passed the empty basin across to the opposite side. Although this practice effectively checked drunkenness and was approved by the medical officers, it was regarded as contrary to Service procedures. Moreover, it seriously interfered with the time allotted for dinner, since the issue in a large ship took up to 25 minutes. It was, therefore, mostly used as a form of punishment.

Although the ration of spirit had been reduced in 1824 from one half-pint to one gill (quarter pint), the reform was largely neutralized by the substitution of the imperial for the wine measure, which added one-fifth to the ration. The excesses became intolerable after the evening serving. Men could not go about the ship in safety. In 1850 a committee was appointed to enquire into the problem, and found that the majority of crimes and offences were attributable to the second 'tub.' They recommended that the allowance be cut by half, the evening serving be abolished, no ration be given midshipmen and boys, and the issue of neat (un-mixed) spirit stop altogether.

In 1881, the issue of the spirit ration to officers, other than warrant officers, ceased, while in the ship's company, the issue was limited to men over twenty.

The rum used in this mixture was British Navy Pusser's rum. (The name 'Pusser' is a corruption of the word 'Purser.' For centuries sailors have referred to the 'purser' as the 'pusser,' and anything which came from the 'purser' was known as 'pusser's' and still is today).

The rum was a dark blend of five rums from Demerara and Trinidad which had been blended and bottled on the island of Tortola in the Crown Colony of the British Virgin Islands. The colour was also in keeping with tradition, since this naturally golden rum was always darkened to camouflage any cloudiness in the water when it was mixed with the rum to produce the grog.

The issue of Pusser's rum was finally abolished in the Royal Navy in August 1970. The reasons for its abolition were much the same as in the past; men were much more efficient without it, and in a highly technical and sophisticated Navy, no risk or margin of error which might be attributable to alcohol could be allowed. So, on 1 August, 1970, the last tot of 'Pusser's' was drunk in HM ships.

The issue of the 'tot' ceased in the Canadian Navy on 30 March, 1972, and on each of HMC ships glasses were raised in a final salute. "The Queen" was toasted and many a man was saddened at the passing of such an old and a heart-warming tradition.

Splicing the Main Brace

The expression to 'splice the main brace,' meant to serve out an extra ration of grog to celebrate an occasion. No one knows when it first came into use. The custom probably originated as a reward to those who were required to splice the brace of the mainsail, the largest and heaviest piece of running rigging in the ship. Historians have concluded:

> "There are many different explanations concerning the origin of this expression, but it is generally considered that this operation was one of such rarity that it merited the serving out of an extra tot. The main brace, being one of the heaviest pieces of running rigging in the ship, was probably seldom spliced, but presumably renewed instead."[10]

Today, the order to "Splice the main brace" is only given by:

A member of the Royal Family; His/Her Excellency, the Governor-general of Canada; or the Chief of the Defence Staff.

When the order is given, every member is entitled to receive a special issue of 2 ½ fluid ounces of spirits.

Navy Rum Terminology

Following is a list of naval rum terminology with which every aspiring seaman should be familiar:

Grog: Traditionally, 2 parts water, 1 part Pusser's rum...

Tot: ⅛ pint rum, the standard daily ration...

Neat: Rum without water...

Splice the Main Brace: A double tot for a job well done...

The Framework of Hospitality: Where 3 sippers equal 1 gulp, 3 gulps equal 1 tot...

Sippers: A small gentlemanly sip from a friend's rum issue...

Gulpers: One, but only one, big swallow from another's tot...

Sandy Bottoms: To see off whatever's in a mug when offered by a friend...

Bob's-a-Dying: In Nelson's day, it meant a 'stupendous drunken bash.'

Drink Measures

1 dash = 8 to 10 drops
1 tablespoon = 3 teaspoonfuls
1 jigger = 1 ½ ounces
1 'Tot' = 2 Imperial ounces or 2 ½ US ounces
6 dashes = 1 teaspoonful
2 tablespoons = 1 fluid ounce or 1 pony
1 large jigger = 2 ounces
1 cup = 8 ounces or ½ pint

18th Century Royal Navy Drinks

Flip

A favorite below decks during the 1800s — especially while in port where plenty of fresh beer was available.

2 ounces Pusser's
1 pint cold beer or ale

Pour into tall glass or mug, the rum first, and do not stir.

Bombo

This was a favorite when the men were ashore in the West Indies. It later became popular as an afternoon drink on the southern plantations in the United States.

Fill tall glass with ice cubes
2 ounces Pusser's
½ ounce sugar syrup

Fill glass with water, stir, and garnish with orange slice and cherry. Sprinkle nutmeg and cinnamon on top.

Navy Punch

This was a drink for the officers and those who came from the quarterdeck. It was popular at dinner parties and balls.

Shaker filled with ice cubes
1 ounce lime juice
2 ounces liquid sugar
3 ounces Pusser's

Shake well, and pour into tall glass or large old fashioned glass partly filled with ice.

Garnish with fruit and sprinkle nutmeg on top.

Hot Toddy

This was often issued under conditions of cold and fatigue when rounding Cape Horn — or 'Old Cape Stiff' as it was often called during the many years before the Panama Canal.

2 ounces Pusser's
1 tablespoon brown sugar

Place ingredients in a heavy earthenware mug, pour in hot water, and top off with nutmeg and stick of cinnamon.

Grog

Old fashioned glass
1 tot (2 ½ ounces) Pusser's
2 tots good water

Squeeze a wedge of fresh lime and stir
Float the expended lime on top.

Modern Pusser's Drinks

Tortola Orangeade

For those who miss breakfast on a hot day.

Fill a tall glass with ice cubes
2 ounces Pusser's
Fill glass with orange juice
Juice from lime wedge to taste
Stir, and garnish with cherry and orange slice.

Modern Navy Grog

This drink isn't anything like the old 'grog,' but it is tasteful and refreshing.

Blender with 1 cup cracked ice
3 ounces Pusser's
1 ounce lime juice
1 ounce orange juice
1 ounce pineapple juice
1 ounce passion fruit nectar
½ ounce Falernum

Blend briefly and pour into old fashioned glass with a few ice cubes. Garnish with fruit and serve with a straw.

P & P

'P & P' or Pusser's and Pepsi, a more modern version of 'Rum and Coke' which was the most popular drink of World War II.

Tall glass filled with ice cubes
2 to 3 ounces Pusser's
Pepsi Cola
Fresh juice from a lime wedge
Stir, and float the expended wedge on top.

Pusser's & Tonic

Fill tall glass with ice cubes
1 ½ ounces Pusser's
Tonic water
Squeeze slice of lime
Stir

Pina Colada

1 to 1 ½ cups shaved or cracked ice
2 ounces Pusser's
3 ounces unsweetened pineapple juice
2 ounces cream of coconut
½ ounce Cointreau

Combine in a blender and blend briefly. Pour into a large cocktail glass and serve with a straw. Garnish with a cherry.

Planter's Punch

Shaker with 1 cup cracked ice
3 ounces Pusser's
1 ounce lime juice
1 ounce sugar syrup
3 to 5 dashes Angustora bitters
soda water

Shake well and pour unstrained into tall glass with several ice cubes. Top off with soda water, stir and garnish with lime slice. Serve with a straw.

Royal Navy Fog Cutter

Shaker filled with ice cubes
2 ounces Pusser's
½ ounce gin
2 ounces lemon juice
1 ounce orange juice
½ ounce orgeat syrup

Shake well, and strain into tall glass filled with ice cubes. Float 1 teaspoon dry sherry on top, garnish and serve with a straw.

Bloody Pusser's

Fill tall glass with ice cubes
1 ½ ounce Pusser's
1 ounce lime juice
fill with tomato juice
1 or 2 dashes Worcestershire sauce
1 dash Tabasco sauce

Sprinkle 'Tortola Salt' (pepper and spices) to taste, then stir and garnish with slice of lime.

The Big Dipper

Popular on Atlantic crossings just before star time.

Shaker filled with ice cubes
1 ounce Pusser's
1 ounce brandy
1 tablespoon lime juice
½ teaspoon sugar
dash of Cointreau

Shake well, strain into an old fashioned glass with several ice cubes, fill with club soda and stir slightly.

Pusser's Teatotaler

Tall glass filled with ice cubes
2 ounces Pusser's
3 level teaspoons iced tea mix
Fill glasses with water, stir, and garnish with slice of lime or lemon.

Force 12

The test for good sea legs.

Shaker filled with ice cubes
2 ounces Pusser's
1 ounce vodka
½ ounce grenadine
2 ounces pineapple juice
Shake well and pour into tall glasses. Garnish with fruit slices.

Tortola Cooler

This drink started on Main Street in Road Town, Tortola, a sailor's delight.

Tall glass filled with ice cubes
1 ½ ounces Pusser's
4 ounces orange juice
Top off with 7-Up
1 teaspoon fresh lime juice
Stir and garnish with orange wedge and cherry.

The Deep Six

This is an unusual drink: smooth, flavorful, expensive and powerful.

Tall glass filled with crushed ice
2 ounces Pusser's
1 tablespoon lime juice
½ ounce sugar syrup
champagne
Combine the rum, lime juice and sugar, and stir well. Then fill the glass with champagne and stir gently. Garnish with a slice of lime.

Pusser's Daiquiri

More flavor than the standard Daiquiri.

Fill shaker with ice cubes
1 ½ ounces Pusser's
½ ounce lime juice
½ ounce sugar syrup
Shake well and strain into chilled cocktail glass.

Admiral Vernon's order which created 'grog,' read in part... "and limes to make (the rum) more palatable to them...(when mixed with water)." And so it was that 'grog' (rum and water) mixed with lime juice came to be known as a 'Limey' and the British ships as 'Limejuicers.' The modern version of the 'limey' is given below; it uses soda water in place of water.

Limey

Fill tall glass with ice cubes.
2 ounces Pusser's
Top off with soda water
Squeeze the juice from one-half lime.
Sugar to taste if desired, but it is not traditional. Stir, and float the expended one-half lime on top.

III
Naval Commissions and Warrants

The "Commission" and the "Commissioned Officers"

The earliest commissions were issued to a selection of the great barons when the King wanted to call out his forces. Land was held in return for military service and when the lords received their 'commission of array,' they mustered their vassals and tenants at a specified place and time to await the King's command.

The same system applied to the fleet. The "Black Book of The Admiralty" contains an article on the office and duties of Admirals that was probably written before 1351 (in the time of King Edward III).

An Admiral, after receiving his commission, had to immediately appoint his lieutenants, deputies and other officers, who were required to find out what ships and seamen were available in the Kingdom. He then requisitioned the vessels he needed, with their mercantile crews, had fore- and after-castles fitted, and sent soldiers on board to do the fighting. The mariners were only required to navigate the ship.

Captain and lieutenant came with the soldiers — a company to each ship. Later, when sailors and fighters had been amalgamated, the officers were appointed by commission, each to a particular post in a named ship for a specified cruise; a permanent rank in the Navy did not exist.

Between commissions these men were civilians rather than naval officers — they went to sea as merchant officers, served with the Army, pursued a political career, or found some other form of employment. Experience in the wars of the eighteenth century taught the Admiralty the advisability of retaining the services of experienced sea officers. To this end they adopted the method of paying officers half the usual rate when they did not hold an office in a ship. Then, when they received their commissions, they received full pay.

The commissions of the 1660s were worded as follows:

"James, Duke of York and Albany, Earl of Ulster, Lord High Admiral of England and Ireland, Constable of Dover Castle, Lord Warden of the Cinque Ports, and Governor of Portsmouth.

To Captaine Pakington Broke, Captain of His Ma'ties Ship the *Foresight*, for this present expedition.

Whereas I have appointed you to be Captaine of His Ma'ties said shipp, and the charge and command of Captain in her accordingly, hereby willing and charging the Maister, and all other officers and company in His Ma'ties and shipp, jointly and severally in their said employments, to behave themselves with all due respect and obedience unto you, their said Captaine. And you likewise shall so obey and follow such orders and directions as you shall from time to time receive from myself, or any other your superior officer, for His Ma'ties service; hereof nor you nor any of you may fail, as you will answer the contrary at your perils; for which this shall be your warrant. Given under my hand and seal, at St. James,' this ninth day of August, 1662.

James

By command of His R. Highness,

W. Commyns."[11]

Until 1790, when the Admiralty finally altered the way commissions were granted, a lieutenant would be appointed by his commission to "the fourth lieutenant of His Majesty's ship *Lion*, or the first lieutenant of His Majesty's ship *Victory*." After 1790 a commission no longer specified the rank, but indicated 'seniority' (the date of his first commission in the rank). When the officers joined their ship they determined, by their seniority dates, the positions they would hold in the ship.

It was not until 1860 that the decision was made to grant one commission for each rank held, in spite of the fact that the principle of permanent rank was accepted in 1790.

After the turn of the century, one commission for all ranks from sub-lieutenant to captain came into effect.

When the Canadian and Australian Navies were established in 1910 it was intended that their officers should be interchangeable with their opposite numbers in the Royal Navy. One of the necessary steps to be taken to ensure this was to word their commissions identically so that all were appointed "in His Majesty's Fleet." However, for some years, because of a legislative delay, the King was not in a position to make an Order in Council authorizing the Governor-General of Canada to issue such commissions. At first, officers were commissioned "in Our Naval Service of the Dominion of Canada," but this was changed in 1912 to "in His Majesty's Canadian Fleet." Finally in 1920, the commission was changed to read "in His Majesty's Fleet" as had been originally intended.

A further change was made in 1950 as a result of the National Defence Act being passed. It defined the three categories of officers being "a person who holds His Majesty's Commission in the Royal Canadian Navy...." But commissions made no mention of the Navy by name, only of "Her Majesty's Fleet." Since the relationship between the RCN and other navies of the Commonwealth was no longer governed by the 1911 agreement, it was possible to change the commissions to fit the new act. They read "In Her Majesty's Canadian Fleet" in the heading, and "Royal Canadian Navy" in the body of the letter:

3.25 Commission scroll.

3.26 CPO warrant.

In the Canadian Armed Forces, the commission is signed by His/Her Excellency, the Governor-General of Canada, as Her Majesty's representative, and by the Minister of National Defence. Officers are commissioned, and continue to exercise command by right of their commissions, at the pleasure of the Sovereign.

Commission has always entrusted an important task to its recipient. In the days of sail, the captain was also the chief engineer, since he and the bo's'n were responsible for setting up the rigging and staying up the spars. He and the master also navigated and manoeuvred the ship, and also took charge of the men handling the canvas in storms or battle. Now, however, he no longer has to fit out and man his ship with little assistance beyond his own professional and personal resources, because the large Navy organization is there to help him. But the tasks are no lighter. His job has become more difficult because of the sophisticated machinery placed below hatches which requires the skills of a specially trained agent, the engineer officer. At the same time, many other devices have come aboard — fire control gear, radio, radar and sonar for instance, all requiring special skills for proper management. The captain, through his officers, is responsible for all of them.

When a young man is first commissioned as a sub-lieutenant, his task is to learn the skills required for leadership and command. His training has given him the technical background, but he must learn, on the job, to apply his training to the realities of a ship at sea. But mastering his specialty, (or even all specialties if that were possible) would not guarantee that he would rise far in the service — to complete his training he must learn, as well, the more difficult skills of leadership. It is this opportunity that is afforded the sub-lieutenant through his commission.

A naval officer receives a second commission when he reaches 'flag' rank (the rank of commodore or above).

The "Warrant" and the "Warrant Officers"

The 'warrant' or 'executive' officers (the old 'ship officers'), ran the ship before the advent of the 'fighting officers,' after which they held less responsible positions. Yet these men, although not of 'commission' rank, never quite lost their claim to being 'executives.' When the regulations introduced in the eighteenth century began to specify the order of command on board ship, in the event of accidents, the four old 'ship-officers' figured quite prominently. After 1746 the second master also slipped into the list, and the order of 'command' became: captain, lieutenants (first, second, third, etc.), master, second master, bo's'n, gunner and carpenter. No one else is mentioned. (The regulations did not specify what should happen if they all became casualties.) Apparently the other 'officers,' even old-standing ones like the purser and the surgeon, were regarded as altogether too "civilian" to be considered for the command of a ship of war. The same principle holds to this day, for the "order of command" of a ship goes from top to bottom through the executive branch down through the commissioned officers, warrant and petty officers to ordinary ratings. Non-executives, even of flag-rank, do not figure at all in the order.

The old warrant executives were the master, the bo's'n, the gunner and the carpenter. Although the master had a higher status on board than the other three, he was not a permanent feature of the ship. He was an officer in 'inconstant employ,' appointed to a ship as commissioned officers were for a commission of a certain duration. The other three were in constant employ — the old 'standing officers' who were not commissioned.

History has consistently taken the 'standing officers' for granted so it is easy to conclude that they had a high standard of efficiency, considering the demands placed on them. The crews changed constantly, were of varying quality and always untrained. This collection of all types, classes and conditions of essentially 'short service men' had to be moulded into a well-organized and trained crew. Though there were occasional failures, these officers usually succeeded in their efforts to co-ordinate their crews' activities.

Although the introduction of the commissioned officer made a tremendous difference, it was the standing officers who 'licked the crew' into shape. They were the mainstay of the whole system of ship economy. Each appeared to have his own particular circle of mates and permanent assistants which formed the core of each department; each had a strong allegiance to their own immediate chief (a trait which newly-commissioned captains often found irritating). This loyalty tended to circumvent the authority of the commission, and forced a captain to consider his ship as a unit.

It was the custom, as soon as the crew of a newly commissioned ship was on board, and before the ship went to sea, for the captain to rate his first-lieutenant, master, bo's'n, gunner and carpenter (assign their duties). After that these individual 'department heads' were responsible for making good seamen out of their part of the ship's company.

When the 'warrant officers' dress was instituted in 1787 the 'old ship officers,' along with the master, the surgeon and purser all went into uniform. They also all achieved the possibility of promotion to commissioned rank when, in 1864, the titles of chief bo's'n, gunner and carpenter were introduced for outstanding individuals in the various branches.

The gunner, the last of the three to make an appearance in the Navy, gradually rose to a position of prominence. This was brought about by the arrival of the great gun, and by the research which was required to improve this important piece of equipment. While the gunner seldom fitted into the 'command' function, the great gun revolution assured him a place among the new commissioned, specialist executive officers who emerged from it. In the early days he was not only responsible for the guns but also for the small arms which were stacked in his own sanctum, the 'gunroom.' He was also responsible for the care of the ammunition, which in an old wooden ship, was a serious charge, requiring a particularly careful individual.

As responsibilities increased in the eighteenth-century ships, certain lower officers began to play the part of lower-class warrant officer, under the head of the department. This process was well on the way in 1808, when the regulations declared that all these inferior departmental officers, as well as the master-at-arms and the cook, "though appointed by warrants, are to be considered as petty officers."[12] There were two such types in the gunner's department, the armourer and the gunsmith, appointed by warrant from the Board of Ordnance in 1731.

The bo's'n, who was next to the master in importance in the seventeenth century, began to lose ground, since the most important part of his former work had been the 'propulsion system' of the ship, along with its associated cables, ropes, flags, colours, pendants, anchors and sails. He also maintained the 'watch' system and meted out punishment as was considered necessary. The appearance of the corporal in Charles I's time, and the promotion of the master-at-arms in 1731 as a full blown warrant officer, relieved the bo's'n of some of the responsibility for discipline. While the master-at-arms and the ship's corporals identified the guilty, the bo's'n still administered the punishment. After 1816 bo's'ns could become 'yeomen of signals,' and by 1889, chief yeomen, but since these individuals could rise to warrant rank, the rank of the bo's'n remained at the same level.

The sail-maker and the rope-maker, obviously important in the sailing ship, were also among the lesser warrant officers in the bo's'n's department. By the end of the eighteenth century, both were appointed by the commissioners of the Navy, and executed their warrants under the bo's'n.

The course of the carpenter's career was also, for the most part, downwards. At one time, he was responsible for the care and preservation of the ship's hull, masts, yards, bulkheads and cabins, and "in an engagement frequently to pass up and down the hold with his crew, and to be watchful against all leaks from shot under water, having Shot-Boards and Plugs of Wood ready and whatever else is necessary to stop them, and likewise to fish or otherwise secure the Masts and Yards."[13]

The carpenter's activities were eventually taken over by the engineering branch, and he lost further ground to the bo's'n when in 1878 he ceased to be 'executive,' and joined the ranks of a non-military or 'civilian' branch of his own. As wood gradually gave way to metal the nature of his work changed and his title was changed to 'shipwright.'

At one time the cook had been a full warrant officer and head of his own indispensible department. However, when those in authority began to divide the ship's company into 'military' and 'civilian' branches, the cook could hardly be considered as belonging to the former. An order of 1704, although well-meant, sealed his doom, since it gave preference in appointments to the post of cook to "such cripples and maimed persons as are pensioners of the chest at Chatham." By the 1740s, when the 'rank of the officers in a ship' was settled (i.e., order of precedence and of taking command), the cook was omitted altogether, and, in the same regulation, the position was relegated to the list of 'inferior officers.' Though no less important today than he was in the past, the cook never recovered his lost status.

Four other professions of significance sprang from the same genre as the 'warrant officer.' They were all essentially 'non-military,' 'non-combatant,' 'civilian,' and 'non-executive.' They existed outside the naval Service itself, but were, and are, quite necessary to the efficiency within the Service. In the Navy of World War II they were called paymasters, surgeons, chaplains and instructor officers. Today, their counterparts are the logistics officers, doctors and the chaplains. The instructor officer has been replaced by the training development officer, who makes decisions regarding the methods of instruction. (Any member of the Navy, after receiving training in instructional technique, may conduct classes.)

When the Royal Canadian Navy was established in 1910, it adopted the rank structure (including warrant officers) and the uniforms of the Royal Navy. When the rank structure and pay scales (but not rank titles) became uniform in the three services in 1949, naval warrant ranks were abolished; but the rank of chief petty officer was divided into two classes and given the same rates of pay as first and as second class warrant officers in the Army and Air Force.

Warrant officers were appointed by warrant of the Minister of the Naval Service, or, after 1922, the Minister of National Defence.

The first warrant officers in 1910 were British personnel on loan from the Royal Navy to assist in the organization and training of the Canadian fleet. They included bo's'ns, gunners, artificer engineers and carpenters. During World War I the ranks of wireless telegrapher (W/T) and skipper appeared.

The W/Ts were an experimental radio branch and were replaced after the war by telegraphists entered on the lower deck. The skippers were temporary officers — professional seamen and fishermen employed in command of small auxiliary patrol craft who appeared during World War II. By the end of the war, the "Canadian Naval List" included chief masters at arms, a head bandmaster, warrant electricians, warrant shipwrights, warrant victualling officers and schoolmasters.

When the RCN acquired destroyers in 1922, the rank of gunner(T), for torpedo, appeared and during World War II there were signal bo's'ns, warrant telegraphists, warrant photographers, warrant engineers (replacing the earlier artificer engineer), warrant mechanician (drawn from the stoker's ranks), warrant ordnance officers, warrant catering officers, warrant writers and warrant officers (special branch).

The tendency of warrant officers to be absorbed into the commissioned ranks had been evident in the Royal Navy since the late eighteenth century, when the master became a 'warrant officer of wardroom rank.' In the late nineteenth century there had been warrant officers and chief warrant officers, but by the time the RCN was established, the chief bo's'n, chief gunner and chief carpenter (the only officers in this category) were commissioned. They later officially became 'commissioned officers,' and bore the title 'commissioned gunner,' etc. In 1949, the remaining warrant officers were commissioned and the King's Regulations listed the following warrant officers:

Executive officers:
  Gunner, gunner(T)
  Bo's'n, bo's'n(A/S), i.e., anti-submarine or asdic, later sonar
  Signal bo's'n, warrant telegraphists, warrant communications officer
  Warrant master-at-arms, warrant photographer, skipper
Engineer officers:
  Warrant engineer, warrant mechanician
Supply and Secretariat officers:
  Warrant writer officer, warrant stores officer, warrant cookery officer, warrant catering officer
Electrical officers:
  Warrant electrical officer, warrant radio officer
Shipwright officers:
  Warrant shipwright
Ordnance officers:
  Warrant ordnance officer
Special branch officers:
  Warrant officer(SB)
  Warrant officer(SB)(E)
Wardmasters:
  Warrant wardmasters
Shore patrol officers:
  Warrant patrol officer.[14]

The ship's company consisted of five individual groups in 1910. These were: the captain, the wardroom, subordinate officers (cadets, midshipmen and acting sub-lieutenants), warrant and chief warrant officers and the lower deck.

Today, the words 'warrant officer' are used to designate the three senior non-commissioned officer ranks in the Navy:
chief petty officer first class;
chief petty officer second class;
petty officer first class.

The word 'warrant' can be traced back to mediaeval times, and the ancient French 'warrant,' is a variant of 'guarant' or 'garant.' There are similar roots in the early German 'warent' and 'wahren.' Today the word still has many meanings but, in the military context, it signifies an authority granted by one person to another to do something which he has not otherwise the right to do. In this respect, it is not unlike the 'commission.'

IV
Naval Decorations and Medals

For everyone except the experts, there is always a bit of mystery associated with the strips of coloured ribbon worn on the uniform of the officers and men of Her Majesty's fighting forces. People associate the pieces of coloured silk with orders, decorations and medals, but few can explain their meaning or significance.

British subjects must wear the ribbons of their orders, decorations and medals in a certain sequence on their left breast, the position of priority being in the centre of the chest.

Though many decorations are given in times of peace, a fairly complete picture of a man's fighting career could be had by noting the coloured strips on his coat or tunic.

Medals were first issued to British seamen by the authority of the Long Parliament of Britain. Pepys notes in his "Naval Minutes" on the second Dutch War (1664):
  "The proclamation called attention to the fact that care would be taken for the sick and wounded and widows, and that medals would be given for eminent service."[15]
Following is a brief description of the naval medals, given in the order of their institution.

The Naval General Service Medal (1793-1840)

This medal was originally intended to be used during the period from 1793 to 1815, but was extended to cover 1793 to 1840 as well. It was authorized in 1847 and issued in 1849. A list was published in 1848 of the actions and boat services for which medals would be given. Those who considered themselves entitled to the medal had to give their names to the staff officer of pensions in the district where they lived by 30 April, 1849. (In those days, many could not read the papers or notices, which in any case would not have had a very wide circulation outside each town.)

An image of Queen Victoria's head with diadem, the usual legend and the date is on one side of this medal. The other side shows a figure of Britannia seated on a sea-horse, with a trident in her right hand and laurel branch in the left. There is a plain silver clasp for suspension. Engagement bars for no less than 230 different engagements, actions and cutting-out expeditions were authorized. These either bore the name of an action, the name of the vessel capturing or defeating an enemy's ship, or the words "Boat Service" with the date.

It is not possible to mention all the bars here, but among those inscribed are:

'1st June, 1794': This for Lord Howe's action on the Glorious First of June

'Camperdown': This for the battle of October 11, 1797

'Nile': This for Lord Nelson's battle in Aboukir Bay, 1 August 1798

'Trafalgar': This for the famous battle of 21 October 1805

Included in the list of the medal's recipients of the bar for the '1st of June, 1794,' was Daniel Tremendous McKenzie, of HMS *Tremendous*. At that time a certain number of the seamen were allowed to take their wives to sea with them, and Tremendous McKenzie was born at sea shortly before the battle took place. In the record of issue, he is officially styled as "Baby."

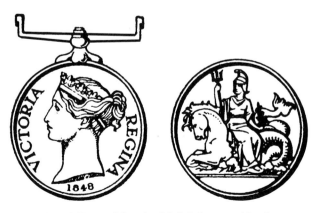

3.27 Naval General Service Medal, front and back.

The Conspicuous Gallantry Medal (Royal Navy, 1855)

Before 1943 this medal was only awarded to petty officers and men of the Royal Navy, and non-commissioned officers and men of the Royal Marines who distinguished themselves by acts of conspicuous gallantry in action with the enemy. It was also made available to men of the Merchant Navy and was the Naval counterpart of the Army medal for distinguished conduct in the field.

It was originally sanctioned specifically for the Crimean War, but was reinstituted in 1874, and was made available for any war. The medal was of silver and on one side had the effigy of the reigning sovereign with the usual legend. On the other, in raised letters, were the words "For Conspicuous Gallantry," with a crown above, and the whole design encircled by laurel branches. Medals awarded before 1874 had an ornamental clasp for suspension, but those issued after that date had a plain clasp. The ribbon, originally blue, white, blue in equal stripes, exactly like that of the D.S.C., was altered in 1921 to the ribbon of the old Naval General Service Medal, 1793-1840.

Left to right:
3.28 Conspicuous Gallantry Medal, back.
3.29 Victoria Cross, front.

The Victoria Cross (1856)

The Victoria Cross, the most highly-coveted decoration possible for any sailor to obtain, was instituted by Queen Victoria in 1856 at the suggestion of the Prince Consort. The decoration consists of a bronze cross pattee, one and one-half inches wide with raised edges. On the obverse, in the centre, is a lion statant gardant standing upon the Royal crown, while below the crown are the words "For Valour," on a semi-circular scroll. The reverse has raised edges like the obverse, and the date of the act for which the decoration is given is engraved in a circle in the centre. The

Cross is suspended by means of a plain link from a 'V,' which is part of the clasp, ornamented with laurel leaves, through which the ribbon passes, and on the back of the clasp is engraved the name, rank and ship of the recipient. The ribbon, one and one-half inches wide, was originally blue for the Navy. Crimson was adopted during World War I for the Navy, Army and Air Forces.

The Victoria Cross was introduced during the Crimean War as a means of rewarding individual officers and men of the Navy and Army who might perform some act of valour and devotion to their country in the presence of the enemy. Clasps to the ribbon could be awarded for any subsequent act of gallantry.

The first distribution of the Victoria Cross was made on 26 June, 1856, when Queen Victoria personally decorated 61 recipients, 14 of whom were members of the Royal Navy.

In 1902 King Edward issued an order to the effect that Victoria Crosses earned by soldiers and sailors who had been killed should be delivered to the relatives. Before this date, when officers or men had been recommended for the V.C., but had died before they could receive it, the recipients' names appeared in the *Official Gazette*, but the decoration was never actually given. The order was made retroactive, so that the surviving relatives of men who had won the Cross as far back as the Crimean War, or the Indian Mutiny, but who had died while performing their act of valour, received the coveted token.

If any unit is engaged in an action of outstanding gallantry (for instance, the blocking of Zeebrugge on 23 April, 1918), recipients for the V.C. could be chosen by ballot from among the whole number engaged. If less than 100 persons are present, one officer may be chosen by the officers; one petty officer by the petty officers; and one seaman by the others in the group.

The Victoria Cross takes precedence over all other orders and medals. Only 1,343 Crosses (of which 290 have been posthumous), and three bars have been awarded from the date of institution in 1856 until the present time. Ninety-four of these are Canadians by birth, and of these, four were sailors. These individuals are:

William Hall, Naval brigade (Royal Navy)
Born: Horton's Bluff, Nova Scotia
Citation: "...for...gallant conduct at a 24-pounder gun brought up to the angle of that Shah Nuggiff, at Lucknow, on the 16th of November, 1857."[16]

Rowland Richard Lois Bourke, Royal Naval Volunteer Reserve
Born: London, England, 28 Nov. 1855, entered Canada, 1902.
Citation: "Volunteered for rescue work in command of M.L. 276, and followed *Vindictive* into Ostend, engaging the enemy's machine guns on both piers with Lewis Guns. After M.L. 254 had

3.30 William Hall, Naval Brigade, Royal Navy.

3.31 Rowland Richard Lois Bourke, Royal Naval Volunteer.

backed out, Lt. Bourke laid his vessel alongside *Vindictive* to make further search. Finding no one he withdrew, but hearing cries in the water he again entered the harbour, and after a prolonged search eventually found Lieutenant Sir John Alleyne, and two ratings, badly wounded, and in the water, clinging to an upended skiff, and he rescued them.

During all this time the motor launch was under very heavy fire at close range, being hit in fifty-five places, once by a 6-inch shell — two of her small crew being killed and others wounded.... This episode displayed daring and skill of a very high order, and Lieutenant Bourke's bravery and perseverance undoubtedly saved the lives of Lieutenant Alleyne and two of the *Vindictive*'s crew."

10 May 1918 [17]

Frederick Thornton Peters, Royal Navy
Born: Charlottetown, P.E.I., 17 September, 1889
Citation: "Captain Peters was in the 'suicide charge' by two little cutters at Oran. *Walney* and *Hartland* were two ex-American Coast Guard cutters which were lost in a gallant attempt to force the boom defences in the harbour of Oran during the landings on the North African Coast. Captain Peters led his force through the boom in the face of point-blank fire from the shore batteries, destroyer and cruiser — a feat which was described as one of the great episodes of naval history. The *Walney* reached the jetty disabled and ablaze, and went down with her colours flying. Blinded in one eye, Captain Peters was the only survivor of the seventeen men on the bridge of the *Walney*. He was taken prisoner but was later released when Oran was captured."

8 November 1942 [18]

Robert Hampton Gray, Royal Canadian Navy Volunteer Reserve
Born: Nelson, B.C., 2 November, 1917
Citation: "For great bravery in leading an attack to within fifty feet of a Japanese destroyer in the face of intense anti-aircraft fire, thereby sinking the destroyer although he was hit and his aircraft was on fire and finally himself killed.... The actual incident took place in the Onagawa Wan on 9 August, 1945. Gray was leader of an attack which he pressed home in the face of fire from shore batteries and at least eight warships. With his aircraft in flames he nevertheless obtained at least one direct hit which sank its objective.... Lieutenant Gray did not return. He had given his life at the end of his fearless bombing run."

9 August 1945 [19]

3.32 Frederick Thornton Peters, Royal Navy.

3.33 Robert Hampton Gray, Royal Canadian Navy.

The Distinguished Service Cross (Late Conspicuous Service Cross)

The Conspicuous Service Cross was instituted by King Edward VII as a means of "recognizing meritorious or distinguished services before the enemy," performed by warrant officers, acting warrant officers, or by subordinate officers of His Majesty's Fleet. In October 1914, the name of this decoration was altered to the 'Distinguished Service Cross,' and its award was extended to all naval and marine officers below the relative rank of lieutenant-commander, "for meritorious or distinguished services which may not be sufficient to warrant the appointment of such officers to the Distinguished Service Order.

The decoration, which is suspended from its ribbon by a ring, is a plain silver cross pattee convexed with the reverse side plain. On the obverse it bears the cypher of the reigning monarch surmounted by the crown. Bars are awarded for further service. Only eight Conspicuous Service Crosses were awarded from the date of its institution in 1901 until the beginning of World War I, when it was renamed the Distinguished Service Cross.

The D.S.C. is the only purely naval decoration, as opposed to medals, and was awarded to the town of Dunkirk for the gallant behaviour of its inhabitants during World War I.

Left to right:
3.34 Distinguished Service Cross, front.
3.35 Distinguished Service Medal (RN), back.

The Distinguished Service Medal (RN)

This medal was established on 14 October, 1914. It was designed to be awarded in the numerous cases of courageous service in war by petty officers and men of the Royal Navy, and non-commissioned officers and men of the Royal Marines, and all other persons holding corresponding positions in the naval forces, who "may at any time show themselves to the fore in action, and set an example of bravery and resource under fire, but without performing acts of such pre-eminent bravery as would render them eligible for the Conspicuous Gallantry Medal."

The medal bears on one side the effigy of the Sovereign with the usual legend, and on the reverse the inscription "For distinguished service," surmounted by a crown, and encircled by a wreath of laurel. It hangs from the ribbon by means of a straight silver clasp. Bars are awarded for further service.

Navy Gold Medals (1794-1815)

The Navy Gold Medals were instituted on the occasion of Lord Howe's victory over the French Fleet on the 'Glorious First of June,' 1794, and their award continued until 1815.

The large medal, conferred only upon Admirals, was circular and measured two inches across. On the obverse was part of an antique galley, on the prow of which was the winged figure of Victory placing a wreath on the head of Britannia, who stands on the galley with the right foot on a helmet, and holding a spear in her left hand. Behind her is the Union shield. The reverse was engraved with the name of the recipient and the event for which the medal was conferred within a wreath of oak and laurel. The medal was suspended by a plain gold ring and was worn around the neck from a ribbon, one and three-quarter inches wide, of white with blue borders.

Similar medals were later awarded for various fleet actions, including the battles of Cape St. Vincent, 1797; Camperdown, 1797; the Nile, 1798; and Trafalgar, 1805, as well as for a number of outstanding single ship actions, up until 1815.

Their award ceased after the expansion of the Order of the Bath into three classes in 1815.

Left to right:
3.36 Navy Gold Medal, front.
3.37 Naval General Service Medal, back.

Naval General Service Medal (1915)

Instituted by King George V in 1915 for "service in minor operations whether in the nature of belligerency or police, which may be considered of sufficient importance to justify the award of a medal in cases where no other medal would be awarded." It was first issued with a bar or clasp with the inscription "Persian Gulf 1909 — 1914" to officers and men of HM ships employed in the suppression of the arms traffic in the Arabian Sea or Persian Gulf between 19 October, 1909 and 1 August, 1914.

The obverse bore the image of the head of King George V in naval uniform with the usual legend, and the reverse a striking representation of Britannia and two sea-horses travelling through the sea.

Clasps were also awarded for Palestine, 1940; S.E. Asia, 1945-46; Minesweeping, 1945-51; Bomb mine clearance, 1945-53; Palestine, 1945-48; Yangtse, 1949 and Malaya, 1948.

Naval personnel who already held the Naval General Service Medal (1915) for service before the war of 1939-45 and later qualified for another clasp, continued to wear the ribbon before those of the campaign stars, etc., 1939-45. The single oak leaf emblem is worn on the ribbon of the Naval General Service Medal to denote the award of a Mention in Despatches, or the King's or Queen's Commendation.

1914-1915 Star

The award of this Star was approved in 1917 for all those officers and men of the British and Indian Expeditionary Forces, and to officers and men of the Royal Navy, Royal Marines, Royal Naval Reserve and Royal Naval Volunteer Reserve who served on the establishment of a unit landed for shore service in France or Belgium between 5 August, 1914 and midnight 22-23 November, 1914.

This decoration was a four-pointed star in bright bronze. The reverse was plain, and stamped with the name and unit of the recipient. The bar was of the same material as the star, and was of simple design with the inscription '5th Aug.-22 Nov. 1914' on a frosted ground.

The 1914-1915 Star was sanctioned in 1918, and was of similar design and shape as that of the 1914 Star. The only difference was that the date '1914-1915' appears on the centre scroll, while the smaller scrolls bearing the words 'Aug' and 'Nove' were omitted. The ribbon is identical to that of the 1914 Star.

British War Medal (1914-1920)

This medal was approved by King George V in 1919 to record the bringing of the war to a successful conclusion, and the arduous services rendered by His Majesty's Forces.

The medal, which hangs from its ribbon by a straight clasp without swivel, bears on the obverse the effigy of His Majesty — with the legend *Georgius V: britt: omn: rex et ind: imp:*. The reverse represents St. George on horseback trampling underfoot the eagle shield of the central

Left to right:
3.38   1914-1915 Star, front.
3.39   British War Medal, back.

powers and a skull and cross-bones, the emblem of death. Above is the risen sun of victory. The male figure, rather than a symbolic female one, was chosen because man had born the brunt of the fighting. The figure was mounted on horseback as symbolical of the man's mind controlling a force (represented by the horse) or greater strength than his own.

The medal was granted to officers, warrant officers, petty officers, non-commissioned officers and men of the Royal Navy, Royal Marines, Royal Naval Air Service, Royal Indian Marine, Royal Naval Reserve, Royal Naval Volunteer Reserve and the Dominion and Colonial Naval Forces. Clasps were never issued because of excessive cost, although forty-seven individual clasps had been proposed by the Royal Navy and were approved by the King. These covered naval operations around the world.

Victory Medal

This medal, of bronze, bears on the obverse a winged figure of Victory. On the reverse is an inscription "The great war for civilization." The rim is plain, and the medal hangs from a ring. Any officer or man who had been "mentioned in despatches" was allowed to wear a small bronze oak leaf on the ribbon of this medal. Only one oak leaf was worn, no matter how many times the individual was mentioned.

The medal was approved for all officers and men of the RN, RM, RNAS, RNR, RNVR, RNASBR, and Dominion and Colonial Naval Forces who had rendered approved service either at sea between midnight 4-5 August, 1914 and midnight, 11-12 November, 1918, or on the establishment of a unit within a theatre of military operation.

3.40   Victory Medal, front, and oak leaf.

1939-1945 Star and Atlantic Star

The eight campaign stars awarded for service in World War II were all of similar design and were made of a yellow copper-zinc alloy form of a six-pointed star measuring one and three-quarter inches between opposite points. The Royal and Imperial cypher is in the centre, surmounted by a crown. The cypher is surrounded by a circlet bearing the name of the particular star.

The 1939-1945 Star was awarded for service in operation from 3 September, 1939 to 15 August, 1945, the date on which active operations against Japan ceased in the Pacific. Approved naval service was six months afloat in areas of active operations.

The Atlantic Star commemorates the Battle of the Atlantic and was designed primarily for those serving in convoys, escorts and anti-submarine forces and for fast merchant ships sailing unescorted. It was awarded for six months service afloat between 3 September, 1939 and 8 May, 1945, in Atlantic or home waters, and to personnel employed with the convoys to North Russia and in the South Atlantic.

The Africa Star, Pacific Star, Burma Star, Italy Star and France and Germany Star were also awarded for approved naval service.

Left to right:
3.41   Star and Atlantic Star, front.
3.42   Defence Medal, back.

Defence Medal (1939-1945)

The Defence Medal was awarded for three years' service at home, or six months' overseas in territories subjected to air attacks or closely threatened. This medal was awarded in addition to the previously mentioned Campaign Stars.

The medal was in cupro-nickel with a straight bar suspender, and had on the obverse the uncrowned effigy of King George VI with the usual legend. The reverse had the design and inscription shown in the illustration.

Canadian Decorations, Medals and Awards

Canada General Service Medal (1866-70)

The issue of this medal, which was presented by the Canadian Government, was not authorized until January 1899. It was given to soldiers of the British Army, and to those of the Canadian Militia including most likely the Provincial Marine, who were employed on active service during the Fenian Raids of 1866-1870, and the Red River Expedition of 1870.

The medal bears on one side the effigy of Queen Victoria, crowned and veiled, with the legend "Victoria Regina et Imperatrix," and on the other the Canadian flag surrounded by a wreath of Maple. The word "Canada" appears at the top, and the medal is hung from a straight clasp. The same ribbon was used for the 'Canada Medal' established in 1943.

Left to right:
3.43   Canada General Service Medal, back.
3.44   Canada Medal, back.

The Canada Medal

This medal was established in October, 1943, with the approval of His Majesty, King George VI, on the recommendation of the Canadian Government. It was the first distinctly Canadian decoration intended for the recognition of "Meritorious service above and beyond the faithful performance of duties" by Canadian citizens, whether as civilians, or as members of the Armed

Forces. It could also be given to the Merchant Navy and to citizens of other countries.

The medal is silver with the effigy of the Sovereign on the obverse, and on the reverse the Arms of Canada with the word "Canada" on the scroll beneath. A spray of Maple Leaf is on each side.

The award confers no individual precedence, but the recipients are allowed to use the letters 'C.M.' after their names. Though the Canada Medal officially took precedence over all war medals, it is believed never to have been actually awarded.

Canada Volunteer Service Medal

This medal was authorized in 1943 for men and women of all ranks in the Canadian Armed Services who volunteered for service during World War II. A minimum of eighteen months service must have been honourably completed, though those honourably discharged or retired after having proceeded outside territorial limits of Canada received the medal irrespective of time served. Recipients who served abroad were entitled to wear a silver maple leaf on the ribbon. The medal could also be awarded posthumously to those of any rank in the Naval, Military or Air Forces of Canada who had been killed, or died of wounds sustained in action or on duty.

The medal is silver, and has on the obverse seven marching figures representing the Services (men, women, and nurses), with the inscription "Canada" above and "Voluntary Service Volontaire" below, while the reverse bears the Canadian Coat of Arms.

3.45   Canada Volunteer Service Medal, front and back.

Decorations for Bravery

Qualities of heroism have always commanded admiration and respect; those who risk their lives to save or protect others defy the instinct of self-preservation. In doing so, they exhibit a generosity of spirit which is an inspiration to all and it is fitting that such service and sacrifice should be acknowledged and acclaimed. Decorations for bravery are a means of expressing symbolically the nation's gratitude and the high esteem in which those who receive such awards are held.

In order to provide that form of recognition the Canadian honours system was enlarged in 1972 to include the following decorations for bravery which are awarded in the manner and on the basis outlined below:

Cross of Valour
Star of Courage
Medal of Bravery

No two incidents in which bravery is exhibited are the same in all respects; every meritorious action is conditioned by the circumstances in which it is performed. Consequently, a series of three decorations has been created so that the hazards encountered in widely differing situations will be fairly reflected in the level of award made.

Cross of Valour

The Cross of Valour is awarded for acts of the most conspicuous courage in circumstances of extreme peril and may be awarded posthumously. It consists of a gold cross of four equal arms. The obverse is enamelled red and edged in gold with, superimposed in the centre, a gold maple leaf surrounded by a gold wreath of laurel. On the reverse, the Royal cypher and crown and the words "Valour-Vaillance" appear.

The decoration is worn by male recipients from the neck suspended from a red ribbon. It is worn by women, when in uniform, in the same fashion and otherwise on the left shoulder suspended from a ribbon fashioned into a bow.

Recipients are entitled to have the letters "C.V." placed after their surnames on all occasions when the use of such letters is customary.

Star of Courage

The Star of Courage is awarded for acts of conspicuous courage in circumstances of great peril and may be awarded posthumously. It consists of a silver star of four points with a maple leaf in each of the four angles. On the obverse, superimposed in the centre, is a gold maple leaf surrounded by a gold laurel wreath. On the reverse, the Royal Cypher and Crown and the word "Courage" appears.

The decoration is worn by male recipients on the left breast suspended from a ribbon of red

3.46   Cross of Valour.

3.47   Star of Courage.

3.48   Medal of Bravery.

with two blue stripes. It is worn by women, when in uniform, in the same fashion and otherwise on the left shoulder suspended from a ribbon fashioned into a bow.

Recipients are entitled to have the letters 'S.C.' (E.C. in French) placed after their surnames on all occasions when the use of such letters is customary.

Medal of Bravery

The Medal of Bravery is awarded for acts of bravery in hazardous circumstances and may be awarded posthumously. It consists of a circular silver medal. On the obverse, there is a maple leaf surrounded by a wreath of laurel. On the reverse, the Royal cypher and crown and the words "Bravery-Bravoure" appear.

The decoration is worn by male recipients on the left breast suspended from a ribbon of red with three blue stripes. It is worn by women, when in uniform, in the same fashion and otherwise on the left shoulder suspended from a ribbon fashioned into a bow.

Recipients are entitled to have the letters 'M.B.' placed after their surnames on all occasions when the use of such letters is customary.

The Order of Canada

Desiderantes Meliorem Patriam

The granting of honours is a gracious way for any country to pay tribute to those who exemplify the highest qualities of citizenship and whose contributions enrich the lives of their contemporaries. It was timely that Canada should have adopted this practice on the 100th anniversary of Confederation. On 1 July, 1967, the Order of Canada was established as the centrepiece of our system of honours. Its Latin motto proclaims the aspirations of its members who, in their lives and their work, have shown that "they desire a better country."

The Order confers no special privileges on its members and brings them no monetary rewards; it is solely a fraternity of merit. The three levels of membership — Companion, Officer, and Member embrace the full spectrum of achievement and service in fields as diverse as biology and ballet, philanthropy and folklore. Persons who strive for the betterment of their communities, or devote their talents to special causes, stand with those who have gained distinction on the national scene.

The Queen of Canada is the Sovereign of the Order. The Governor General is the Chancellor and Principal Companion and presides over the affairs of the Order, in accordance with the terms of its constitution. An advisory council, under the chairmanship of the Chief Justice of Canada, has the task of assessing the relative merits of the persons nominated for the Order, and recommending to the chancellor the names of those considered to be worthy of appointment.

Although its ranks are closed to no one, the number of persons who can be appointed to the Order is governed by the Constitution. By limiting membership in this way, high standards of admission are maintained and the prestige of the Order is ensured.

Companions of the Order of Canada

1. Appointments as Companions and Honorary Companions of the Order shall be made for outstanding achievement and merit of the highest degree, especially service to Canada or to humanity at large.

2. Notwithstanding Subsection (1), any distinguished person who is not a Canadian citizen, but whom the Government of Canada desires to honour, may be appointed as an Honorary Companion of the Order.

3. Where a Governor General ceases to hold that office, he(she) shall, notwithstanding Section 7, continue, by virtue of his(her) having held that Office, to be a Companion of the Order.

4. Notwithstanding Section 7, the spouse of a Governor General who serves with the Governor General during any period when he(she) holds that office shall be appointed to be a Companion of the Order and shall cease to be a Companion by reason only of the Governor General's death or retirement.

5. Subject to Sections 6, and 7, the Governor General may appoint to be Companions of the Order, other than Honorary Companions, a maximum of fifteen persons in any year.

6. Membership, other than honorary membership in the Order, is limited to one hundred and fifty Companions in addition to the Principal Companion, his(her) spouse and any former Governor General and his spouse or surviving spouse.

7. When the maximum number of Companions of the Order have been appointed, a person may be appointed as a Companion of the Order only where a vacancy occurs.

Officers of the Order of Canada

1. Appointments as Officers and Honorary Officers of the Order shall be made for achievement and merit of a high degree, especially service to Canada or to humanity at large.

2. Notwithstanding Subsection (1), any distinguished person who is not a Canadian citizen, but whom the Government of Canada desires to honour, may be appointed as an Honorary Officer of the Order.

3. The Governor General may appoint to be Officers of the Order, other than Honorary Officers, a maximum of forty persons in any year.

Members of the Order of Canada

1. Appointments as Members and Honorary Members of the Order shall be made for distinguished service in or to a particular locality, group or field of activity.

2. Notwithstanding Subsection (1), any distinguished person who is not a Canadian citizen, but whom the Government of Canada desires to honour, may be appointed as an Honorary Member of the Order.

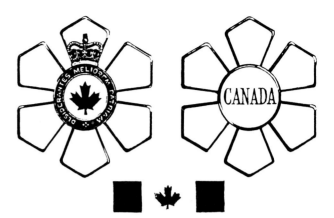

3.49 Companion of the Order of Canada Medal.

3.50 Officer of the Order of Canada Medal.

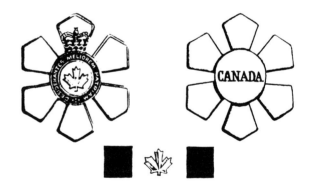

3.51 Member of the Order of Canada Medal.

3. The Governor General may appoint to be Members of the Order, other than Honorary Members, a maximum of eighty persons in any year.

The Order of Military Merit

During Canada's Centennial Year, when the Order of Canada was established as a means of honouring those who rendered meritorious service to the Nation, the Cross of Valour, the Star of Courage and the Medal of Bravery were instituted to reward acts of bravery performed in saving or attempting to save a life or property. It was also decided to include in Canada's honours system a means of recognizing conspicuous merit and exceptional service by the men and women of the Canadian Forces, both regular and reserve. Accordingly, on 1 July, 1972, the Order of Military Merit was established.

As with the Order of Canada, the Order of Military merit confers no special privileges on its members and brings them no monetary rewards. It is a society of honour with three degrees of membership Commander, Officer and Member.

The Queen of Canada is the Sovereign of the Order and the Governor General is the Chancellor as well as being a Commander of the Order. The Chief of the Defence Staff is the Principal Commander of the Order. Appointments to the Order are made by the Governor General on the recommendation of the Minister of National Defence.

The insignia of the Order worn by its members are the visible marks of honour, along with the post-nominal letters to which each is also entitled. When the names of members of the Order are published and when they are addressed in correspondence, it is customary to place after their names the following initials: CMM for Commander; OMM for Officer and MMM for Member.

The full range of insignia are illustrated below: The badge of Commander is worn suspended from a ribbon which passes around the neck, the badges of Officer and Member are worn suspended from a point above the left breast pocket of service uniforms where the ribbon of the Order is worn on all occasions when it is not appropriate to wear medals.

For each badge, there is a corresponding 'miniature' or small replica, suspended from a narrow ribbon and worn on the left breast with mess kit or evening dress. Small lapel badges are available for wearing with civilian clothing.

Commanders of the Order of Military Merit
1. Appointments as Commanders of the Order are made for outstanding meritorious service in duties of great responsibility.
2. Appointments as Honorary Commanders of the Order are made for outstanding meritorious service to Canada or the Canadian Armed Forces in military duties of great responsibility.
3. Where a Governor General or a Chief of the Defence Staff ceases to hold such office, he(she) continues, by virtue of having held that office, to be a Commander of the Order.
4. The Governor General may appoint to be Commanders of the Order, in any one year, a number of eligible persons that most closely approximate six percent of the total number of persons that he(she) may appoint to all catego-

3.52 Commander of the Order of Military Merit Medal.

Left to right:
3.53 Officer of the Order of Military Merit Medal.
3.54 Member of the Order of Military Merit Medal.

ries of membership, other than honorary membership, in the Order in that year.

Officers of the Order of Military Merit
1. Appointments as Officers of the Order are made for outstanding meritorious service in duties of responsibility.
2. Appointments as Honorary Officers of the Order are made for outstanding meritorious service to Canada or the Canadian Armed Forces in military duties of responsibility.
3. The Governor General may appoint to be Officers of the Order, in any one year, a number of eligible persons that is not greater than the number of persons that most closely approximate thirty percent of the total number of persons that he(she) may appoint to all categories of membership, other than Honorary membership in the Order in that year.

Members of the Order of Military Merit
1. Appointments as Members of the Order are made for exceptional service or performance of duty.

2. Appointments as Honorary Members of the Order are made for exceptional service to Canada or to the Canadian Armed Forces in the performance of military duty.

3. The Governor General may appoint to be Members of the Order, in any year, a number of eligible persons that is not greater than the difference between the total number of persons that he(she) may appoint to all categories of membership, other than Honorary membership in the Order in that year, and the aggregate of the number of persons appointed as Commanders and Officers of the Order in that year.

The Canadian Forces' Decoration

The Canadian Forces' Decoration may be awarded to officers and men of the Canadian Forces who, in an approved capacity, have completed a period of twelve years' service in accordance with the regulations set out below.

The decoration is gilt in colour and in the form of a decagon, each of the ten sides being representative of a province of Canada. It bears on the obverse the uncrowned effigy of the Sovereign encircled by the Canadian Royal Title with the word "Canada" on the lowest side. On the reverse appears a crown, maple leaves and an eagle representative of the Navy, Army and Air Force respectively. The name of the recipient is engraved around the edge of the decoration.

The decoration is worn on the left breast pendant from a ribbon one and one-half inches in width. The ribbon is of the colour gules broken into equal divisions by three narrow vertical stripes of the colour argent.

Reproduction in miniature, which may be worn on certain occasions by those on whom this award is conferred, is of a standard size as for all other miniatures.

3.55 Canadian Forces' Decoration medal, front and back.

All officers and men of the Canadian Forces are eligible for The Canadian Forces' Decoration provided they have completed the required period of service, have undertaken all required phases of training and duty, and are certified by the responsible Service authorities as efficient and in every way deserving of the award.

Chief of the Defence Staff Commendation

The Chief of the Defence Staff Commendation may be awarded to any member of the Canadian Forces (CF) who has performed a deed or activity that is considered to be beyond the demands of normal duty. It may also be awarded to a member of the Armed Forces of a country other than Canada for an achievement or meritorious service that is of benefit to Canada or to the CF.

The Chief of the Defence Staff commendation is a framed, gold-embossed scroll that is inscribed with the member's name and an appropriate narrative, and that is signed by the CDS.

The symbol of the Chief of the Defence Staff Commendation, adopted for wear below the button on the left breast pocket of the CF uniform, is a gold bar with three maple leaves.

3.56 Chief of the Defence Staff gold bar.

The Maritime Commander's Commendation

The Commander, Maritime Command established the Maritime Commander's Commendation and the Certificate of Achievement to ensure that meritorious or exceptional service which deserves formal recognition at the command level, but which does not meet the criteria for national awards, is recognized.

The Maritime Commander's Commendation recognizes achievement of Maritime Command personnel who have made an exceptional contribution to Maritime Command and the Canadian Forces by their personal effort and example. This award is always signed by the Commander of Maritime Command.

The Certificate of Achievement recognizes Maritime Command personnel who have made a significant contribution to Maritime Command through their personal effort and example. This award is signed by an officer of flag rank.

Orders, Decorations and Medals

Precedence

The protocol for wearing the insignia of Canadian orders and decorations, separately or together with senior British orders and decorations, is prescribed in Order in Council P.C. 1972-1206 of 1 June, 1972 which reads as follows:

"1. This Directive may be cited as the Canadian Orders and Decorations Directive.

2. The correct sequence for wearing the insignia of Canadian Orders and Canadian decorations is as follows:

(a) Cross of Valour — CV;

(b) Companion of the Order of Canada — CC;

(c) Officer of the Order of Canada — OC;

(d) Commander of the Order of Military Merit — CMM;

(e) Star of Courage — SC;

(f) Officer of the Order of Military Merit — OMM;

(g) Medal of Bravery — MB;

(h) Member of the Order of Canada — CM; and

(i) Member of the Order of Military Merit — MMM.

A person who, prior to the coming into force of this Directive, was a member of an Order or the recipient of a decoration referred to in this section should wear the insignia of the Order of the decoration, together with the insignia of any Canadian Order or any Canadian Decoration that he is entitled to wear, in the following sequence:

(a) Victoria Cross — VC;

(b) George Cross — GC;

(c) Cross of Valour — CV;

(d) Companion of the Order of Canada — CC;

(e) Officer of the Order of Canada — OC;

(f) Order of Merit — OM;

(g) Companion of Honour — CH;

(h) Order of the Bath (Companion) — CB;

(i) Order of St. Michael and St. George (Companion) — CMG;

(j) Royal Victorian Order (Commander) — CVO;

(k) Order of the British Empire (Commander) — CBE;

(l) Commander of the Order of Military Merit — CMM;

(m) Distinguished Service Order — DSO;

(n) Order of the British Empire (Officer) — OBE;

(o) Imperial Service Order — ISO;

(p) Order of the British Empire (Member) — MBE;

(q) Royal Red Cross (Member) — RRC;

(r) Distinguished Service Cross — DSC;

(s) Military Cross — MC;

(t) Distinguished Flying Cross — DFC;

(u) Star of Courage — SC;

(v) Officer of the Order of Military Merit — OMM;

(w) Medal of Bravery — MB;

(x) Member of the Order of Canada — CM;

(y) Member of the Order of Military Merit — MMM;

(z) Air Force Cross — AFC; and

(aa) Royal Red Cross (Associate) — ARRC."

Authorized orders, decorations and medals are worn only by personnel entitled to do so. Where doubt exists as to the entitlement of an individual to wear a badge, the matter is referred to NDHQ, by the command concerned, for clarification.

Decorations, etc., may be worn as follows:

Loose mounting — The ribbons of medals, with the required length of ribbon exposed, are sewn over a pin bar with the medals hanging free.

Court mounting — The ribbons and medals are mounted on a panel, its size determined by the number of ribbons. The lower edge of the panel is in line with the centre of the medals. Commencing from the lower edge, each ribbon runs up the front of the panel to the top and back down to the medal. The medals are stitched to the panel so that they do not swing loosely.

Medals are worn so that no part of the mounting bar is visible, with their lower edges in a straight line. Each medal is suspended by its ribbon from the bar, beginning with the senior medal at the end furthest from the shoulder (inner end), with its obverse worn outwards.

Medals are to be hung so that they are fully visible. If this is not possible because of the number worn, they are overlapped with the senior medal showing in full. Normally, six or more standard size medals and more than eight miniatures will require overlapping. The maximum width of the mounting is governed by the physique of the individual. The bar must not project beyond the edge of the lapel or the arm seam of the jacket.

Occasions for Wearing Orders, Decorations and Medals

Orders, decorations and medals are worn with the Service dress uniform on the following occasions:

(a) State ceremonies;

(b) Investitures;

(c) Royal and vice-regal escort duties;

(d) When in attendance on Royal or vice regal personnages of heads of foreign states;

(e) Guards of honour;

(f) Courts martial;

(g) Parades and inspections;

(h) Church services;

(i) Funerals and memorial services;

(j) Officer of the guard when boarding ships of war; and

(k) Service and civilian ceremonial occasions. Orders, decorations or medals are not worn at Royal or vice-regal garden parties unless specifically requested by the host.

V
The Canadian Touch

HM Canadian Ships (HMCS) and Their Forebears

During the Middle Ages there was no permanent National Maritime Fighting Force. The 'old' or 'Mediaeval' Navy of England was an emergency measure, formed only as the country's needs dictated. As such, it was an aspect of feudalism. The King, in mediaeval days, ran the State in his own way and out of his own revenues. It was only in national emergencies that he was entitled to ask his people for help, which he received in the form of service — military rather than monetary help; this held true whether he required help on land or sea.

The British Navy is considered to have had a considerable number of "Fathers." King Alfred is one. So are Edward III, Henry V, Henry VIII and so on.

King Alfred's 'Navy' spent only 15 days out of 365 doing what might be called 'quasi-war work'; for the remaining 350 days they were simple merchantmen, owned by the trading companies of England, not by the Crown. When ships were needed, they were acquired on 'short loan,' and returned to private service when the crisis had passed.

Both Edward III and Henry V firmly advocated that the Crown should be responsible for the maintenance of ships. Unfortunately, after Edward III's resounding success at Sluys in 1340 and at Espagnols-sur-mer in 1350, his interest waned. The effect of this disinterest was a crushing naval defeat at La Rochelle in 1372 and the subsequent demise of his Navy and his naval policy. Henry V, however, who was intent on making good his claim to the French throne, realized that he would:

"...want many ships often. It will therefore be much better and cheaper to build or buy my own rather than hiring them all the time."[20]

Henry, however, made his fleet ancillary to his army, so that it was little more than an army transport department. He died before he could make good his claim and his ships were sold to pay his debts.

Henry VIII built the Crown's first 'fighting' Navy to protect himself from the Pope's supporters. This policy was so successful that his successors desired a 'fighting fleet,' as did all the other crowned heads of Europe.

The first British Navy, of a purely national nature was that of Charles II. When he regained power in 1660, both he and Parliament agreed to retain the new maritime fighting force and the method of 'parliamentary' financing. Although he no longer owned the fleet in the old proprietary sense he was anxious to retain as much of the semblance of ownership as was possible. Perhaps he anticipated the movement toward a constitutional monarchy in which all state functions, offices and services are 'under the Crown.'

In the early seventeenth century, ships were referred to as 'His Majesty's Ship.' During the later part, the word 'Majesty's' began to be abbreviated in reference to a ship. An extract from instructions issued by James, Duke of York, Lord High Admiral in 1663 read:

"That before any of ye said cloathes be sold on board any of his ma't's shippes, ye prices thereof be rated..."[21]

The abbreviation took several forms, including "ma'ties," a term used by Captain Charles Wylde in reference to "His ma'ties Shipp *Bristol.*"[22]

By 1725, His Majesty's Ships were unofficially referred to as 'H.M..' William Franklyn, who was supplying sloops to the fleet, addressed the following letter to the Navy Board:

"Right Honourables,

In pursuance of my contract, on Tuesday last I sent on board H.M. sloop *Happy*, Captain Cottrell,..."[23]

The earliest example of what might have been official use of the abbreviation 'H.M.S.,' appears in a National Maritime Museum file, RCL/7, in a 1789 reference to H.M.S. *Phoenix.* H.M.S. *Alfred* and H.M.S. *Diadem* are referred to in the 1795 *Spencer Papers*, Vol. 1.[24]

When Canada's first ship was commissioned, she was named HMCS *Rainbow* — HMCS representing the abbreviation for His Majesty's Canadian Ship. This tradition continues to the present day.

During World War II the cap tallies of the Canadian sailor bore only the four gold letters: HMCS. This was adopted as a means of protecting the identity of the various ships entering and leaving ports, but the letters clearly stated that the bearer was a member of one of His Majesty's Canadian Ships in commission.

The Barber Pole Brigade

During World War II, when all ships were painted the same bleak camouflage gray, efforts were made to produce distinguishing marks and symbols for individual units, and for the groups in which they served. The crews were becoming entities in themselves, each one with its own recognizable personality. The various groups of ships were larger families of these entities. HMCS *Saguenay* and HMCS *Skeena* were among the first ships to distinguish themselves in this way.

A favourite rendezvous for the Atlantic warriors was 'The Crow's Nest,' located in St. John's, Newfoundland, where the first lieutenants of these two ships decided to paint a band of red and white oblique stripes around their funnels to suitably distinguish their ships. Consequently, the ships of the Fifth Escort Group (C-5), the destroyers HMCS *Saguenay* and HMCS *Skeena*, along with the corvettes HMCS *Galt*, HMCS *Sackville*, HMCS *Agassiz* and HMCS *Wetaskiwin* became known as the "Barber Pole Brigade."

The Brigade was part of the Mid-Ocean Escort Force, escorting convoys across the North Atlantic from St. John's, Newfoundland (Newfiejohn) to Londonderry (Derry), Northern Ireland. Like all naval formations, its complement of ships changed from time to time. A plaque in the "Crow's Nest," presented in October 1942, bears the names of its original members.

When the *Barber Pole* Song was written in the summer of 1943, C-5 consisted of HMCS *Ottawa*, HMCS *Kootenay* (destroyers), and HMCS *Arvida*, HMCS *Kitchener*, HMCS *Wetaskiwin* and HMS *Dianthus* (corvettes).

The lyrics to the song were composed by Surgeon-Lieutenant W.A. Paddon, who described its conception:

> "The song was written in a period of about four hours in Londonderry between voyages, while my corvette, HMCS *Kitchener*, was refuelling and taking stores and ammunition... The air "Road to the Isles" was much in my mind as the convoys usually broke up off the Western Isles (of Scotland), and their beauty and permanence in a very troubled time impressed itself deeply on anyone who had spent two or three weeks on convoy duty and suddenly saw the land and smelt the heather. One really knew one had survived a convoy trip and come again to land, and it was an emotional experience." [25]

The song was first sung in the wardroom of one of the newly completed destroyers and from then on, it spontaneously and quickly spread throughout the escort groups. It embodies the mixture of tension, high spirits and intense group loyalty common to all crews in those days when six small ships were the only protection against the U-boats for several dozen merchantmen.

The tradition was revived again in 1958, when, on commissioning, the *Restigouche* class Destroyer Escorts were formed into the Fifth Canadian Escort Squadron. When the fleet was reorganized in 1965, the destroyers HMCS *Gatineau*, HMCS *Columbia*, and HMCS *St. Laurent*, along with the frigate HMCS *Swansea*, the new Fifth Escort Squadron, continued the 'Barber Pole' tradition.

Today, the Fifth Canadian Destroyer Squadron consists of HMCS *Iroquois, HMCS Huron* (DDH 280's), HMCS *Annapolis*, HMCS *Nipigon* (Annapolis Class DDH's), HMCS *Fraser* and HMCS *Saguenay*. (St. Laurent Class DDH's).

Battle of the Atlantic

On 3 September, 1939, SS *Athetia* was sunk off the coast of Northern Ireland. One week later, Canada was at war with Germany and her allies. From that day until the last of the German U-boats had surfaced and surrendered, the Allied Navies maintained their vigilance.

Battle of the Atlantic Sunday, celebrated the first Sunday in May, commemorates the sacrifices of sailors and merchant seamen who gave their lives for their countries while valiantly plying the convoy routes of the North Atlantic. The Canadian Navy lost 1,797 men and 32 ships; there were 319 wounded. The intensity of the battle reached its peak during July 1942 (referred to by German submariners as "The happy time"), when the Allies were losing 10,000 tons of shipping every ten hours.

The elements were often as cruel as the foe, with raging storms, pack-ice, bitter cold, fog, and the blackness of the Atlantic night. Success only came as the result of indefatigable courage and determination, co-operation and skill. From the western anchor of the Atlantic Convoy system, over 26,000 merchant ship voyages were made during the 2006 days of war, and they provided over 90,000 tons of war supplies a day to the battlefields of Europe.

On 'Battle of the Atlantic Sunday,' remembrance services are held across the country in naval bases, individual units and HMC ships at sea. The National ceremony is held in Halifax, where the men of the fleet parade to Point Pleasant Park, the site of the Naval Memorial. The service held in Esquimalt on Sunday, 2 May, 1982, is typical of other services held on that day:

BATTLE OF THE ATLANTIC SUNDAY
PRELUDE
UNVEILING AND DEDICATION OF SAILOR'S MEMORIAL

LAYING OF WREATH
O CANADA

O Canada! Our home and native land!
True patriot love in all thy sons command.
With glowing hearts we see thee rise
The true North strong and free;
From far and wide, O Canada,
We stand on guard for thee.
God keep our land glorious and free!
O Canada, we stand on guard for thee.
O Canada, we stand on guard for thee.

SCRIPTURE SENTENCES

Proclaim with me the greatness of God, together let us extol his name. He shall judge between many peoples, and shall decide for strong nations afar off; and they shall beat their swords into plowshares and their spears into pruning hooks; nation shall not lift up sword against nation, neither shall they learn war any more. (Micah 4:3)

THE RESPONSIVE READING

Chaplain: Give thanks to the Lord, for he is good; his love is everlasting.

All: God is inside the city, she can never fall, at crack of dawn God helps her; to the roaring of nations and tottering of kingdoms, when he shouts, the world disintegrates.

Chaplain: Let us thank God for his love, for his marvels on behalf of men; satisfying the hungry, he fills the starving with good things.

All: Come, think of God's marvels, the astounding things he has done to the world; all over the world he put an end to wars, he breaks the bow, he snaps the spear, he gives shields to the flames.

Chaplain: Then they called to God in their trouble and he rescued them from their sufferings; releasing them from gloom and darkness, shattering their chains.

All: Pause a while and know that I am God, exalted among the nations, exalted over the earth! Let these thank God for his love, for his marvels on behalf of men; breaking bronze gates open, he smashes iron bars.

Chaplain: Let these thank God for his love, for his marvels on behalf of men. Let them offer thanksgiving sacrifices and proclaim with shouts of joy what he has done.

All: Others, taking ship and going out to sea, were plying their business across the ocean; they too saw what God could do, what marvels on the deep!

Chaplain: He spoke and raised a gale, lashing up towering waves. Flung to the sky, then plunged to the depths, they lost their nerve in the ordeal, staggering and reeling like drunkards with all their seamanship adrift.

All: Then they called to God in their trouble and he rescued them from their sufferings, reducing the storm to a whisper until the waves grew quiet, bringing them, glad at the calm, safe to the port they were bound for.

Chaplain: Let these thank God for his love, for his marvels on behalf of men. Let them extol him at the Great Assembly and praise him in the Council of Elders.

All: If you are wise, study these things and realise how God shows his love.

SCRIPTURE READING

I Corinthians 15: 50-58

HYMN

Faith of our fathers! living still
in spite of dungeon, fire, and sword;
O how our hearts beat high with joy
whene'er we hear that glorious word!
Faith of our fathers, holy faith,
we will be true to thee till death.

Faith of our fathers! God's great power
shall soon all nations win for thee;
and through the truth that comes from God
mankind shall then be truly free.
Faith of our fathers, holy faith,
we will be true to thee till death.

SCRIPTURE READING

Romans 8: 31-39

ADDRESS
PRAYERS

Almighty God from whom true peace comes, open our minds and hearts to a true love of peace. Guide those who are in authority to listen well to your wisdom and to forego expediency, to work, instead, only for justice, and charity which is the only true path to peace in the world. May your kingdom come so that the earth will be filled with your knowledge and your love and your peace — we ask this through your Son and Holy Spirit.

O Eternal Lord God, who alone spreadest out the heavens, and rulest the raging of the sea; who has compassed the waters with bounds until day and night come to an end; be pleased to receive into thy almighty and most gracious protection the persons of us thy servants, and the Fleet in which we serve. Preserve us from the dangers of the sea, and from the violence of the enemy; that we may be a safeguard unto our most gracious Sovereign Lady, Queen Elizabeth and her Dominions, and a security for such as pass on the seas upon their lawful occasions; that the inhabitants of our Commonwealth may in peace and quietness serve thee our God; and that we may return in safety to enjoy the blessings of the land, with the fruits of our labours, and with a thankful remembrance of thy mercies to praise and glorify thy holy name; through Jesus Christ our Lord. Amen.

THE NAVAL HYMN

Eternal Father, strong to save,
Whose arm hath bound the restless wave,
Who bidd'st the mighty ocean deep
Its own appointed limits keep:
   O hear us when we cry to Thee
   For those in peril on the Sea.

O Christ, whose voice the waters heard,
And hushed their raging at Thy word,
And walkest on the foaming deep,
And calm amid the storm didst sleep;
   O hear us when we cry to Thee
   For those in peril on the Sea.

O Holy Spirit, who didst brood
Upon the waters dark and rude,
And bid their angry tumult cease
And give, for wild confusion, peace:
   O hear us when we cry to Thee
   For those in peril on the Sea.

O Trinity of love and power,
Our brethren shield in danger's hour;
From rock and tempest, fire and foe,
Protect them wheresoe'er they go:
   Thus evermore shall rise to Thee
   Glad hymns of praise from land and sea.

LAST POST
ROLL CALL OF HMC SHIPS
SILENCE
REVEILLE
GOD SAVE THE QUEEN

God save our gracious Queen,
Long live our noble Queen,
God save the Queen.
Send her victorious,
Happy and glorious,
Long to reign over us;
God save the Queen.

THE BLESSING

May the God of all consolation bless you in every way and grant you peace all the days of your life.

May he enrich you with his gifts of faith, hope and love, so that what you do in this life will bring to thee happiness of everlasting life. Amen.

POSTLUDE

Therefore, let us remember those of our brothers who have gone before in the service of God, Sovereign and Country, those whose names are kept alive through the remembrance of their ships; those lost by the RCN in World War II.

Those Lost through Enemy Action — 15
Levis, Spikenard, Racoon, Charlottetown, Ottawa, Louisburg, St. Croix, Athabascan, Valleyfield, Regina, Alberni, Clayoquot, Trentonian, Guysborough, Esquimalt

Those Lost through Unknown Causes — 1
Shawnigan

Those Lost through Marine Causes — 2
Bras D'Or, Skeena

Those Lost through Collision — 4
Fraser, Margaree, Windflower, Chedabucto

Those Lost through Mines — 4
Weyburn, M.T.B. 460, Mulgrave, M.T.B. 463

Those Lost through Fire — 6
Otter, M.T.B. 461, M.T.B. 465, M.T.B. 459, M.T.B. 462, M.T.B. 466[26]

Trafalgar Day

Trafalgar Day commemorates 21 October, 1805, the day when Admiral Horatio Nelson defeated Napoleon's reluctant fleet in the decisive victory which is an important event in the proud record of Britain's Naval Forces.

The Canadian Navy celebrates Trafalgar Day because of its roots in the Royal Navy and because of the coincidence of outstanding events on that date in its own history. On 21 October, 1910, the cruiser *Niobe* arrived in Canada. The original 'Atlantic command' was formed in October, and it was on 21 October, 1944, that HMCS *Uganda* was re-commissioned, becoming the first cruiser in RCN service since *Niobe*, 34 years previously.

On the Friday closest to 21 October, there are several events which traditionally mark Lord Nelson's victory at Cape Trafalgar in 1805. For example, the officers (past and present) of HMCS *Star* gather at a mess dinner; HMCS *Cataraqui* celebrates with a ceremonial parade in Kingston, Ontario; and 'weepers' are held in both Stadacona and Naden. In Halifax, 'super weepers' are the order of the day for the officers of *Subron One*, and the base officers enjoy 'penny beer.' In Naden, the dress for 'weepers' is usually a variation of the dress actually worn by Nelson's men at Trafalgar. [27]

VI
And What About...?

There is always a selection of nautical lore that does not quite fit into any specific category. Although those items discussed here cannot be considered strictly Canadian, they are of interest because of their nautical significance.

Nail the Colours to the Mast

This expression refers to an act of great gallantry, and is originally related to the Battle of Camperdown on 11 October, 1797. During that battle, a sailor, John Crawford, serving in HMS *Venerable*, climbed aloft and actually nailed the English colours to the mast when the flag halliards had been shot away.

Three years earlier, on the Glorious First of June, 1794, a similar act of heroism was performed which is recorded as follows:

"At the time of the engagement, the 1st of June 1794, William Fitz-Gerald was a midshipman on board the *Marlborough*, not more than sixteen years of age. His ship had been driven nearly on shore by a French vessel, and in this position was cruelly raked fore and aft by the enemy's fire. The last remaining mast was shot away, and a cheer was given by the Frenchmen under the impression that she had struck her colours, as it was the one which carried the flag. The men had been ordered, after firing, to lie flat on the deck to escape the enemy's fire, but when the Frenchmen raised their exultant cry, young Fitz-Gerald sprang to his feet, tore the flag from the wreck of cordage, etc., and nailed it to the stump. In a short time after, some other ships came to their aid and the splendid vessel came out triumphant."[28]

Unfortunately, this gallant midshipman was taken prisoner by the enemy, and died in a French prison. In commemoration of his daring, a handsome plaque was awarded to this brave sailor. It reads:

"A tribute of respect from his Country to Mr. William Fitz-Gerald, Midshipman of His Majesty's Ship the *Marlborough*, for his gallant conduct on the ever memorable 1st of June 1794, when the French Fleet was defeated by the British Fleet under the command of Admiral Earl Howe.

John Julius Angerstein, Chairman
Lloyd's Coffee House"[29]

The Hammock

This item is not mentioned in the official Establishment of Stores of 1686, but appears in the supplementary Establishment of 1693 for flagships only. Among the bo's'n's stores are 400 'Hammaccoes swinging' for the Admiral of the Red, 300 for the Admiral of the Blue, and 200 for the other flagships.

Apart from rum, the hammock was the only thing the Royal Navy received from the New World, and for a long time was exclusively a naval monopoly. In the Bahamas Columbus saw the suspended beds in which the inhabitants slept, which they called 'hamacs.' The new word became 'hamaca,' and later made its way into the English naval vocabulary during the reign of Queen Elizabeth I as 'hamaco.'

At the time of the Armada, hammocks were taken from the captured Spanish ships by English sailors. They were officially introduced in the Navy in 1597; a warrant in that year authorised payment for 300 bolts of canvas "to make hanging cabones or beddes for the better preservation of their healths." They were limited to a breadth of 14 in. since to work the guns it was necessary to crowd as many men as possible in the space. During the Crimean War, spare oars were cut up on board H.M.S. *Agamemnon* and fitted to the canvas hammocks, fashioning the first litters.

Hammocks were always made of brown canvas until well into the nineteenth century, and a ship usually prided herself on the whiteness of her hammock cloths. After a battle more sails than were actually damaged by the enemy's fire were invariably requisitioned to obtain canvas for more hammock cloths (as well as new white trousers for the ship's company).

In the days of Nelson, it was a common jibe at the French that they could not give orders for getting hammocks up and down, for they said 'up' when slinging, and 'down' when stowing.

In 1957, the Royal Navy announced that it would be discarding the hammock for sleeping purposes in its future warships. This was similar to the change which began in the Royal Canadian Navy in 1949, when HMCS *Sioux* began a major refit. Since then, all new and modernized warships in the Canadian Navy have been fitted with bunks, as well as other furnishings and facilities designed to make life at sea more livable!

The First Woman in the Navy?

The following is an account of the discovery of a woman soldier on board a ship enroute to Guinea in 1693. The extract reads:

"Saturday the 18th (November 1693) ... This

morning we found out that one of the *Royal African* company's soldiers, for their castles in *Guiney*, was a woman, who had entere'd herself into their service without the least suspicion, and had been three months on board without any mistrust, lying always among the other passengers, and being handy and ready to do any work as any of them; and I believe she had continued undiscover'd till our arrival in *Africa*, had she not fallen very sick, which occasion'd our Surgeon to visit her, and ordered her a glister (sic); which when his mate went to administer, he was surprised to find more sally-ports than he expected, which occasioned him to make a further enquiry; which, as well as her confession, manifesting the trust of her sex, he came to acquaint me of it, whereupon, in charity, as well as in respect to her sex, I ordered her a private lodging apart from the men, and gave the taylor some ordinary stuffs to make her woman's cloaths; in recompence for which she prov'd very useful in washing my linnen, and doing what else she could till we deliver'd her with the rest at Cape Coast Castle. She was about twenty years old and a likely black girl."[30]

This is the first known occasion of a woman going on board a ship as a member of the crew. On certain occasions, women were able to travel with their husbands, and as in the case of 'Tremendous' Mackenzie, who was born onboard HMS *Tremendous* in 1794.

Some Old Beliefs and Superstitions

Beside customs and tradition, seafarers have always been prone to belief in signs and omens; a fact due in part to the perilous nature of a seaman's calling, and the mystery and uncertainty of the sea. Sailors have always been inclined to attribute supernatural causes to natural phenomena, and to constantly watch for signs and portents of troubles to come.

Among the earliest nautical superstitions, is one attached to 'St. Elmo's Fire,' or the 'Corposants' as English sailors called it. This phenomenon is the glow accompanying the slow discharge of electricity to earth from the atmosphere. It usually appears on the extremities of the masts and yards of ships, and is often accompanied by a crackling noise. It is most frequently seen during and after snowstorms, but may occur at any time. The phenomenon was well known to the mariners of ancient Greece, who, when they observed two lights, called them Castor and Pollux and invoked them as gods.

The name St. Elmo comes from St. Erasmus, or Ermo, a martyr of the fourth century, and the patron saint of Mediterranean sailors, who regard St. Elmo's fire as the visible sign of his guardianship. They believed that when St. Elmo's fire was seen during a storm it was a good omen for the safety of the ship. Fernando Columbus, the son and biographer of the great Christopher, mentions it in his account of his father's second voyage to the West Indies:

"...on that night was seen St. Elmo with seven lighted tapers at the topmast, there was much rain and great thunder; beholding which the sailors chanted many litanies and orisons (prayers), holding it certain that in the storms in which he appears none are in danger."[31]

The famous Magellan, a well-educated man of his day, also mentions the feeling of comfort and hope he experienced from seeing these lights in time of danger.

Quite naturally, waterspouts have been regarded with superstition and fear by sailors of all times. Columbus' crew in the *Santa Maria* were terrified of them, and discovered an 'infallible' charm against their powers which consisted in repeating passages from the Gospel of St. John. To this day Levantine sailors, at the approach of a waterspout, will kneel down and, holding a blackhandled knife (kept for this specific purpose) in one hand, read aloud from the Gospel of St. John. On coming to the words "et verbum caro factum est," etc., they cut the air in the direction of the waterspout, believing that the spout will collapse.

The power of the little Remora or Sucker Fish *(Echeneis remora)* to stop or retard ships, was one of the most widely spread beliefs in ancient and mediaeval times. They are said to have delayed Mark Antony from getting into action at the battle of Actium, despite the exertions of several hundred sailors. The force of tempest, tide and current, together with oars and sails could, so some believed, be checked by one small 'remora' fish, compelling a vessel to become motionless in the midst of the ocean.

The belief in the power of witches to adversely influence wind and weather conditions at sea, was common in days gone by. An incident is reported in the Isle of Man, where the fisher folk discovered that the foul weather was caused by an old woman who raised the tempest by whirling water round and round in a basin. She was caught in the act and condemned to death by being put in a barrel filled with spikes and rolled down a hill. The grass there is said to have never grown again.

It is still believed that whistling for the wind in a calm will sooner or later conjure up a breeze. There are stories of ancient mariners who, during a calm, keep one eye cocked on the weather leach of the maintop-gallant sail and whistle for hours at a time. Having a parson stick a knife in the mast was thought by some to be effective, although many old 'shellbacks' believed that the presence of a clergyman on board at all was unlucky, and would bring contrary winds and foul weather.

Another superstition is that striking a glass or bowl, and allowing it to ring, without stopping the vibration with the hand, will result in some person drowning. 'Ring a glass and drown a sailor' the saying goes. A curious instance of support for this belief occurred some years ago:

"I was sitting one evening in a cafe, and at an adjoining table sat a friend of mine, a submarine officer, accompanied by a lady. The latter was idly amusing herself tapping a glass on the rim and making it ring, to the evident annoyance of her companion, who at each tap placed his fingers on the rim to stop the ringing, and presently said rather testily 'for heaven's sake, stop! Don't you know the saying to ring a glass is to drown a sailor?' The lady chaffingly persisted, till at last the officer, losing his temper, got up from the table and marched out of the room. The next day, the submarine which he commanded was lost, and he and all his crew perished."[32]

It was also considered unlucky to drink the health of any person in water. This was tantamount to a curse, as though expressing a wish that the person so toasted might drown.

To put to sea on Friday has always been regarded as inviting the worst kind of luck. On Good Friday in Southern ports, the yards of square-rigged ships were 'scandalized' or canted crosswise. (This practice was forbidden in the British Navy as an example of 'popery!')

Another superstitious practice that persists to this day in sailing ships is throwing a pack of playing cards overboard to bring a fair wind. A few years ago a large sailing ship with many of her crew sick with scurvy lay becalmed outside Melbourne Heads. Two men were on the point of death with not a whisper of a breeze in sight. Suddenly the second mate, a Finn, scattered a new pack of playing cards over the taffrail. Within half an hour, a breeze sprung up and carried the ship into Port Phillip. One of the sick men died as the ship dropped anchor, but the other was rushed to hospital and recovered.

Warming the Bell

This expression appears to have come from the phrase 'warming the glass'; the half-hour sand-glass by which the sounding of a ship's bell was timed. The belief was that when the glass was warm the sand ran through quicker, thus shortening the watch. Midshipmen on watch were reputed to nurse the glass between their hands, or under their jackets, to stimulate the flow of sand.

Dead Horse Ceremony

The following description of the 'Dead Horse Ceremony,' held on board Messrs. Devitt and Moore's clipper ship *Sobroan*, on 14 November, 1890, is taken from the manuscript journal of one of the saloon passengers, Mr. Thomas Parkin, M.A., of Fairseat, High Wycombe, Hastings, Sussex.

"7 p.m. *Burial of the Dead Horse.* The ceremony known as burying the dead horse is a curious one and was still practiced (in 1890) in many Australian ships. Sailors, before they join their ships, have an advance note given them for a month's wages. This they usually spend so that the first month they may be said to be earning no wages. They therefore symbolise the first month's work by the dead horse and speak of it as 'working the dead horse.' The procession with R. Bradley as jockey of the dead horse, left the fo'castle or seaman's quarters a little after seven in the evening. The crew dressed up in different characters, amongst which was that of a soldier and two policemen. The procession made the tour of the main deck singing a dismal chant, consisting of a solo chorus, one of the refrains being "Poor Old Horse." The horse was then put up to auction, and was knocked down for 10 pounds 10 shillings, which was the amount collected from the passengers. The horse, with the rider on his back, was then hauled bodily from the deck to the mainyard, and illuminated during his ascent by blue lights burnt on the yard and from one of the boats near the poop. As soon as the yardarm was reached the ride detached the horse from the line and it fell with a splash into the water. "Rule Britannia" was then sung and after hearty cheers had been given for the Captain, the officers, the passengers and the crew the proceedings terminated.

"Captain J.A. Elmslie will not allow the usual shaving and larking which takes place on board Australian vessels when 'crossing the line' but has the ceremony of the Dead Horse instead, which is much better as we have several invalids on board."[33]

The Jaunty

The word 'jaunty' was apparently the closest the British 'tar' could come to the French 'gendarme.' As the head of the Navy's police or former regulating branch, the master-at-arms was a well known figure. Although there were lieutenant-commanders-at-arms and lieutenants-at-arms, it was the master-at-arms who was ever present in the minds of young seamen.

His history and title date back to the mid-1600s when he was a junior officer responsible for the training of all men in the ship in the use and care of small arms.

The master-at-arms was rated as one of the 'inferior' officers in the ship, appointed by warrant from the Navy Board. However, as the years passed his duties changed and he gradually became the disciplinarian or ship's policeman.

When the Royal Canadian Navy came into being in 1910, the master-at-arms was a chief petty officer, the most powerful figure on the lower deck. He was responsible for the seamen's discipline ashore and afloat. He seldom served in ships smaller than a cruiser, and before World War II, the Canadian Navy's master-at-arms usually performed his duties. Up to World War II he was the only non-commissioned officer privileged to wear a frock coat and sword on ceremonial occasions. Other chief petty officers wore their ordinary uniforms and carried sabres on such occasions.

The master-at-arms was many things to many men. As the ship's policeman he was held in awe; as a disciplinarian, he was the right hand of the officers; as a master he was also a friend to wrong-doers and protected the sailor's rights. In effect, he was a buffer between the officers and men. No official inspection took place without the master-of-arms. He always attended divisions and was present at the commander's and captain's defaulters parades every day.

But the 300-year tradition of the master-at-arms was replaced by an even older tradition when the RCN was revamped. The boatswains were first recorded in the British Navy over 400 years ago and were known as 'standing officers'; they remained with the ship, and were appointed by Admiralty Board.

Shore Leave

Every novel ever written about the Navy mentions 'shore leave,' but there is doubt as to whether the expression was used in the old days of the Navy. Obviously a 'leave' would not be granted unless the crew could go ashore, so the term itself is redundant. Old signal books refer to such things as 'general leave to the watch,' 'special leave to the watch,' 'the usual leave may be granted to officers,' and so on. Station or port orders referred to arrangements for such things as 'paying-off leave,' and 'Christmas leave.' Nowhere is there any reference to 'general shore leave to the watch,' or arrangements for paying-off leave, or the like.

The only sort of leave which did not connote going ashore was the questionable invention of the executive officers called the 'lower deck leave.' It was sometimes indulged in on board a vessel in drydock, during which the ratings spent their general leave in their messes and did no work.

It seems likely that the phrase 'shore leave' is a civilian invention and its usage, unlike the activity itself, should be avoided.

The Luck Coin in Ships

The discovery in 1963 of a Roman bronze coin in what appears to have been the mast-step of a second century barge in the Thames, at Blackfriars, in London, has led historians to examine the modern custom of placing a coin in the construction of a ship, and to consider the antiquity of the custom.

An inquiry made of a number of boat-building and boat-owning companies in England revealed that the custom was indeed well known, and that it was commonly practiced until early 1930. In large wooden ships, where the mast was a fixture, the general practice was to place a new sovereign in the mast-step of the vessel, both for luck and to date the vessel's construction.

Had the coin been placed underneath the mast in wooden sailing vessels where the mast was lowered, it would probably have been stolen, so the tenon of the stem or sternpost was favoured.

The origin of this custom is not known, but the apparent luck motive suggests a pagan origin. Possibly in ancient times a sacrifice was made to the gods to bring good fortune to a new ship, but after coins were invented a money payment was substituted.

A similar custom existed during the Roman period in the Mediterranean and in England, for three wrecks of that period, each of which contained a coin in a mast-step, have been discovered. The first was in the wreck of a Roman merchant ship, called *Chretienne A.*, found off the coast in the Mediterranean in June, 1962. The coin was found in a mast-step situated in a keelson. It had been minted in Cossura in 217 B.C., but the wreck itself has been dated to the first century B.C. The second discovery was made in July 1963, in the Roman barge discovered at Blackfriars, London. The coin was of the Emperor Domitian, and had been minted in Rome in 88-89 A.D. Significantly, the coin lay reverse uppermost, showing the figure of Fortuna, goddess of luck, holding a steering oar. The third discovery was made in November 1963, in a mast-step of the wreck at Port Vendres in the Mediterranean, off the coast of France. The coin was of the Emperor Constantine, and had been minted in London during the early fourth century A.D.

General Drill

The activity known as 'general drill' would look like mass confusion to the uninitiated: a sudden flurry of activity, masts being climbed, sailors pounding over the deck, boats being lowered and other apparently aimless activities.

However, to a sailor raised in the tradition of the Royal Navy or the Royal Canadian Navy, it is a highly organized and competitive form of activity designed to test the seamanship and ingenuity of the ship's company.

Orders such as: 'lay out the kedge anchor,' 'rig deck tackle,' 'away (number) seaboats, pull around the ship,' 'prepare to abandon ship,' 'operate a foam gun on the fo'c'sle,' 'fire a gun,' and so on are given simultaneously.

Even more demanding 'drills,' such as ordering the cook of the watch to deliver a serving of bacon and red lead to the captain, who could be doing 25 push-ups on the flag deck, were thought up by imaginative squadron commanders or training officers. Such activity generated humorous anecdotes by the score.

"On one occasion, while a group of ships was working up in Bermuda during World War II, general drill reached a glorious climax with the final drill of the day:

'Away boats and floats: Abandon ship.'

One of the ships won handily and wished she hadn't. Boats and floats hit the water in record time and the ship's company worked far into the night replacing slashed lashings and hoisting the heavy floats and boats back into place."[34]

If a senior officer thought he could make things difficult for his competitors, the ship's companies would often try to outwit him.

"A few months before World War II, on the West Indies Station, a Royal Navy cruiser resorted to the fiendish stratagem of fashioning a bower anchor out of balsa wood, leading it with a gantline and shipping it to the port hawse. Now they were ready for the signal:

"Send a bower anchor to the flagship."

This would be a gruelling experience if one had to move a real anchor. It was, however, not to be the signal they would receive.

"Let go the port anchor."

There was nothing to do but let the fake anchor go, and to watch ruefully as the anchor floated slowly away, bobbing gently in the light sea — much to the glee and amusement of the competing ships in company."[35]

Speed was of the essence, and the ship who completed her drills in the least amount of time was considered the winner of the evolution. Today, the purpose of the 'general drill' remains unchanged, and though radio communication has taken the place of signal flags, this exercise brings out the best in ingenuity, skill and speed.

Notes

1. Paymaster Lieutenant H.R.H. Vaughn, "The Boatswain's Whistle," *The Naval Review*, Vol. 10, (n.p., The Naval Society, n.date), p.373.

2. Ibid., p.377.

3. Ibid.

4. Ibid., p.378.

5. Ibid.

6. Ibid.

7. Ben W. Blee, Commander, USN, "The Story of Grog in the Royal Navy," United States Naval Institute of Proceedings, (Maryland, U.S. Naval Institute, 1959), p.63.

8. F.H. Miller, "Grog," *The Navy and Army Illustrated, Vol. II, (n.p., 1896), p.89.*

9. "Whiskey in Place of Beer," Excerpts from the Admiralty Minute Book, *The Mariner's Mirror*, (St. Albans, Staples Printers Ltd., 1957), p.154.

10. Captain W.N.T. Beckett, R.N., *A Few Naval Customs, Expressions, Traditions and Superstitions*, (Portsmouth, Gieves Ltd., 1953), p.64.

11. J.G. Brighton, *Admiral Sir P.B.V. Broke, Bart., A Memoire*, (London, n. pub., 1866), pp. 480-481.

12. Michael Lewis, *England's Sea officers, the Story of the Naval Procession*, (London, George Allen and Unwin, Ltd., n. date), p.235.

13. Michael Lewis, *The Navy of Britain, a Historical Portrait*, (London, George Allen and Unwin, Ltd., 1949), p.178.

14. E.C. Russell, "Warrant Officers," N/Hist Memorandum 1440 1 dated 28 Oct. 1964.

15. J.R. Turner, *A Descriptive Catalogue of the Naval Manuscripts in the Pepsyian Library*, Vol. I, (London, The Naval Records Society, 1903-1904), p.122.

16. George C. Machum, *Canada's VCs*, (Toronto, McClelland and Stewart, Ltd., 1956), p.19.

17. Ibid., p.103.

18. Ibid., p.175.

19. Ibid., p.197.

20. Michael Lewis, *The Navy of Britain, A Historical Portrait*, p.36.

21. Dudley Jarret, *British Naval Dress*, (London, J.M. Dent and Sons, Ltd., 1960), p.18.

22. W.E. May, "HMS," *The Mariner's Mirror*, Vol. 58, No. 2, (St. Albans, Staples Printers Ltd., 1972), p.102.

23. Dudley Jarret, *British Naval Dress*, p.24.

24. W.E. May, "HMS," *The Mariner's Mirror*, p.102.

25. "Beneath the Barber Pole," from an unknown source included by letter from the Commander, Fifth Canadian Destroyer Squadron (1000 - 2(D-5)), dated 23 Dec., 1980.

26. "Memorandum on the Losses of RCN ships," (Ottawa, Chief of Naval Staff, 11 Dec. 1947), n. pag.

27. Edward C. Russel, *Customs and Traditions of the Canadian Armed Forces*, (Ottawa, Deneau and Greenburg, 1980), p.201.

28. "Nail the Colours to the Mast," Answers, *The Mariner's Mirror*, (St. Albans, Staples Printers, Ltd., 1973), p.107.

29. Ibid.

30. *A Collection of Voyages and Travels, Vol 6*, ed. by Awnsham and John Churchill, (London, John Walthoe et. al., 1732), p. 179.

31. A. MacDermott, "Some Old Beliefs and Superstitions of Seamen," *The Mariner's Mirror*, (St.Albans, Staples Printers Ltd., 1956), p.254.

32. Ibid., p.255.

33. Allen E. Bax, "Dead Horse Ceremony," *The Mariner's Mirror*, (St. Albans, Staples Printers Ltd., 1957), pp. 344-345.

34. "General Drill," *The Crowsnest*, Vol. 13., No. 6, (Ottawa, Queen's Printer, 1961), p.16.

35. Ibid., p.17.

4 The Wardroom

I
Humble Beginnings

There are many different theories regarding the origins of the 'wardroom' and its association with the ship's officers but there is general agreement that the word did not derive from the word "wardrobe." "Ward" is apparently from the Anglo Saxon word "weardian" which meant "guard." "Guard" is from the French and means "garder," or earlier, "warden." "Room" is self-evident. Used together in this context, the words mean: "a space set aside for the weardian or a division of space for the military." Most older dictionaries give one word, "wardroom," as a mess room for senior officers in a warship.

There is no specific reference to a naval officers' mess before the mid 1750s when the two separate words 'ward room' were used. In a typical British "ship of the line," beginning aft on the middle deck, stands the wardroom, with two galleries opening onto the ship's sides, called "quarter-galleries," and occasionally, a stern gallery. This is the military officer's mess. By the end of the eighteenth century, this compartment had become the lieutenants' living-room; their cabins and storerooms, which were little more than screened-off corners, led from it or were immediately forward of it.

The 'gunroom,' now closely related to the wardroom in function, had a somewhat different beginning. In a typical British ship of the line, the midshipmen were divided into two areas. Midshipmen messed in the 'after cockpit,' sharing it with the master's mates, whose descendants are the sub-lieutenants, and the surgeon's mates. The original 'gunroom' was located on the deck above, but was referred to as the 'lower deck.' This compartment, located in the stern, was the home of the gunner, the youngest 'young gentlemen,' then called 'volunteers,' and, sometimes, the more junior midshipmen. As a 'young gentleman' one shared a fairly spacious area, but when promoted, ended up cramped in the bowels of the ship. The gunroom probably became the perview of midshipmen, and junior sub-lieutenants, when the 'new guns' appeared and modern ships were designed to accommodate them. In the new ships the main armament was placed in turrets on the upper deck. The lower deck gun space disappeared, leaving only the name and perhaps some senior 'snobs' behind to find a new place to mess.

II
The Purpose of the Wardroom

The wardroom has existed in the Navy for nearly 250 years as a living and recreational area for the ship's officers. It is the only compartment in a ship for the exclusive use of its members, and others may not enter unless invited, or unless they have the express permission of the mess president: the executive officer. Officers use the wardroom as a place to relax and enjoy themselves, to entertain guests and be entertained. It is the centre of a social life in HMC ships and its success in this regard depends on the contributions of its members.

The captain of a ship is a full member of the wardroom in vessels where he is not provided with a particular place for his own use. It is customary for him to be invited to become an honorary member. Although he has no vote in the government of the wardroom and does not normally interfere with any decision, he has power to issue any instructions concerning it that he chooses, and may veto any ruling of the mess, should he see fit.

The wardroom, as the home of a group of responsible citizens, conforms to the rules and customs adhered to in good society. As in life, where special circumstances require special behaviour, certain additional rules and customs are in force in an officers' mess, but these do not replace the code of manners recognized in good society. The mess is the only "democratic institution" in the service, and like all democratic organizations, it requires that all members take an active interest and part in its operation.

III
Dining in the Wardroom

General

An important function of the wardroom is to provide a place for its members to enjoy their meals in a congenial atmosphere.

Breakfast, luncheon and supper are normally served informally at the wardroom or gunroom table. These meals are served by the stewards to each officer as he arrives at the table. There are brunch routines on weekends and holidays in some wardrooms.

Naval shore establishments usually provide a sandwich bar in a separate room of the wardroom complex at noon on working days, in addition to the normal table service. Courtesy dictates that sandwiches be consumed in the designated seating areas, and space at the wardroom bar is not used for that purpose.

Dinners in the wardroom are formal affairs, arranged for special occasions. There are three types: 'mess dinners'; 'dine-the-ladies'; and 'dining-in.'

'Dine-the-ladies' is mixed and a 'dining-in' is less formal than a 'mess dinner' although the procedures for all three are similar.

The procedures outlined here are those used in the wardrooms of HMC ships and naval establishments. When the wardrooms of naval establishments are used for mess dinners by other units these procedures are not followed.

The 'mess dinner' is a special or ceremonial occasion, carried on from the days when officers dined formally every evening. The traditions and ceremonies observed during the dinner have evolved over time but the basic rules of conduct observed are those of other gentlemen (and ladies) in polite society. The sequence of events, and the customs and traditions observed when dining in a naval mess, (whether ashore or onboard one of HMC ships) are outlined below.

Army Regiments, Air Force Squadrons, and the Services of other nations have unique customs and traditions quite different from those of a naval mess dinner. When entertaining guests, it is a normal courtesy to give a brief explanation beforehand of the rules and idiosyncrasies of the dinner.

Terminology

In this chapter, the following terms and meanings are used:
(a) Dinner: A formal function, formerly known as 'dining-in-the-mess' or 'dining-in';
(b) Supper: A less formal meal. A duty officer who cannot dress for dinner or is likely to be called away may have supper rather than dinner;
(c) President: The president of the dinner;
(d) Black tie: Black or white dinner jacket worn with a black bow-tie; and
(e) White tie: Civilian evening dress consisting of a tail-coat, wing collar and white bow-tie.

Dress

The dress to be worn at dinner is specified well in advance and is shown on the invitation.

Naval officers wear either RCN or CF pattern mess dress at dinner. The specific order of dress depends on the occasion and the season or latitude.

Retired officers wear mess dress or appropriate civilian formal attire with miniature medals. Officers of other services wear the appropriate equivalent of mess dress.

Civilian guests wear appropriate formal attire. Lady guests wear formal evening dress.

The President and Vice-president

The mess president (i.e., the executive officer or base administration officer) is usually the president of the dinner, although any officer may be called upon to act as president. The president is in charge of the proceedings regardless of his rank, seniority or classification. During the dinner the president may discipline any diner for misbehaviour. He occupies the head of the table; at a large table this is in the centre and at a small table it is the end nearest the door.

The vice-president is subordinate to the president during dinner whatever their relative ranks and seniorities, but he can fine or warn the president for any infraction of the rules. In a large mess with more than one table, there is provision for a vice-president to be seated at each table.

The vice-president sits on the president's right farthest away from him (if the president is in the centre); at the opposite end of a single table (if the president is at the head of the table); or at the end of each table farthest from the president when several tables are used.

Before Dinner

Arrival

Invitations to dinner are worded "1930 for 2000." This half hour is set aside for cocktails, and to allow those officers acting as hosts to review the seating plan, find their guests and introduce themselves. The remainder of the time can be spent sharing a before dinner drink with friends.

Sherry is the normal pre-dinner drink, chosen by generations of sagacious officers, because it comes in small quantities, and being a fortified wine, serves as a 'warm-up' for the wine that follows.

Seating Plan

The seating for a naval mess dinner is usually formally arranged and a plan is drawn up and displayed. Individual places at the table are marked with a name card. The following rules apply:

(a) Shifting places is not permitted;
(b) Guests sit to the right of their hosts. If an officer is hosting two guests he sits between them. If he has more than two guests, the host should have them disposed on either side of him in two groups;
(c) Guests should not sit beside each other if it can be avoided; and
(d) The president is host to guests of the mess. If there are many guests, the vice-president or other members act as hosts, with the president host to the guest of honour.

The success of a dinner is often related to the amount of time spent on the seating plan. Therefore the organizer:

(a) Carefully considers each person attending the dinner;
(b) Avoids concentrating junior officers or senior officers;
(c) Considers the personalities involved and distributes the more witty and outgoing individuals to help liven up the entire group;
(d) Avoids placing long-winded or boring individuals as vice-presidents; and
(e) When ladies are present, considers the group and determines how best to separate couples, if it seems desirable to do so.

If no seating plan is provided, or if the seating plan provides only for the president and mess guests, officers take their places at the table without regard to rank or seniority.

Entry

At 1955, the senior steward enters the ante-room and reports to the president:

"Dinner is served, Sir."

The president and his guest then leads the way into the dining room. The band strikes up "The Roast Beef of Olde England" (the tune which Nelson and his officers went to dinner by in the flagship on the eve of Trafalgar), thereby signalling the remaining officers to escort their guests in to dinner.

When 'dining-the-ladies,' each officer seeks out and escorts the lady to be seated to his right.

On entering the dining room, the president goes to his place and sits down immediately. The others then take their seats as they arrive at their places.

Dining

Grace

When all diners are seated, the senior steward reports to the president:

"Officers seated, Sir."

The steward also informs the President of the Mess Committee if a chaplain is present. The president then taps the table for silence. If there is a chaplain present, he will say 'Grace.' If there is more than one chaplain present, they arrange beforehand who will ask the blessing. It is generally said at the beginning of dinner, and at the end. If the chaplains are guests, the president asks them before dinner if they will agree to say 'Grace.'

If there is no chaplain present, the president says 'Grace.' Although the person saying 'Grace' may use his own wording, the prayer normally used by presidents (though not often by chaplains) is: "For what we are about to receive, thank God." (The popular idea that the normal 'naval grace' is simply "Thank God" is entirely incorrect.)

The Menu

The organizer, with the chief cook's assistance, decides the menu. In doing so he tries to choose a menu that will satisfy a wide range of palates. The menu should be balanced and interesting, and provide an opportunity for the cooks to demonstrate their talents.

As a general rule, he avoids:

(a) Dishes that may be unfamiliar or risky (e.g. Haggis)
(b) Dishes which cannot be eaten by members of various religious faiths (e.g., pork)
(c) Dishes which are difficult or undignified to eat (e.g., game hens or boiled lobster); and
(d) Dishes which are difficult to serve to a large number of people (e.g., filet mignon)

Following is a typical menu:

Appetizer: Crab Cocktail
Soup: Consomme Royal
Fish: Filet of Sole
Joint: Veal Cordon Bleu
    Potatoes
    Fresh Vegetables
Sweet: Lemon Parfait

Savoury: Welsh Rarebit

Dessert: Cheese, mints, nuts, fruit

Appropriate wines are served with the various courses. Sherry is sometimes served with the soup; white wine accompanies the fish or poultry, and red wine is served with other meats.

Service

Mess guests are served before the president and other guests before their hosts. The president does not delay starting a course, since other diners wait to follow his lead. No dish is removed until the last diner has finished eating each course.

If a diner has been granted permission to sit down late, or to return to the table, he continues with the course then being served, unless he has the president's permission to eat the course he missed.

Wine and other beverages are always served and removed from a diner's right.

When the last course has been finished, the stewards clear the table of everything except the table decorations, sweep up all the crumbs and remove the napkins. Finger bowls may be provided when fresh fruits or other such desserts are served. Each diner is provided with an individual bowl of warm water for rinsing his fingers. The bowls are removed when the table is cleared.

Table Settings

Though the table service provided at a formal dinner party may initially appear formidable, the basic rule of thumb for silverware is simply "start at the outside and work in." The arrangement of utensils corresponds to the courses that will be served, and are placed in the order in which they will be used. On the right beginning at the outside — is the soup spoon, fish knife, and dinner knife. On the left is the fish fork, salad fork and the dinner fork. The dessert spoon and fork are placed above the plate. A bread knife and teaspoon may be added.

4.01   Table setting for a formal dinner in the wardroom.

The stewards ensure that the right wine gets to the right wine glass for each course. The accompanying illustration shows the proper service for a formal dinner. A bare table is often used, but a cloth may or may not be used depending on the quality of the table.

Table Manners

Diners sit up straight at the table with their hands on their lap when not using table utensils.

The table napkin is laid across the lap (not tucked in the tunic). At the end of the meal, the napkin is laid on the table so that it can be taken away by the stewards when the table is cleared.

Soup is taken from the side of the spoon. A knife is never lifted to the mouth, or used for cutting bread or rolls. (These are broken with the hands.) The fork is held in the left hand for the meat, and may be transferred to the right hand for vegetables. The knife and fork are placed side by side on the plate to indicate that the plate may be removed.

Other fine points of manners followed are:
(a) Lumps of sugar are removed with tongs or a clean spoon;
(b) Tea or coffee cups are not held in the hand for long periods; after a short sip, they are returned to the saucer;
(c) Teaspoons are not used to taste the tea or coffee, but rather to stir the ingredients; and
(d) Toothpicks are only used in private.

Rules of Order

The tap of the president's gavel for 'Grace' signals that the dinner has officially begun. Between then and the 'loyal toast' the following rules apply.

Without the president's permission, no one may:
(a) Come in and sit down at the table;
(b) Leave the table;
(c) Return to the table;
(d) Read (except the menu or the musical programme);
(e) Write; or
(f) Speak to anyone not dining (this does not apply to giving an order to a steward or receiving a message from him).

If a diner is near enough to the president to ask his permission regarding any item listed above, he does so; if he is too far away, he sends a steward to the president with the request. When he is coming to the table late, or is returning having left it, he always asks the president's permission.

Diners are not allowed to:
(a) Commence a course before the president;
(b) Smoke;
(c) Utter an oath or use foul language;

(d) Place a bet or wager;

(e) Discuss political or other controversial subjects;

(f) Talk 'shop';

(g) Speak in a foreign language (except when foreign guests are present;

(h) Tell 'off-colour' stories;

(j) Mention a woman's name unless she is a celebrity (The president's decision on the matter, as on all others is final. This rule does not apply when ladies, other than female officers, are present);

(k) Mention a specific sum of money; or

(l) Propose a toast ("Cheers" or similar remarks or raising the glass as in greeting constitutes a toast).

Whenever the president or vice-president taps the table there must be silence until he has finished speaking.

Discipline

Misbehaviour or breaking the rules of order generally results in disciplinary action. The president has three options: order the culprit to leave the mess; fine him an appropriate number of drinks; or warn him.

The punishment will usually fit the crime. A diner is ordered to leave for a serious offence such as gross rudeness. For other offences, more light-hearted in nature, the offender is given a chance to exonerate himself by the use of his wits.

An officer coming to dinner late may have his excuse accepted; he may be refused permission to dine, or he may be fined. Fines vary from a single drink to drinks for all present. The president may award drinks to any diner or diners he chooses to name, including himself. If there is an offended party he is generally mollified by receiving payment of a fine. The vice-president may warn or fine the president. Fines imposed on a guest must be paid for by his (or her) host.

It is permissible for any diner to call the president's attention to a misdemeanour, but wise is the man who first obtains the president's permission to do so since without such permission, he himself may be fined.

The procedure for warning or fining is for the president to tap the table for silence, and say, for example:

"Mr. Watson will have the honour of giving the navigating officer a glass of port," or

"Mr. Gunn will have the honour of passing the port."

There is no set phrase, but the expression "will buy a drink" is avoided. If the president wishes to warn someone, he merely says:

"Mr. Tremblay is warned."

The president enlarges upon any of these remarks whenever he wishes. Fines are nearly always levied in terms of port or other wine in which toasts are drunk. They are never paid until after the toasts have been drunk, and no diner who has not drunk the toasts in wine may accept payment of a fine. Toasts may never be drunk in wine that is served in payment of a fine. Offenders honour fines in the wardroom ante-room after the dinner is over, and in the beverage of the recipient's choice. If a diner who was named as the recipient of the payment of a fine does not accept payment, the fine is considered paid.

When the table has been cleared, the senior steward reports to the president:

"Table cleared, Sir."

The president taps the table for silence and calls on the chaplain to 'give thanks.' If no chaplain is present the president 'gives thanks' in the customary way:

"For what we have received, thank God."

Repartee, speeches and explanations are normally left until the end of dinner, after the toasts, when everyone has been well-wined and dined. This is not the time for a serious or lengthy speech, unless the speakers' itinerary precludes another opportunity to address the group.

The guest of honour normally makes the final speech of the evening, and everyone is expected to listen attentively.

Since points of order may be confusing to non-military guests, speakers usually use common sense and good taste in consideration for them.

Toasts

Passing the Port

After 'Thanks' are given, port glasses are brought around by the stewards and set before each diner. Decanters of port, stoppers in, are set before the president and each vice-president. Other dessert wines such as Madeira or Marsala may be used instead of, or in addition to, the port.

When the decanters are in place, the senior steward reports to the president:

"The wine is ready to pass, Sir."

The president then unstoppers the decanters in front of him, as do the other officers with decanters. The president passes his decanters to the left, and other officers do the same without serving themselves.

The decanters are kept at least one place apart as they move around the table. If no one is seated at the end of the table, the stewards move the decanters across it. Any officer who forgets to help himself before passing the port is out of luck since decanters move only to the left. The port is passed by sliding the decanters along the table, reducing the risk of dropping them or spilling their contents. They may be raised from the table to pour. The practice of never lifting the decanters, even to pour, is an exaggeration of the passing method. It is not a tradition, should not be practiced, and getting caught is a good way to get fined.

No-one is required to take wine if they do not want it, but it must be taken on the first round of the decanters, or not at all. In civilian toasts, if you do not take wine, your glass is filled with water. In the Navy, however, toasts are never made with water, as superstition says that the person toasted will die by drowning.

When a set of decanters arrives in front of an officer who has charge of it, he serves himself and keeps the new set in front of him. The stewards then bring the decanters' stoppers to the officer so that the sets remain matched.

No one touches their wine until the 'loyal toast' has been proposed.

When the wine has been passed and the decanters are in place the senior steward reports:

"The wine has been passed, Sir."

The president then stoppers the decanters in front of him and the other officers do the same.

The Loyal Toast

The health of Her Majesty the Queen is honoured while diners remain seated in the wardrooms of HMC ships and designated naval establishments, except:

(a) When a band is present, and "God Save the Queen" is played;

(b) When foreign guests, other than foreign exchange officers, are present; and

(c) When Her Majesty the Queen, or another member of the Royal Family is present (unless they have specifically expressed a wish that those in attendance remain seated.)

The privilege accorded to the Navy of remaining seated while drinking the Sovereign's health is long-standing but obscure in its origin. There are several popular beliefs about these origins: one is that King Charles II when on board the *Royal Charles* bumped his head on rising to reply to the toast; and that King William IV, Lord High Admiral, did the same as he stood up during a dinner on one of HM ships. Another is that King George IV, while dining on board one of HM ships said, as the officers rose to drink the King's health: "Gentlemen, pray be seated, your loyalty is above suspicion."

The Department of History and International Affairs, Royal Naval College, supports the theory regarding the Lord High Admiral. [1] It was almost impossible to stand upright between decks in many older wooden ships, except between the deck-beams, and in ships having a pronounced 'tumble-home' (steeply-sloping sides), anyone seated close to the ship's side would find it difficult to stand at all.

The late Marquis of Milford Haven (Lord Louis Mountbatten's father) when First Sea Lord, drew attention to the fact in Admiralty orders that, although the Navy had the privilege of sitting when honouring the 'loyal toast,' the privilege did not apply when the National Anthem ("God Save the Queen") was played. This was in strict accordance with the wishes of His Majesty, King George V. Thus Admiralty Instructions read:

"The underlying idea is that whenever the anthem is played, when the King's Health is proposed, everyone stands up. If it is not played, people remain seated." [2]

This is the custom followed today by the Royal Navy.

At mess dinners in HMC ships and designated naval establishments, the following procedure for the 'loyal toast' is observed:

(a) The president taps the table for silence and says:

"Mr. Vice — the Queen."

(b) If a band is in attendance, it plays the first six bars of "God Save the Queen."

(c) After the anthem, the vice-president responds:

"(Madam/Ladies and) Gentlemen, The Queen."

If the anthem is played, the toast is taken standing. If there is no anthem, the toast is taken sitting. Guests, male or female, military of civilian, follow the customs of the naval mess that they are visiting, just as naval officers dining in other messes observe the traditions of that particular institution.

Toasts to Other Nations

When a foreign (non-Commonwealth) officer or official is being entertained officially on board or ashore, the protocol for toasts changes. (The rules set out below do not apply when the foreign officer is on exchange duty with the Canadian Forces or is being privately entertained.

At mess dinners in HMC ships and designated naval establishments, the following procedure for toasts to other nations is observed:

(a) President: "Mr. Vice — The King of Alpha."

(b) Band: Alpha National Anthem (diners stand);

(c) Vice-president: "Madam/Ladies and Gentlemen, The King of Alpha."

(d) Diners: Drink toast standing;

(e) Band: Royal Anthem ("God Save the Queen");

(f) Senior foreign officer/official: Madam/Ladies and Gentlemen, The Queen of Canada."

(g) Diners: Drink toast standing.

When more than one guest is present, a collective toast may be proposed. To this toast the senior and highest rank of the foreign officers or officials present will respond on behalf of all foreign guests by proposing the health of Her Majesty the Queen. No national anthems are played. Arrangements for toasts should be discussed with foreign guests beforehand.

At mess dinners in HMC ships and designated naval establishments, the following procedure for collective toasts is observed:

(a) President: "Mr. Vice — The Heads of States here represented."
(b) Diners: Stand;
(c) Vice-president: Madam/Ladies and Gentlemen, the Heads of State here represented."
(d) Diners: Drink toast standing;
(e) Band: Royal Anthem ("God Save the Queen");
(f) Senior foreign officer/official: "Madam/Ladies and Gentlemen, The Queen of Canada."
(g) Diners: Drink toast standing.

This procedure may be modified slightly by the president. If, for example, only two foreign guests are present, he may wish to toast the heads of their respective States. The toast then may be:

(a) President: "Mr. Vice — The King of Alpha."
(b) Band: Alpha's National Anthem (Diners stand);
(c) Vice-president: "Madam/Ladies and Gentlemen, The King of Alpha."
(d) Diners: Drink toast standing.
(e) President: "Mr. Vice — The president of Bravo."
(f) Band: Bravo's National Anthem (diners stand);
(g) Vice-president: "Madam/Ladies and Gentlemen, The president of Bravo."
(h) Diners: Drink toast standing;
(j) Band: Royal Anthem ("God Save the Queen");
(k) Diners: Drink toast standing.

Presidents are careful not to allow short versions of foreign anthems to be used unless they have ascertained that their use would not offend the guests.

Toasts of the Day

Once the 'loyal toast' has been proposed, and the health of the Sovereign drunk, the formalities of the dinner are over. Cigars and cigarettes are passed, though no one may smoke until the president is smoking or has given permission to smoke.

At this point, the president will call upon a member (often the most junior officer present), to propose the 'toast of the day.' There is a different toast for each day of the week, and getting them confused is dealt with strictly! The president is within his autocratic right to call for any 'toast of the day,' regardless of the day on which the dinner is being held.

Although it is customary for the officer giving the toast to preface it with an applicable brief and witty preamble, those who can be neither witty nor brief are cautioned against attempting the effort.

Some early versions of the 'toast of the day' were:

Sunday: Absent friends and those at sea; absent friends
Monday: Our native land; Queen and country
Tuesday: Our mothers; health and wealth
Wednesday: Ourselves; our swords; old ships (i.e., shipmates)
Thursday: The King; honest men and bonnie lassies
Friday: Fox hunting and old port; ships at sea
Saturday: Sweethearts and wives;

The 'toasts' used today are:

Sunday: Absent friends
Monday: Our ships at sea
Tuesday: Our men
Wednesday: Ourselves (The remark "Since no one else is likely to think of us" often follows the toast but is not actually part of it
Thursday: A bloody war or a sickly season
Friday: A willing foe and sea-room
Saturday: Sweethearts and wives ("May they never meet" is often a response to this toast.)[3]

Other Toasts

At a 'dine-the-ladies,' a graduation mess dinner, or when a group of mess members 'dine-out,' the group being honoured is often toasted. It is appropriate to do so either just before or after the 'toast of the day,' and should be done before any miscellaneous toasts.

Another custom in the Service is for the president to invite the bandmaster (if present) and the chief cook to join him in a glass of port. Chairs are provided and a toast may be proposed, after which they stay for the rest of the evening. (The senior steward is not invited since he will still be busy with his duties.)

Wine Guardians

After the toasts, anyone who wishes may leave the table with the exception of officers in charge of wines. If they wish to leave they must pass the decanters on to the officer on the left. If an officer in charge of wine, whether the president himself or another, leaves the table without finding a new guardian, the wine may be passed at the offender's expense until the decanters are empty.

The president may order the wine removed after toasts are drunk, but the decanters are usually passed at least once more. After the decanters are passed a second time the stoppers are left off until the wine is finally removed on the president's order.

The president or other officers guarding the wine are not at liberty to pick up the decanters in front of them to refill their glasses. Guardians may not pass the wine to the left without waiting for the president to set the example or asking his permission. When the wine has been passed again the president and other officers guarding the wine may then fill their glasses from the decanter that has been passed.

Adjournment

The president may suggest to the guest of honour and others at the head table that they adjourn for coffee and liqueurs. When he rises the diners stand and remain standing until he has left the room. Diners may sit down again to finish their port at their leisure, but are expected to join the president in the ante-room without undue delay.

Notes

1. "Canadian Naval Customs and Traditions (Correspondence)," (Royal Naval Staff College, NOTC 1210 - 1, Greenwich, 1981), n. pag.

2. Captain W.N.T. Beckett, *A Few Naval Customs, Expressions, Traditions and Superstitions*, (Portsmouth, Gieves Ltd. Bookshop, 1953), p.35.

3. "Canadian Naval Customs and Traditions (Correspondence)," (Royal Naval Staff College, NOTC 1210 - 1, Greenwich, 1981), n.pag.

5 Naval Uniforms

I
Naval Swords

Little is known of the swords worn by naval officers prior to 1805. The only evidence that they existed is found in some illustrations dating before that time. The swords shown were dress swords, and were not used for fighting. The naval fighting 'sword' was the cutlass, a crude cutting weapon unlike the delicate thrusting blade of the straight sword. Though it would inflict a less deadly wound than the straight edged sword would, the cutlass was well suited for fighting in the close confines of a ship.

In 1805, the Board of Admiralty and Lord Nelson jointly submitted sealed patterns of swords that were to be deposited at Portsmouth and Plymouth. Unfortunately, no record of the design of these swords exists today.

On 1 January, 1825, the Board issued "Uniform Regulations" with lithographic illustrations.

The commissioned officer's sword was a straight 32-inch blade with ivory grip, lion-head pommel, simple knuckle-bow and langets engraved with anchor and cable. The scabbard was of black leather with gilt mounts.

The swords of masters of the fleet, masters, second masters, mates, gunners, bo's'ns and carpenters were of the same pattern as those of commissioned officers, except that the backpiece of the handle was plain with a flute round the top and down the back. The grip was black fish skin bound with three gilt wires.

Midshipmen were to carry similar swords, but of "such length as may be convenient," perhaps because there was once a midshipman shorter than his sword.[1]

Medical officers who had been given a regulation pattern sword in 1805 discarded it in favour of a "small sword with a plain brass handle, according to pattern, ornamented with the appropriate device."[2]

In 1827, the Navy adopted the 'gothic hilt.' The escutcheon bears the crowned anchor. The lion-

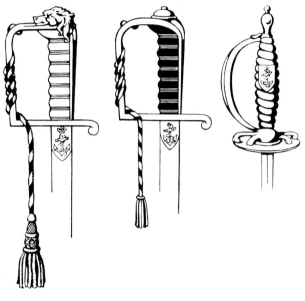

Left to right:
5.01 (1825-1827). Sword hilt and knot for warrant officer.
5.02 (1825-1827). Sword hilt and knot for commissioned officer.
5.03 (1825-1837). Sword hilt for medical officers.

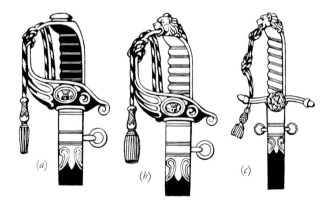

5.04 (1879). Sword hilts and dirk hilt showing knots.
A. Warrant officers; B. Commissioned officers;
C. Midshipmen.

head pommel and white grip were retained. The midshipmen's sword had the same grip and pommel, but without cross-guard or Gothic hilt; the swords of warrant officers had no lion head and the grips were of black leather.

In 1842, officers were given the "liberty to wear dress swords."[3] As a result, some Admirals adopted the 'mameluke' hilt of the Generals of the Army, except that they used the crowned anchor on the langets instead of badges of rank. The actual pattern of this hilt is preserved by the Wilkinson Sword Company, and colour plates of uniform purveyors of the period show this sword.

Evidently the 'Naval Field-Marshal' was a novelty at the time, for a spirited caricature shows a mounted Admiral at full gallop with the new sword flying at his back.

In the Regulations of 1856, midshipmen were required to give up their swords and returned to using the dirk. It was not until 1879, however, that it was officially described. It was gilt mounted with a white fish-skin grip. The total length of the dirk when in its black leather scabbard was 23 ¼ inches. The knot was of blue and gold cord with a small gold bullion tassel.

5.06 Sword and dirk knots.

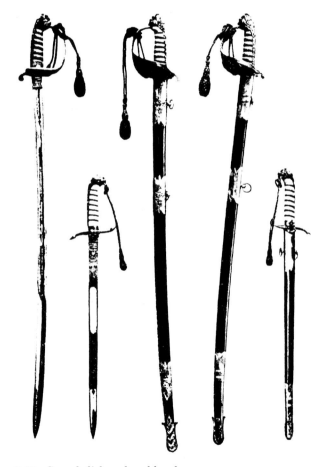

5.05 Sword, dirk and scabbards.

All these swords are in use today with the exception of the 'mameluke' which only lasted about ten years.

The naval cutlass was, and still is, a simple weapon. The handguard of sheet steel had at first a scalloped edge. In 1828 a new pattern was ordered in which the handguard was of plain steel very similar to that of the heavy cavalry of 1840. In 1841, a new pattern with special 'grip handles' was introduced and all the old patterns were sent to the Tower for alteration, but were destroyed in the great fire at the storehouse in October of that same year.

In 1845 there was an effort to make good this loss by converting ten thousand Cavalry swords into naval cutlasses. In 1848, 25,524 blades were ordered at a cost of five shillings each. In 1860 the blades were 25 ½ inches long, and in 1875 they were changed to 27, then 29 inches in length. In 1877 the blade length was again shortened to 27 inches.

In all these swords, which were supplied by the Board of Ordnance, the handguards were blacked. In 1900 the grips, at first moulded in cast-iron, were made of two-piece leather riveted onto the tang, like the Cavalry sword of 1853. In 1889 the guard was of bright steel, the inner edge turned down to prevent chafing the clothing, and the blade altered again to 28 inches in length.

Under an Admiralty order of 22 October, 1936 (No. 4572) it was stipulated that "the cutlass is no longer to form part of the equipment of men landed for service"; it was, however, retained for ceremonial parades.

During the first half of the eighteenth century the sword was usually suspended by two short slings from a waist belt, worn under the coat with the sword coming out through one of the plaits in the tail of the coat. The belt was occasionally worn over the coat and, of course, was worn over the breastplate by anyone old fashioned enough to wear one. The belt was ornamental and measured about 1 ½ inches wide.

By 1750, when the coat was beginning to be cut away slightly in front, a similar belt was still being worn, but under the waistcoat with the sword protruding under its 'skirt.' The sword was worn in front of the coat tail which was folded back to accommodate it; sometimes the sword was suspended from slings hooked to the waistband of the breeches.

About 1790 it became common to wear a broad belt with a brass buckle having a foul anchor embossed or engraved upon it. It was worn over the right shoulder, sometimes outside the waistcoat and under the coat; sometimes over the coat.

When the regulation sword was introduced it came with a narrow belt, usually with an S-hook connection. It had two unequal slings attached, one to the top locket near the upper end of the scabbard, the other to the mid-locket about a quarter of the way down, so that the sword almost trailed. The various buckles usually had a lion's head embossed on them. They were leather belts but senior officers had them embossed in gold for dress purposes. This practice was probably due to the influence of the Duke of Clarence, who earned the displeasure of the Board of Admiralty by issuing his own dress regulations in 1814. He decided that the belt should be worn over the waistcoat and under the coat with breeches, but over the coat with pantaloons.

In 1825, one-and-a-half inch sword belts with an anchor buckle were introduced. These were of white silk for lieutenants and above in full dress, and blue silk for officers in undress and for all other officers on all occasions. A black leather belt could be substituted for the blue silk. Anchors also ornamented the buckles which attached the slings to the belt.

In 1827 these belts were changed for plain two-and-a-half inch black patent leather shoulder belts which were intended to be worn under the waistcoat. But since this belt could not be worn under the buttoned up frock coat it was supplemented in 1829 by a black leather waist belt in which the sword was worn in a frog.

In 1832 the Admiralty prescribed a one-and-a-half inch waist belt with two slings of different lengths. The undress belt was of plain black patent leather, while the full dress belt and slings for lieutenants and above was embroidered in gold. Lieutenants had two lines of embroidery, captains and commanders three lines, while flag officers had a design of acorns and oak leaves. These features have been retained ever since. The belt was to be worn outside the coat on all occasions, but when tunics and monkey jackets were introduced the sword belt was worn underneath.

In 1847 the two slings of different lengths were replaced by two short ones seven inches long. In this way, the sword was able to hang up and down. The width of the belt was increased to one-and-three-quarter inches. In 1856 the old pattern was reverted to, with the exception that the slings of undress belts were round instead of flat.

When the dirk was restored to the midshipmen in 1856, they were ordered to wear it in a frog, but within a few years it was exchanged for two short, equal slings.

There are conflicting explanations for why the slings of the naval officer's sword belt are so long. Some experts say that the trailing sword was easier to handle when on a horse, and others feel that it was meant to be a mark of disgrace. It may, however, simply have been the fashion of the times.

There is some foundation in the 'horse theory' because long slings were a cavalry fashion. They originated with the light horse of central Europe (Hussars and Lancers from Hungary and Poland) and spread westwards to the Prussian, French and British Armies during the eighteenth century. In the French Army, the slings were peculiar to the horsemen, while the long slings were adopted by most, if not all, corps in the British Army between 1795 and 1820. They have remained a part of full dress uniforms ever since.

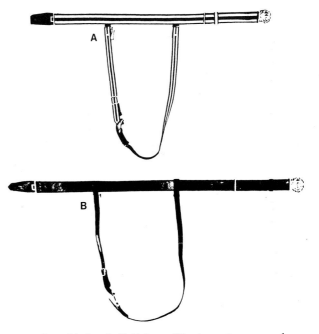

5.07 Sword belts. A. Full dress: Lieutenant-commander, lieutenant and sub-lieutenant; B. Full dress: Commissioned officer from warrant rank or warrant officer.

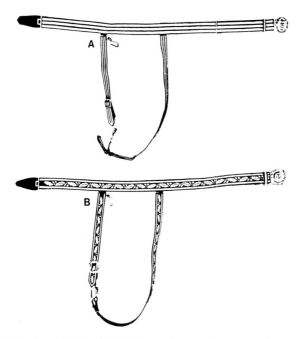

5.08 Sword belts. A. Full dress: Commodore, second class, captain or commander. B. Full dress: Flag officer or commodore, first class.

In the eighteenth and nineteenth centuries, when every gentleman could ride, many naval officers were, no doubt, capable horsemen, but it is likely that the 'tarpaulin' officer was not. In any case, a seaman on a horse would have been considered a funny sight. Horse marines probably existed only in myths, although the US Marine Corps had mounted units. At any rate, it is doubtful that the Admiralty would recommend any change in uniform that would bring ridicule on the Royal Navy.

It is most improbable that trailing one's sword was a mark of disgrace. It was the great discovery of the seventeenth century that the 'esprit de corps' and fighting spirit of a body of troops could be greatly increased by drilling them together and clothing them alike. Any mark of disgrace worn under order would contravene this principle. Moreover, the history of uniform shows that any item of clothing not approved of by those who wear it doesn't survive.

The trailing sword was, unquestionably, a sign of pride. In fact, the sword would have been no mark of distinction at all unless it was trailed, for all arms wore the same pattern belt. The cavalry regiments have always been splendidly dressed, with the light horse being the most dashing. To draw attention to themselves while on foot, troopers and officers alike let their spurs jangle and their steel-shod scabbards rattle over the cobblestones. This is the origin of the phrase 'sabre rattling,' which denotes a swaggering, bullying attitude.

Since Army officers have hooked up their swords or worn them with the 'Sam Browne' for over 100 years, Naval officers have become conspicuous by carrying theirs in the hand.

II
Distinction Colours

By 31 December, 1959, following a decision made by the Board of Admiralty in 1955, the distinction colours worn by non-executive officers between the stripes on their coats and shoulder-boards were gone forever. In the modern Navy, specialization had reached the point that it had become illogical to attempt to distinguish between categories of officers.

This move to simplify the complicated officer structure by dispensing with the colours was a return to the practice of the seventeenth and eighteenth centuries, when there were only two kinds of naval officer: 'executive' or combatant officers who were appointed by commission of the Crown, and 'non-executive' or sailors, appointed by warrant of the Admiralty. Complications, however, crept in during the nineteenth century, when engineers appeared on the scene, and men like the purser, surgeon and the parson assumed officer status.

Under the term 'branch distinctions,' coloured bands of cloth or velvet were introduced in 1863. These were worn on the sleeve in conjunction with distinction lace. Navigators wore pale blue, medical officers scarlet, accountants white and engineers purple. Navigators discarded their newly acquired light blue cloth in 1867 after they became members of the executive branch.

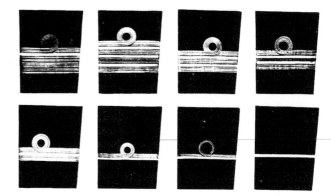

5.09 Distinction marks of rank and branch on sleeve. Left to right: Paymaster Rear-admiral, right sleeve; paymaster captain, right sleeve; paymaster commander, right sleeve; paymaster lieutenant-commander, left sleeve; paymaster lieutenant, left sleeve; paymaster sub-lieutenant or commissioned writer, right sleeve; warrant writer, left sleeve; paymaster midshipman or paymaster cadet.

The rank of 'engineer student' was created in 1877, and to distinguish between the student, and the midshipmen and cadets, students wore a quarter-inch purple stripe on each sleeve.

In 1879, the instructor branch became an integral part of the RN. Their uniform was similar to that of other non-executive branches (with straight gold stripes) and with light blue cloth between the gold lace.

By December 1918, the list of 'branch colours' had grown and included:
Shipwright — silver grey
Wardmaster — maroon
Electrical — dark green
Armourer/ordnance — dark blue

At that time the remaining branches of the Navy received the 'curl,' the decorative design seen on coat sleeves, shoulder, etc. To distinguish them from other officers, 'executive officers' began to wear badges, cap peaks and epaulets.

5.11   Shoulder straps. Left to right: Paymaster Rear Admiral; paymaster captain, left shoulder; paymaster commander, right shoulder; paymaster lieutenant-commander, right shoulder; paymaster lieutenant, right shoulder; paymaster sub-lieutenant or commissioned writer, right shoulder; warrant writer, left shoulder; paymaster midshipman or paymaster cadet.

By 1924, the dental surgeons' orange was added to the list of distinction colours.

In 1937, officers were distinguished as follows:
Executive officers: By absence of distinction cloth
Engineer officers: By purple cloth
Medical officers: By scarlet cloth
Dental officers: By orange cloth
Accountant officers: By white cloth
Instructor officers:By light blue cloth
Shipwright officers: By silver grey cloth
Wardmasters: By maroon cloth
Electrical officers:By dark green cloth
Ordnance officers: By dark blue cloth

Apart from the 'distinction cloth' of the branch, midshipmen(E) differed from midshipmen by wearing shoulder straps and not wearing the dirk and dirk-belt. Paymaster midshipmen and paymaster cadets differed from midshipmen and naval cadets by wearing shoulder straps.

When serving afloat, assistant constructors of the Royal Corps of Naval Constructors and electrical engineering officers wore the uniform prescribed for a lieutenant, with assistant constructors wearing silver grey 'distinction cloth' and electrical engineers dark green between the rows of distinction lace.

Canadians accepted the distinction colours of the various branches as they had accepted the RN uniforms. But by the time dress regulations for the RCN were printed in 1951, slight modifica-

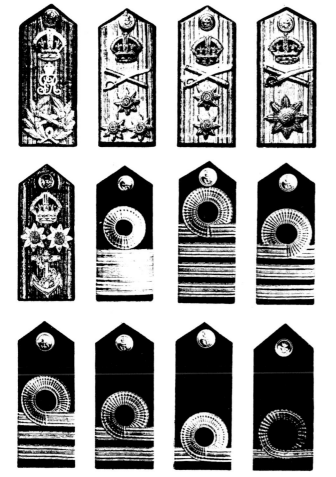

5.10   Shoulder straps. Left to right: Admiral of the Fleet; Admiral; Vice-Admiral; Rear Admiral; commodore, first class; commodore, second class; captain, left shoulder; commander, right shoulder; lieutenant-commander, left shoulder; lieutenant, left shoulder; sub-lieutenant, mate or commissioned officer from warrant rank, left shoulder; warrant officer, left shoulder.

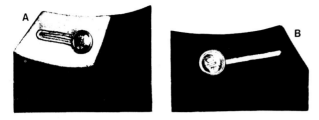

5.12 A. White turnback and button-hole for midshipman.
B. Button-hole for naval cadet.

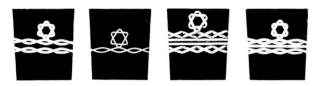

5.13 Royal naval reserve cuffs. Left to right: Lieutenant,
RNR; skipper, RNR; paymaster-lieutenant-commander,
RNR; paymaster-lieutenant, RNR.

5.14 Royal naval volunteer reserve cuffs. Left to right:
Lieutenant-commander, RNVR, right sleeve; Lieutenant,
RNVR, right sleeve; paymaster-lieutenant-commander,
RNVR left sleeve; paymaster-lieutenant, RNVR, right
sleeve.

tions had been made to the list of distinction
colours.

Medical officers were divided into two categories. Doctors retained their scarlet distinction
cloth, but medical administrative officers, nurs-
ing officers, and medical technical officers were
given the colour maroon, thereby expanding the
Canadian wardmaster branch. The 'special
branch' consisting of intelligence, information,
firefighting and law was added, and finally, the
civil engineers received the colour 'brick red' but
used it for only four years, from 1955 to 1959.

Distinction colours were also used within the
reserve organizations.

III
No Baton for the Admiral

In the table of the relative ranks of the three
Armed Services, an Admiral of the Fleet is
equated with a Field-Marshal and a Marshal of
the Royal Air Force. Since the Navy is traditionally the senior service, if three such officers
received their promotion on the same day, the
Admiral of the Fleet would take precedence over
his colleagues. Yet, curiously enough, only the
rank of Field-Marshal carries with it the award of
the baton.

As far back as Roman times a ceremonial
staff, or baton, was used as a symbol of leadership and authority. In the sixteenth century
French generals all had batons. In the seventeenth and eighteenth centuries a baton in the
form of a short plain staff of polished wood was
carried by British Generals and Admirals who
were Commanders-in-Chief. The distinguishing
insignia of the highest English naval rank was
from very early times a jewelled whistle, usually
suspended around the neck by a massive chain.
But by the time of Charles II the whistle had
fallen into disuse as part of the regalia of high
naval rank or office, and nothing has replaced it.

Field-Marshals were first instituted in England in 1736 when the rank was conferred upon
John, Duke of Argyll, and George, Earl of Or-
kney, by George II. In 1747 the rank of Admiral of
the Fleet was equated with that of Field-Marshal.
Although the Duke of York, the son of George III,
is said to have received a baton in 1795, the first
ceremonial baton to be presented to a British
Field-Marshal was that given to the Duke of
Wellington by the Prince Regent in 1813. After
the Battle of Vittoria on 21 June, 1813, in which
Wellington defeated Marshal Jourdan, the latter's baton was discovered among the loot captured on the battlefield. The Duke forwarded this
trophy to the Prince Regent. According to Sir
James Barrie, the baton greatly interested His
Royal Highness and inspired him with the idea of
designing one for British Field-Marshals. The
Prince must have worked quickly, for on July 3,
less than a fortnight after the battle, he des-
patched the newly designed baton with the
following letter to Wellington:

"My Dear Lord,
Your glorious conduct is beyond all human
praise and far above my reward. I know no
language the world affords worthy to express
it. I feel I have nothing left to say, but devoutly
to offer up my prayers of gratitude to Provi-

dence that it has in its omnipotent bounty blessed my country and myself with such a general. You have sent me, among other trophies of your unrivalled fame, the staff of a French Marshal, and I send you in return, that of England. The British Army will hail it with enthusiasm, while the whole universe will acknowledge these valorous efforts which have so imperiously called for it. That uninterrupted health and still increasing laurels may continue to crown you are the never ceasing and most ardent wishes of, my dear Sir,

Your very sincere and faithful friend,
G.P.R."[1]

The baton probably differed little from the original except that the French eagles were replaced with British lions.

The present day design of a Field-Marshal's baton consists of a wooden rod 23 inches long covered with crimson velvet, studded with 18 golden lions 'statant' (standing on all four legs). At each end of the rod is a flat boss of gold ornamented with a circle of laurel leaves and another chased with a rose, shamrock and thistle. Surmounting the top boss is a model in gold of Saint George slaying the dragon. From Wellington onwards, Army officers promoted to the rank of Field-Marshal have received, from the Sovereign, a baton as part of the insignia of their rank.

On the occasion of his coronation in 1821, however, George IV presented a baton to the Duke of Clarence as Admiral of the Fleet, who was then the solitary holder of that rank. Later on, in the same year, Earl St. Vincent, as the senior Admiral of the Red, became Admiral of the Fleet, and he too, was presented by the King with a baton "as a token of His Majesty's personal esteem." These two batons were exactly the same as that of a Field-Marshal except that they were covered with blue instead of crimson velvet. Both are now preserved in the National Maritime Museum in Greenwich. In those days Admiral of the Fleet was not an ongoing position. Appointments to the rank seem to have been the prerogative of the Sovereign, and for a long time there was only one.

When William IV came to the throne in June 1830, he renounced his position as Admiral of the Fleet, and two days later promoted William Peere Williams-Freeman, who by then had become Senior Admiral of the Red, in his place. He also promoted two more elderly Admirals in recognition of their long service. All were presented with batons, which have been passed down to their descendants.

As time went on, more Admirals of the Fleet were being promoted, but the rank was granted more or less as a reward for long service, and few ever commanded at sea. No question of the award of a baton arose until December 1880, when Admiral of the Fleet Sir Thomas Symonds wrote to the Secretary of the Admiralty stating that he had heard a baton had been presented to an Admiral of the Fleet many years ago, and asking if he could have one. The Admiralty refused, although their records must have shown that in 1821 a deputation from the Board had presented St. Vincent, Admiral of the Fleet with a baton awarded by George IV, and there was, therefore, a precedent. But they appear to have considered that the presentation had been made "in token of Royal esteem" and not by virtue of promotion to the rank. A few months later another Admiral of the Fleet wrote to the Admiralty suggesting that as he ranked above a Field-Marshal of equal seniority, he too, should have a baton. Again the Admiralty refused.

In 1890 a committee on naval officers' uniforms, presided over by the Duke of Edinburgh, an Admiral, suggested to the Board that Admirals of the Fleet should wear an aiguillette and be presented with a baton as were Field-Marshals. The aiguillette was approved, but the baton was not. Seven years later, on the occasion of her Diamond Jubilee, Queen Victoria asked that her son, the Duke of Edinburgh, now an Admiral of the Fleet, should be presented with a baton by the Admiralty. But once more the Board refused, their decision obviously being reinforced by the opinion of the Garter King of Arms that "the first two batons should not cause a precedent and not be given as a right of appointment." It was never the custom, he declared, for an Admiral of the Fleet to receive a baton by virtue of his rank as were Field-Marshals. The Queen was determined, however, that the Duke of Edinburgh should receive a baton, and she ordered one to be made by the crown jewellers, and paid for it herself. Although the Board of Admiralty asked that the presentation not be connected with the Duke's naval rank, the Queen flouted them by wording the announcement in the *London Gazette* that "on the occasion of her Jubilee Queen Victoria was pleased to present to her dear son, H.R.H. the Duke of Saxe-Coburg and Gotha, Duke of Edinburgh, KG, a baton as Admiral of the Fleet."

Despite the insistence of past Royalty that naval batons were bestowed by them to the recipients as Admirals of the Fleet, only five holders of the highest naval rank have ever received one. Today, only one of all the Admirals of the Fleet, HRH Prince Phillip, the Duke of Edinburgh, possesses a baton, and only because he is also a Field-Marshal.

IV
Ranks and Badges of Rank

The efficiency of every Navy depends largely on how well it is directed, organized and supplied. The Navy is run by professionals who man her ships and shore establishments, the necessary bases for all naval operations. Over the span of naval history, a structure of 'rank' has evolved in order that homogeneous control is maintained and orders are properly executed at all levels.

This section traces the evolution of this rank structure, and discusses the various ranks and ratings which have played an important role in this evolution.

There was little, if any, idea of rank (or its sister, seniority) in the days of Samuel Pepys. There were no lieutenants or captains per se; temporary appointments to the 'post' of a lieutenant or captain were made to a specified ship for a specified commission. This explains why officers appear, in Pepys' lists, to fluctuate widely in their naval titles, sometimes even going backwards. For instance, Thomas Berry held the following consecutive posts: Lieutenant, captain, second lieutenant, first lieutenant and captain.

Such treatment would seem inappropriate to an officer serving in a Navy organized by rank; however, regarded as 'posts' occupied by the same officer in various ships, (which, in fact, they were), it would be entirely acceptable. Thus, a modern Mr. Dawson, appearing in the 'seniority list' as a fairly junior lieutenant, might in three successive commissions be the captain of a minesweeper, first lieutenant of a destroyer, and finaly second lieutenant of a cruiser. 'Rank' and 'post' mean entirely different things.

In 1860 titles of rank became official. By then, confusion had worked itself out and the term 'Admiral' or 'captain' etc., connoted naval rank in its modern sense. It meant that a man had reached a certain rung on the ladder of promotion, and that his name was safely logged, in its correct place, among his fellow captains and Admirals. However, the terminology of an individual's appointment still had to be altered. Until 1860, one was appointed as an 'Admiral of' some named squadron, or 'captain of' some named ship for the period of the ship's or squadron's commission. When that particular commission was ended, the individual's commission also ended. This was changed in the twenty-third year of Queen Victoria's reign. An individual was 'commissioned' as 'Admiral' or 'captain' of Her Majesty's Fleet for as long as he lived or until the commission was expressly cancelled.

Foundations for the evolution from 'part time post holders' to 'full time rank holders' were laid by Samuel Pepys between 1673 and 1688, when he was Secretary of the Admiralty. He made certain qualifications compulsory for the would-be holders of specific posts, thus creating certain well-defined classes of persons who alone were qualified to hold these posts. They were not at first 'ranks,' but soon became so.

Volunteer Officers

As long as 'fighting' and 'seamen' officers existed as separate entities, there was no way of determining who was a volunteer. Even in Henry VIII's time, almost all the 'gentlemen' commanding ships were in no sense seamen. They were simply ordinary fighting men with leadership qualities whom the King called on for military service anywhere. Sometimes these individuals volunteered for sea service; at others they were ordered to it. Henry VIII's captains were divided, for the most part, into two classes: ordinary soldiers, usually knights or peers, who were paid one shilling and sixpence a day — the other group was composed of members of a curious, all-officer force of horseguards known as the 'King's Spears.' Members of this elite troupe provided many captains, but they were only paid as 'King's Spears' regardless of where or how they were employed.

The true volunteer became distinguishable in Queen Elizabeth I's time, and began to be referred to by that title. Individuals were either called 'gentlemen volunteers' or 'volunteer gentlemen' and their names are generously sprinkled throughout the pages of Elizabethan sea chronicles.

These men were primarily all from the class referred to as 'landowners' although it was seldom the landowner himself who volunteered to serve the Queen when the need arose. The actual owner was usually preoccupied with over-seeing his tenants and with civil responsibilities; his eldest son was also exempt because of his ties with the estate. This left the younger son to exchange his gentleman's 'ruff and doublet' for a dark blue uniform when an emergency call to serve the Crown afloat was sounded. Once the emergency was over he returned to civilian life.

The Naval Cadet

By making and applying a series of rules Samuel Pepys was able, to some extent, to convert the 'volunteers,' who were hardly seamen, into something much like the modern naval cadet. Pepys did not approve of the chaotic approach to entering the naval service. It was his opinion that there must be an 'ordered' form of entry into an 'ordered' service, and that the rate of entry and quality of person entering the service should be regulated.

Before Pepys' time, 'young gentlemen' usually entered the service by being appointed as 'captain's servants,' usually by a commanding captain or master who had the authority to make such postings, and usually the young gentlemen had some connection (or knew someone who did) with the officer in question. Captains were allowed a large number, by our standards, of servants — four to every hundred of the ship's company, or eight if they were knights or from the nobility.

Mr. Pepys, however, felt strongly that the responsible authority who paid the wages should make the appointment. He approved of the premise of 'captain's servant,' but wanted their appointments regulated. He therefore ordered that no volunteer be above the age of sixteen, or under thirteen unless he was an officer's son, in which case age eleven was acceptable. For further control, he instituted a new class of volunteers, the 'volunteers-per-order.' Also called the 'King's letter boys,' these individuals were presented with a letter from the King commanding the captain of a ship to take them on board and train them. These lads were the first 'naval cadets' and their title as such became official in 1843. They were also the first to be appointed by Admiralty nomination.

The 'King's letter' was abolished in 1729 being immediately succeeded by a Naval Academy in which the volunteer was called a 'college volunteer,' and actually received training before going to sea. Most of those destined to glory, however, entered by way of the 'captain's servant' method, although after 1794 the title was changed to 'volunteer of the first class.'

Curious as this procedure was, it produced nearly all the great naval names of the nineteenth century. Rodney was a volunteer-per-order, almost the last of the old 'King's letter boys,' and Rooke, Shovel, Vernon, Anson, Hawke, Boscawan, Howe, Hood, Jervis, Duncan, Cornwallis, Collingwood and Nelson himself never held a 'King's letter' in their hands, or saw the inside of an Academy. All entered the Navy as 'captain's servants,' the forerunner of the naval cadet.

Midshipmen

It is not clear why this title was considered appropriate for young gentlemen training for commissioned rank, especially since history describes them as of "little or no consequence," ranking below the master gunner, carpenter and bo's'n. The original midshipman was probably an apprentice who had become useful in assisting with the working of the ship and may have been qualified to take a mate's navigator's berth when the opportunity arose.

It is unlikely that the title 'midshipman' was related to the duty being performed since only the helmsman was positioned amidships. The title was likely given to these apprentices because they commonly messed together and slept in the after cockpit situated in the 'orlop,' the lowest of the decks proper, below the water line, without portholes — where the suns rays never penetrated. They shared this stale and gloomy atmosphere with the master's and surgeon's mates.

Whether these young men entered the service as 'King's letter boys,' 'first class volunteer' or 'captain's servant,' they underwent much the same training as a favoured apprentice would receive from his master on board a merchant vessel. They learned the skills of an able seaman, and later might serve as assistants to the officer-of-the-watch.

Before the middle of the eighteenth century, the idea was so firmly fixed that midshipmen would inevitably become commissioned officers that they were among the first to receive uniform. This distinguished them to the ranks of 'gentlemen.'

The Master and his Mate

The 'master' had always been the most important of the ship's officers in a class distinctly above the rest. As long as his duty was the navigation of the ship, even the captain could not overrule him. Although the captain had the King's orders in his pocket, and decided when to leave and where to go, he never attempted to tell the master how to go. This is a longstanding practice in the Naval Service.

For centuries the master waivered between 'commission' and 'warrant' status, although he was officially classed as a 'warrant officer,' and was always appointed by warrant from the Navy office. He finally achieved appointment by commission in 1843.

Under the Stuarts, masters advanced from the merchant skipper of Tudor times into skilled specialists, and after 1675 became increasingly well-educated. By the end of the eighteenth century, they had achieved official status of 'warrant officers of wardroom rank,' an anomalous title which meant that while they were not lieutenants, they lived and messed with them.

The specialization of the nineteenth century which gave rise to the specialist navigator (the naval lieutenant), led to the demise of the naval 'master,' the officer with the longest continuous record in the Navy. He was not suddenly disposed of, however. Appointed by commission in 1843, advanced to 'staff captain' in 1864, then deprived of that title and subsequently referred to as 'navigating lieutenant' (members of a complete navigating branch) in 1867, he died a lingering death until 1913 when the last old school navigator retired from service.

The 'master's mate' managed, in the end, to secure a regular and permanent position in the hierarchy of the commissioned executive branch. He became the 'sub-lieutenant.' Even before the permanent or National Naval Service made its appearance, his post, like the midshipmen's, had become a stepping-stone for the clever, ambitious and well-backed merchant seaman from the 'lower' to the 'upper' deck. It remained so even after the Royal Navy was formed. The 'master's mate' remained the normal way onto the quarter-deck. He exists today even though his title and place have changed; instead of being an alternative step to midshipman, his post became an extra one on the way toward it.

The Sub-Lieutenant

The evolution of the ranks of 'mate' and 'sub-lieutenant' are very closely linked. During the Napoleonic Wars, when there was no shortage of volunteers, midshipmen waited a long time to be appointed to lieutenants. For the sake of extra pay they often took their certificates as 'master's mates' instead. Eventually this became the normal procedure, and 'mate' became an accepted grade between 'midshipman' and 'lieutenant.' In 1840 it became a substantive with appointment by commission and the title was changed to 'sub-lieutenant' in 1861. In the early nineteenth century a lieutenant might command a brig or sloop, requiring an officer of higher rank than a midshipman to be his second in command, which is probably why the rank of sub-lieutenant was created. (According to the Admiralty Papers of Lord Keith, Commander-in-Chief North Sea, the title 'sub-lieutenant' was officially recognized in 1804, and those holding it wore the undress uniform of lieutenants at all times.) The rank disappeared for a time and was revived in 1861 replacing the old rank of 'mate.'

Meanwhile the old style 'master's mate,' the navigational understudy to the master achieved officer status as 'second master' as far back as 1746. The title was changed to 'navigating lieutenant' in 1867 when the master became the 'navigating lieutenant'; and later disappeared with the rest of the branch.

The Lieutenant

When Samuel Pepys reorganized the naval structure he carved a niche for the class called 'lieutenant,' the lowest commissioned officer.

At that time no one was appointed to a lieutenant's rank unless he had served at least three years at sea. One of these must have been spent as a midshipman (service as a master's mate could be accepted in lieu) and two as a volunteer. All prospective candidates were required to pass an examination in practical seamanship and had to be at least twenty years of age. This was later changed to a six year 'probationary' sea service. Even after a candidate had fulfilled all the requirements, his promotion to lieutenant was still not automatic. That was one of the advantages of the rank structure; a commissioned officer had to wait until a position became available for him.

Before Pepys' day, lieutenants were simply young men marking time until some influential friend found them a captain's place. In Pepys' scheme, however, a lieutenant, when appointed, had to be a hard-working professional who knew the jobs of those he was to command, as well as his own. Moreover, he was the captain's 'lieutenant,' or 'locum tenans,' who would replace him if the circumstance required him to do so.

With lieutenants, as with midshipmen and volunteers, Pepys had created a professional class from which those required to serve in the next highest post were selected.

The Commander and the Lieutenant Commander

'Commander' is the modern equivalent 'master commander.' In the early days of the Royal Navy a 'post ship' was sufficiently important to require a fully qualified master in addition to the captain. (In a smaller 'non-post' ship the captain had to qualify as a master, and be responsible for navigation himself. In this case he was often called 'master and commander' and the rank 'commander' developed from this post during the eighteenth century. After 1746 the 'second master' was introduced into the 'non-post' ships to relieve the captain of his navigational duties, and in 1794 the official title became, simply 'commander.'

The rank of 'lieutenant commander' appears to have been introduced into the Royal Navy in 1914. Prior to World War I, a 'lieutenant in command' was called 'lieutenant and commander' and that may simply have been shortened. However, as in the case of the sub-lieutenant rank, the rank of lieutenant commander may have been introduced as an additional step to the rank of commander. Another possibility is that as 'lieutenant' has been described as a 'captain's lieutenant,' 'lieutenant commander' may simply describe the individual qualified to carry out the duties of 'commanders' when the need arose. Since the rank of 'commander' had existed since 1794, and since two existing 'ranks' has never been used to describe one position, this explanation appears reasonable. This is, however, only conjecture 'in lieu' of available fact.

The Captain

The term 'captain' covers both positions a naval officer may hold simultaneously; one a rank, the other a post. One can be the 'captain' of a ship without having reached the rank of 'captain,' or be the rank of 'captain' without being the captain of a ship. One, of course, can be *both*!

The word 'captain' appears to have its origin in the Latin 'caput' or 'head.' The advent of a 'head man' must have raised some very important questions of precedence or command, although experience has always shown that it is disastrous to divide supreme command. But who should wield it, the sailing expert or the fighting expert; the 'master' or the 'captain?' By right of birth as well as by right of appointment, the 'captain' took charge. He was of 'blue blood,' the King's nominee, and, in language both mediaeval and modern, he held the sovereign's 'commission.' What may be termed the 'habit of command' was then far more nearly the monopoly of one class than it is now. The 'captain' quickly assumed that unchallenged position in his own ship and holds it to this day. His authority, however, is limited in one regard: he may not interfere with the navigation of his ship.

The Admiral

Even before the Tudor period, the affairs of state had become extremely complicated, and consequently the Crown found it necessary to entrust various activities to specially selected men, usually drawn from the tenants-in-chief. It placed its monetary affairs in the hands of a Lord Treasurer; the legal and judiciary arrangements went to the Lord Chancellor; and so by the end of the Middle Ages there were nine of these great officers of state, the ninth being 'all sea causes' as the phrase was coined. Its head was the progenitor of the Admiralty, and was called various names at various times. Those better known are 'High Admiral,' 'Lord Admiral' and finally 'Lord High Admiral.'

But long before Admirals had appeared on the scene, every King who possessed ships required some trustworthy servant to administer his fleet. King John (1205) who had four ships, appointed administrators who were referred to as 'custodes' or 'keepers' of the galleys, ships and ports.

In King John's time the Cinque Ports were near their zenith, and their ships played a major role in his wars, sometimes even acting against him. But the administrators of these ships were not directly under the Crown, and it was their dubious loyalty to King John which influenced his son Henry III to bring them under control. As a result the new office of the 'warden of the Cinque Ports' came into existence in 1241.

Henry's son, Edward I realized the danger in relying exclusively on one small section of the sea community to provide him with ships. Consequently he tapped three sources for his Navy: his own ships, ships from the Cinque Ports and private ships from elsewhere, and appointed a 'keeper' of the ships, responsible for administrative functions. But as the need for more and firmer control became obvious he decided to combine the administration and command functions under the position 'captain of the Kings mariners' and appointed William de Layburn, a fighting officer, to fill the post. In 1927 de Layburn was appointed as the King's delegate at a maritime convention of the Low Countries and for the occasion was given the famous title 'Admiral of the Sea of England.'

The word 'admiral' came from the Arabs who among their amirs and chieftains has a chieftain of the sea, the 'Amir-al-Bahr.' As wars began to be fought more frequently on land the word 'bahr' (which meant 'sea') was dropped. When first used in England the title 'Admiral' described, as in de Leyburn's case, an administrative officer and a diplomatic representative of his Sovereign.

In 1303 de Leyburn's successor, Gervase was titled 'Captain and Admiral of the Fleet and of the Cinque Ports and all other Ports from the Port of Dover by the sea coast westwards as far as Cornwallis.' Although he was the leader in battle his title did not necessarily mean that he was commander at sea. Drake's usual title on such occasions was 'General' not 'Admiral,' and even Blake went onboard his flagship with the title 'General at Sea.'

During the fourteenth century the 'keeper of the ships' and the 'captain of the King's mariners' were commonly used but by the end of that century an amalgamation of the two offices resulted in the creation of an office similar to 'Lord High Admiral.' The first person to hold the post was John de Beauchamp in 1360, and the title 'Admiral of England' was first given in 1391 to Edward of York, while in 1403 Henry IV's own son, Thomas of Lancaster received the appointment.

The nobility, of course, delegated most of the

responsibility for 'sea functions' and administration to subordinates. Lieutenants or Vice-admirals took care of judicial matters. This led to the organization of a directive body, the Commission of Admiralty with jurisdictional and disciplinary responsibility.

However it was an incident in 1652 that lead to the title 'Admiral' officially including the title 'Commander at Sea.' During the battle in which Robert Blake (General-at-Sea) was defeated by Adm. Tromp at Dungeness a number of Blake's fleet, commanded by civilian masters, withdrew without permission. The delinquents could not be tried or punished for their actions since only the Admiralty had power to hold a court to try 'sea causes.' This could of course be done but with considerable delay and loss of discipline and prestige to the commander. The result was that the commander-at-sea was empowered to convene court martials afloat, and now, having one important right of Admiralty, they immediately assumed the title of 'Admiral' and have held it ever since.

Eventually the position of Lord High Admiral was replaced by the Commission of the Board of Admiralty. And, as Admirals became more involved in the actual operations at sea, the lieutenant and Vice-Admirals, who had sat in for their superiors on land, were sent to assume a similar function at sea.

The term 'flag officer,' which includes Admirals-of-the-Fleet, Admirals, Vice-admirals, and Rear-admirals, appeared in the seventeenth century. Up to 1743 there had been a total of nine 'flag officers.'

During the Dutch Wars these officers controlled the fleets which, because of their size, had to be divided into three squadrons: the Red, the White and the Blue, occupying the positions of centre, the van and the rear respectively. The squadrons were further divided into centre, van and rear divisions, each large enough to warrant a 'flag man' in charge. Under this arrangement a sizeable fighting force would be divided as follows:

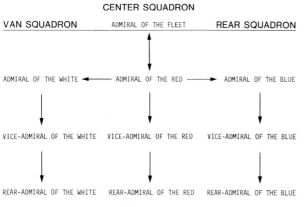

5.15 Squadron organization.

The fleet commander also commanded the red or centre squadron, accounting for the nine rather than ten flag officers. ('Admiral of the Red' as a separate post was introduced in 1805 and only then as a result of an error.)

There is no mention of a 'Rear-admiral' before 1928. But in attempting to distinguish between the commander of the blue squadron and one of the commanders of the blue division, both of whom could be 'Admirals,' the title may have been used to describe the latter, which was always in the rear.

'Commodore,' a title of Dutch extraction was introduced by King William III in the seventeenth century. It was probably an honourary title since dress regulations issued in 1825 included commodores with captain-of-the-fleet and junior captains respectively, and both were honourary positions.

Although the titles 'commodore' and 'commodore-of-the-first (and second) class' have appeared throughout the history of the Royal Navy, as a rank between senior captains and flag officers, there has never been an exact definition of what the job was or why there was a need for two classes. Since at times each class wore the dress and devices of Rear-admirals and senior captains it is reasonable to assume that the commodore had some form of intermediate authority. But there was no shortage of flag officers and senior captains for the size of the fleet so it is difficult to imagine how this authority was exercised.

There was one type of flag officer whose appointment was a badly kept secret. The First Admiralty Regulations of 1781 specified that "there are nine flag officers" and reaffirmed that number until 1808. Yet in Nelson's time flag officers numbered in the hundreds and in the early 1800s there were known to be 70 Admirals, 72 Vice-admirals and 75 Rear-admirals. It appears that to provide turn-over in senior positions and accommodate aging flag officers who could not be employed elsewhere, the Admiralty created a varying number of posts which in fact did not exist. These officers were amusingly referred to as "Yellow Admirals," the nickname given by the public to this ingenious scheme. It was particularly appropriate since yellow was the colour for the 'quarantine flag!'

Ratings

In any ship in the Royal Navy, all the men were carefully appraised as soon as they arrived on board and then assigned as 'forecastlemen,' 'topmen,' 'aftermen' or 'waisters,' as best suited their abilities. They were also rated in the ship's books by the old categories of 'ordinary' and 'able' and as such received different rates of pay.

than the King, and Parliament in its turn, recognizing the contribution made to the nations' welfare by seamen, accepted the challenge. It raised their pay substantially and paid the new wage punctually. The government also distinguished between experienced and inexperienced seamen ('ordinary' and 'able') and differentiated their rates of pay. The Admiralty promptly introduced a rating below 'ordinary seaman' called the 'landman' which was greatly resented by the men; the 1797 mutineers demanded its abolition. The rating survived until 1853, however, when pre-training as seamen was implemented and the rank of 'leading seamen' introduced.

There were no badges of rank for 'ordinary' or 'able' seamen; Good conduct badges were introduced in 1849. The qualifying periods were originally five, ten and fifteen years. They were gradually reduced to four, eight and twelve or more years.

'Leading seamen' received a badge showing the 'fouled anchor' device to distinguish his rank.

5.17 Good conduct badges. Left to right: Four years, eight years, twelve years. Worn on the left arm, below the rating badge. Not worn by chief petty officers.

5.18 Rating badges, worn on the left arm. Left to right: leading rate (1853), leading seaman (1960). Serge jumper showing general position of badges.

5.16 Officers' insignia. Rank collar badges, left to right: Vice-admiral, Rear-admiral, commodore, captain, commander, lieutenant commander, lieutenant, sub-lieutenant and commissioned officers. A. Cap badge. Buttons: B. Flag Officers; C. Other Officers. Classification badges: D. Observer; E. Pilot. Shoulder badges: F. Embroidered; G. Metal. Lapels: H. White turnback and notched hole for midshipmen; I. Notched hole for cadets.

The captain would select from among the best a certain number to act as 'petty officers.'

Seamen

In the early days of the Royal Navy there was no distinction by age, experience or station made between the sailors responsible for 'sailing' the ship and they all received the same pay. By 1629, however, sailors had concluded that Parliament would be a far better employer and paymaster

The Petty Officer

The rate of 'petty officer' was probably established in the early eighteenth century. It is unclear whether the 'first' and 'second' class petty officers were introduced simultaneously, but by 1827, both were in existence. To distinguish between them, 'first class petty officers' wore an anchor surmounted by a crown, and a 'second class petty officer' received the anchor only. The rate of 'chief petty officer' had been introduced by 1853, and in 1860 the rate badges were as follows:

Chief petty officer: Crown and anchor encircled by laurel wreath

First class petty officer: Crown and crossed anchors

Second class petty officer: Crown and anchor

Leading Seaman: Anchor

In the RCN, the rates of 'petty officer' and 'chief petty officer first and second class' were retained.

5.19   Miscellaneous badges. Left to right: Naval patrol armlet, diver, marksman, bugler.

5.20   Rank badges. Cap badges, left to right: chief petty officer, petty officer 1st class. Sleeve badges: chief petty officer 1st class, chief petty officer 2nd class, petty officer 1st class, petty officer 2nd class.

Branch Badges

Branch badges were introduced around 1884. Torpedoes were linked with gunnery at that time, and gunnery instructors wore a Whitehead torpedo crossed diagonally with a gun, encircled with oak leaves and surmounted with a crown and star. A torpedo instructor wore the same badge, but with the torpedo in front of the gun. Simpler versions of the same badges were introduced for seamen.

The next ratings to receive badges were signallers and, as more and more specialists were needed, the number of badges increased. The following badges of the RCN specialists, their trade and qualification apparent from the badge, give a good idea of the amount of diversification.

5.21 Branch badges. Left to right: Seaman gunner torpedo-man, leading torpedo-man.

5.22 Branch badges. Left to right: Pharmacist assistant, laboratory assistant, operating room assistant, physiotherapy aide, radiographer, technical assistant, hygiene assistant, medical assistant, bandsman, sailmaker, control armourer, gunnery armourer, torpedo armourer, physical training instructor, regulating, engine room artificer, stoker mechanic, motor mechanic, plumber, shipwright, electrical technician, radio technician, radio technician (air), electrical technician (air), air-fitter, aircraft controlman, safety equipment technician, meteorologist mate, radar plot, air artificer, plane technician, air rigger, communicator radio, naval storesman, cook, communicator crypto, administrative writer, steward, quarter-master, photographer.

V
The Sailor's Collar

In the Napoleonic era men (including naval officers) wore shirts with three to four-inch high collars supported by a 'stock' so that only a white rim appeared around the top. The height of the stock was sometimes increased to such an extent that the two points of the collar barely showed, probably causing some difficulty in turning the head.

The check shirt made its appearance on the 'slop list' in 1717. This shirt, usually worn by naval ratings, was made with a collar similar to those worn by officers. However, to allow the sailor to turn his head and neck, a knotted handkerchief, usually black, was loosely tied around the collar, which was usually folded over the jacket. Since the collar was part of the shirt, it is unlikely that it was introduced to keep the hair grease from the back of the jacket as some supposed.

In a book published in 1829, entitled *Life on Board a Man-of-War*, the following description appears which confirms that the collar was originally part of the shirt: "The duck frock with the ornamented blue collar showed plainly he was a man-of-war's man."[5]

In a series of prints of sketches by M. Gauci, published in 1829, ratings are shown wearing small blue collars apparently attached to their frocks, and in another set of prints made in 1832 there is a group of seamen unmistakably wearing white shirts and collars. A print by William Spooner of Commodore Charles Napier with his boat's crew from the *Gorgon* landing in Syria in 1840, shows the same shirt collars. The large blue collars which later became traditional, appeared as early as 1845. An engraving, reproduced by the *Illustrated London News* in that year, showed all the seamen on the ship *Hyacinth* wearing large jean collars outside their jackets.

On 13 August 1845, the Admiralty issued a circular adding "materials for making collars" to the slops obtainable in ships, and in 1846 Queen Victoria described, in her diary *Leaves from the Journal of our Life in the Highlands*, the future King Edward VII dressed in a sailor's suit made by the yacht's tailor. A subsequent painting by Winterhalter shows that the suit consisted of white trousers and frock, with blue jean collar attached.

In a series of prints by R.H.C. Ubsdell, published in 1849, and in all subsequent illustrations, seamen are depicted wearing the unmistakable blue collars.

Although separate collars were not authorized until 1890, they were probably worn before that time.

In the various illustrations mentioned, frock coats have been shown with either two or three rows of tape. When the standard uniform was being considered in 1857 captains from Portsmouth and Plymouth were split on the number of rows they recommended, Portsmouth favouring two and Plymouth three. Three won the day probably because draft regulations had previously specified that number.

Notes

1. Dudley Jarret, *British Naval Dress*, (London, J.M. Dent and Sons Ltd., 1960), p.15.

2. Ibid., p.16.

3. Charles Haulkes and Captain E.C. Hopkinson, *Sword, Lance and Bayonet*, (Cambridge, n.p., 1938), n.pag.

4. Cecil Hampshire, *No Baton for the Admiral*, (n.p., June 1959), pp. 150-151.

5. N.E. May, "The Sailor's Collar," *The Mariner's Mirror*, 48, No. 3., (St. Albans, Staples Printers, 1962), pp. 228-230.

6   Badges and Insignia

I
Ships' Badges — Their Origins and Use

Very little has been written about the ship's badge, consequently its origin and use are not well known. It is often confused with the crests which were worn on the helmets of mediaeval knights but which were quite different in origin and use from the heraldic badge.

Badges came into general use about the reign of Edward III and were widely used between the fourteenth and sixteenth centuries. The standard of literacy was very low at that time and the badge was the mark by which the nobles, their partisans and their belongings were recognized by all. In fact the badges of prominent families were so well known that various public figures were referred to in political poems of the day by their badge symbol rather than their name.

For instance Shakespeare wrote of Richard III, (whose badge was a silver boar):
> "The wretched, bloody and usurping boar
>   That spoilt your summer fields and fruitful vines,
>   Swills your warm blood like wash, and makes his trough
>   In your embowelled bosoms, this foul swine lies even now in the centre of this Isle."

And in Henry VI he has the Earl of Warwick exclaim:
> "Now by my father's badge, old Neville's crest
>   The Rampant bear chained to the ragged staff."

Badges often featured a 'word' or 'motto' — for example the feather badge of the Prince of Wales with its motto 'Ich dein' (I serve). Anyone could adopt a badge, (or badges) and use it as he wished.

Whenever feudal lords went into battle, their standards and the coats of their men-at-arms bore the badges of their house. In the chronicles of history reference is made to various badges

6.01   Badge and motto.

such as the standard of the 'Blue Boar,' the 'Bleeding Heart,' the 'Ragged Staff' or the 'Swan.'

A badge was used as a mark of ownership just as the British government marked their stores with a broad arrow. In addition to showing ownership or relation badges had a definite decorative value. There were carved, engraved, painted or embroidered on every conceivable article such as books, drapes, bedspreads, glassware, furniture, rugs, seals, silverware, jewellery, weapons and clothing.

It was only natural therefore, that when a knight put to sea on the King's service his badges and family arms went with him. When Warwick 'The Kingmaker' embarked on one of his expeditions to France, he commissioned William Seburgh, "Citizen and Payntour of London" to provide him with a "grete stremour for the shippe XI yards in length and VIII yards in brede." The size of this banner gave ample room for the Earl's badge with the head adorned with "a great bere (bear) holding a ragged staff" and the rest of its length "powdrid full of raggid staves" (dotted with ragged staves).

The use of badges for ships probably developed

from the idea of a symbol of personal identity since down through the ages mariners have endowed their ships with a spirit or personality. To many sailors a ship was considered a living entity, expected to respond in a certain way, and yet, like a woman, mysterious and unpredictable. So sailors have always decorated their ships, sometimes as an expression of an art form, sometimes as a response to some deeply embedded superstition, and sometimes in the hope of frightening the enemy.

No doubt the ferocious figures that rode the stems of Viking pirate ships struck terror into many a heart as they emerged from the mist. The war galleys of successive Mediterranean civilizations sailed to battle with their bold beaks high at the bows. These, and the great eyes painted on the bows of the Chinese junks, were revived during World War II when massive shark's teeth were painted on the bows of submarines, motor torpedo boats and even on aircraft.

The mariner's ancient practice of giving his ship an individual appearance to make her identity readily known came closest to perfection in the woodcarver's art, particularly in the life-like forms that graced the bows of countless numbers of ships. Sometimes the figurehead was a kingly lion or the mythical griffin, sometimes a mighty warrior in armour, usually symbolizing the ship's name. But often as not it was the figure of a beautiful woman.

The sloop-of-war HMCS *Shearwater* was the only ship in the Royal Canadian Navy to have a figurehead commissioned. She was equipped with both sail and steam power and served Canada from 1914 to 1919. Just below her bowsprit, as part of her stem, she displayed the carved figure of the seabird known as the 'shearwater.'

With the disappearance of the bowsprit and jib-boom and the arrival of the straight-stemmed hull, figureheads were replaced (particularly in steel ships) with another form of bow embellishment. This was gilded scrollwork and armorial images, usually cast in iron. Two examples survived through World War II on the bows of HMC ships *Acadia* and *Cartier* (better known as HMCS *Charny*).

The heraldic ship's badge only came into being officially in the Royal Canadian Navy in 1946. They were patterned after ones used by the Royal Navy. Prior to that time, the commanding officer of a ship was permitted to devise (and pay for) his own ship's badge and the results, while sometimes interesting, were seldom in the best heraldic form.

In the Royal Navy, heraldic badges were first issued officially in 1919, after the end of World War I. They were enclosed in four differently shaped frames according to the class of the ship. Capital ships were assigned a circular frame, cruisers a pentagon, destroyers and submarines, a shield, and aircraft carriers and miscellaneous vessels a diamond-shaped enclosure.

During World War II it was discovered that a name previously held by a ship of one class, say a destroyer, had been given to another, say an aircraft carrier, and the name did not fit the frame. The Admiralty Badge Committee therefore recommended the use of the circular shape for all classes for the duration of the war. In 1945 the Royal Navy decided to permanently adopt this form for all their badges. This policy was applied to the Canadian badge in 1946 when the Director of Naval Reserves, Rear-Admiral H.F. Pullen requested that naval reserve badges be displayed in the circular frame. This was done but with one difference: at the bottom of the rope surround there is a small cluster of three maple leaves.

Before World War II, the insignia used by the famous River Class destroyers of the RCN followed the shield pattern of the RN, and the manner in which the identifying devices within the shield were applied actually made them Coats of Arms. This, for a badge, was improper because arms may only be borne by those granted letters patent of the King of Arms through powers vested in him by the Sovereign. Heraldry is the prerogative of Sovereignty.

Nevertheless, those who served in these early ships of the RCN quite naturally hold their old 'badges' in great affection, and for this reason every effort has been made to adapt the original un-official devices to the requirements of the official heraldic badges used today.

In September 1939, Canada had very few ships. Later they were turned out with such rapidity that it was difficult to find suitable names for them, let alone design appropriate badges.

The Naval Headquarters in Ottawa began to receive numerous requests for information and help on ship's badges. Proposed designs came in for approval almost as fast as ships were built, since the potential value of a good device was generally recognized as being useful in promoting loyalty to a ship and fostering a high level of 'esprit de corps' in the ship's company.

To meet this demand an "Insignia Committee" was formed at naval headquarters, with Dr. Gilbert Tucker, the naval historian, as chairman. The committee adopted the only policy that was practical in war conditions: commanding officers of HMC ships could design their own badges at their own expense! These were, however, to be scrutinized by the Captain of the Port, or in the case of shore establishments, the Secretary of the Naval Board, to ensure that they contained nothing offensive or in bad taste (references to the enemy of course excepted).

6.02 Frames for ships badges. Left to right: Capital ships, cruisers, destroyers and submarines, other ships.

It was understood that these badges should not be regarded as official, and that after the war a permanent policy on ships' badges would be announced with the high probability that wartime insignia would be altered. It was duly recommended that there should be no heavy outlay of funds.

Most of the 'hostilities only' insignia took the form of cartoon paintings on gun shields or bridge structures and there were some astonishing designs produced. An outstanding one was for HMCS *Wetaskiwin* depicting a comely 'Queen of Hearts' seated in a puddle of water, which was fair heraldry if one pronounced the last two syllables of the ship's name 'Queen' — the name that sailors affectionately dubbed the ship. Another for the *Sorel* featured a cartoon style picture of the head of a sorrel mare, with huge teeth and sporting a naval crown, gleefully biting a U-boat.

There were representations of "Popeye the Sailor," "Mickey Mouse," the mounties, cowboys and even Winston Churchill, cigar and all, as well as other lesser known figures doing the most daring things to the enemy, who was usually shown as a U-boat or Hitler. A light-hearted bravado was common to most. The sailors certainly used the opportunity to express themselves in creating these badges, and this tended to draw them together, no doubt bolstering morale and relieving the strain of a new and often frightening life.

Of course not all this wartime 'insignia' was of this type; there were genuine attempts made to create badges in keeping with the dignified form then in use by the RN. One example of this is the HMCS *Algonquin* badge, the only one adopted without alteration in the permanent RCN collection. This shows an Indian's arm rising from the sea holding a spear which is transfixing a snake; the reference is to anti-submarine warfare.

Designs were of mixed quality since some names chosen for ships do not readily lend themselves to representation by symbol. The Garter King of Arms once described heraldry as "an art, a little science and something of a mystery which only those who devote their lives to it can hope to understand and master."

There was often controversy surrounding RCN badges. For instance a design submitted to Clarenceux (Garter King of Arms) from Ottawa for HMCS *Discovery*, named after one of Captain Vancouver's two ships, incorporated the image of a telescope. It was commented that "Vancouver did not discover Canada ... (or) the Maple Leaf" and an alternative suggestion offered was that the current 'Discover-Y' be used instead. The suggested device is an excellent example of a 'rebus,' an ancient and respected form widely used in heraldry, where parts of words are represented by pictures or shapes. The initial reaction to the design was definitely negative, but later the consensus was that this was the best badge in the collection.

A somewhat reserved example of the rebus is on the badge of HMCS *Beacon Hill*; it is simply an illustration of an ancient beacon-light on a hilltop.

The design of heraldry badges, particularly in wartime, sometimes included unofficial insignia to commemorate a past event. For instance the new ship *Athabascan* carries a badge that was presented to the ship by the wife of the executive officer Lt. Lawrence, who, with many of the old ship's company, were lost on 29 April, 1944 when the *Athabascan* was sunk by the enemy. Lawrence had designed a badge for his ship shortly before his death and his father had the carving completed for the new *Athabascan* with only a few changes to the original design.

The *Venture* is a name that has been given to various vessels in British naval history used for training naval officers and the Canadian Navy has followed the tradition. The badge of the current *Venture* illustrates its status and function as a training school for new officers of the Canadian fleet. It features the red maple leaf of the national emblem and the gold naval crown found on the badge worn on the blazers of Canadian naval officers. The 'V' in the design refers, of course, to *Venture* but also represents the process of growth which all young men experience during their training and experience in the Canadian Navy.

Ships' Mottoes

The motto "Toujours gai" was made famous by Mehitabel the cat, but it originated with the English family of Gay many years before.

The motto had the same origin as the Coat of Arms and is probably older. The arms, painted on a knight's shield and embroidered on his pennon and horse's caparison, identified him when his visor was down. His men wore his badge or livery colours to show to which troop they belonged, and in a rout or ambuscade they rallied round his pennon.

To rally his men in a night attack and to encourage them to battle, a knight would also have a battle cry which in the Middle Ages, was usually called his 'word' in English, 'mot' in French, and 'motto' in Italian. Somehow the Italian form was adopted by the English. At first the 'word' was usually the leader's name with an 'A' before it to clear the voice, as in 'Ahoy.' The Saxon hero Wereward chose the particularly apt battle cry 'Awake.' His name meant 'Guard of the Army' and he was nicknamed 'The Wake' meaning 'The Watchful.' His word identified him as the leader and was an exhortation as well!

In pitched battles between kings, national battle cries were used. 'St. George for England' (presumably shortened to 'St. George') was opposed by yells of 'St. Andrew' or 'Montjoie St. Denis,' prior to the Reformation. It was used however, more recently in a signal made by Admiral Sir Roger Keyes on St. George's Eve in 1918 to the force under his command at Zebrugge:

"St. George for England."

Captain A.F.B. Carpenter *Vindictive* replied:

"And may we give the Dragon's tail a damn good twist."

As the use of personal badges diminished after the sixteenth century when education became more widespread, the use of mottoes also diminished. Armies became more organized and the call 'Hurrah' replaced the older slogans. (Slogan is of Gaelic origin and means 'Cry of an Army.') Personal mottoes became long, learned and cryptic and were difficult for the common soldier to understand, much less yell in the heat of action. Latin mottoes became popular and now outnumber the others, while a learned few adopted Greek. Some even appear to reverse the ancient idea behind the motto. For example, 'Auriga virtutum prudentia,' used by one English family is literally translated 'Forethought is the

charioteer of courage,' although it is probably intended to mean 'Common sense is the chief of the virtues.' It could also mean 'Discretion is the better part of valour.' Most modern mottoes, however, simply express a vague piety or a statement of aspirations such as:

"Dum spiro spero" — While I breathe I hope.

Some reflect a bourgeois attitude, such as:

"Industria ditat" — Industry enriches.

Others show a particularly moral spirit as in:

"Fiat justitia, ruat coelum" — Do right though the heavens fall, the motto adopted by the Admiral-of-the-Fleet, Lord Fisher.

The ship's motto, like the badge, is subject to the approval of the ships' badges committee. The commanding officer has responsibility for submitting the proposed motto, and it is the committee's duty to ensure that the motto is appropriate and accurately expressed. In the RCN most of the ships' mottoes are in Latin but some are in English and French. A few, like those of HMCS *Iroquois* and HMCS *Micmac* are in one of the Amerindian tongues. On board, the motto is displayed on the battle honour scroll or board; in naval air squadrons it is part of the squadron badge surround.

Battle Honours

Seamen have always taken pride in the battle exploits of their own ships as well as earlier ships of the fleet that have borne the same name. As a result, the custom developed of displaying battle honours in a conspicuous place in the ship. In 1954, however, the Admiralty took control of this practice, and set up rules for the award of battle honours. Like the rest of Her Majesty's Fleets of the Commonwealth, the Royal Canadian Navy in consultation with the Admiralty subscribes to a common system of battle honours.

Battle honours are awarded to the ship's name rather than to the hull itself, so that the honour lives on in future ships of the same name. HMCS *Bonaventure* proudly displays eight such honours including *Barfleur* 1692, and HMCS *Carleton* the honour *Lake Champlain* 1776. Similarly, several ships of the Royal Navy and the Royal Australian Navy wear honours won in battle by HM Canadian Ships.

Mr. E.C. Russell, the Naval Historian remarked:

"Like many of the cherished traditions of the Royal Canadian Navy, shared battle honours is one more symbol of the ties that bind the nations of the Commonwealth as free and equal realms under one sovereign. These and the ancient devices of badge and motto express the sailor's pride in ship, pride in Service, pride in wearing the Queen's Uniform and satisfaction in a task well done."[1]

The Maple Leaf

The idea of adopting the maple leaf as an emblem of the people of Canada became popular early in the nineteenth century. The maple leaf has become very well known worldwide, mainly through its display by HMC ships. The maple leaf badge was worn on the funnels of Canadian ships of war some sixty years ago.

In a letter to the Naval Secretary, Able Seaman Joseph Stephenson wrote:

"Well, in the first place it all started at Gibralter in March 1918. Forty Canadian ratings were drafted to "Gib" to man these ships (CD 2, CD 7, CD 11 and CD 8) — about ten ratings to each ship. We commissioned the ships in the traditional way of the Navy and flew the pennant, spliced the main brace and off we went ... In order to have them recognized as Canadian and not British we flew the Blue Ensign under the commission pennant. When we got to our destination and settled down our sweeping gear and kites all overboard ready for action I said to my Skipper "Can I paint the maple leaf on the funnel?" He said "Go ahead!" This I did and we knew then that we were meaning business."[2]

During World War II the Naval Board officially authorized the wearing of the green maple leaf on the funnel. In those days all His Majesty's ships, from every country of the Commonwealth, flew the White Ensign. The maple leaf badge readily identified a ship of the Royal Canadian Navy.

This symbol was carried over into peace time, but the colour of the maple leaf was changed from green to red.

The Foul Anchor

The 'Foul Anchor' is the ancient badge of mariners the world over. A century-old dictionary definition clearly explains the symbols: "An anchor is said to be foul or fouled either when it hooks some impediment under water or when the ship [but] the wind shifting entangles her slack cable around the stack or around the upper fluke thereof. The last from being avoided by a sharp lookout, is termed the seaman's disgrace."[3]

If the foul anchor insignia illustrates one of the worst examples of seamanship it is difficult to explain the badge's prestige. The Admiralty, however, offers this opinion: "It seems more than probable that the fouling was originally done for decorative purposes, not for any implied meaning."

No one really knows how the foul anchor originated as the badge of the Admiralty although it is known that it came from various Lord High Admirals.

The earliest known example was in the Arms of Patrick Hepburn, Earl of Bothwell, Lord High Admiral of Scotland in 1488. Lord Howard of Effingham of Armada fame (1588) was the first Lord High Admiral of England to use it. His seal in the British Museum, dated 1601, shows the stock and shank of an anchor fouled by a cable.

In 1633, after the murder of Buckingham, Lord High Admiral of England, his office was put into commission and the Lords Commissioners adopted the Duke of Buckingham's seal for their own.

The Naval Crown

The badges of all air squadrons, most regiments and all bases and stations, are surmounted by the Royal crown, but the badges of HMC ships are all contained within a rope surmounted by the naval crown, a symbol of great antiquity. It is similar to the Rostral crown of Roman origin, and consists of a circlet bearing the sterns of three ships of the line, each with three poop lanterns and two squared sails spread on a mast and yard and fully fitted and sheeted home. The hulls and sails are placed alternately around the circlet.

When first introduced in antiquity, a crown had no regal or royal significance. It started as a simple garland or wreath of leaves and flowers worn round the head by those who had distinguished themselves in the athletic games as a temporary badge of prowess given on the spot.

Laurel, sacred to Apollo, was the symbol of victory among the early Greeks and Romans. There were also myrtle and olive crowns, and the Roman "Corona Obsidionalis," of grass or wild flowers plucked on the site, was given to the general who had won a victory or conquered a city.

The "Corona Civica," of oak leaves and acorns, went to any Roman soldier who had saved the life of a Roman citizen in battle.

Later, among the Romans, some of these emblems came to be fashioned in the more permanent form of gold circlets worn on the head, not unlike the modern coronets worn by peers of the realm. The "Corona Navalis" or "Rostra," a golden circlet decorated with the prows and sterns of ancient galleys, was given for an important victory at sea. It originated, most likely, well before the fifth century, and was the precursor of the naval crown in use today.

In 1666 Sir Robert Holmes received a naval crown as part of the "honourable augmentation" of arms granted to him by Charles II for his brilliant services against the Dutch. Since then, many naval officers of distinction adopted the same emblem on receiving a grant of arms or an augmentation to those they already bore.

The design of the naval crown has varied from

time to time, and at one period showed eight bows or sterns of ancient ships, not the three sterns alternating with the two square sails used at present. But the general design is of very ancient origin, and has been used in England, often as a badge or symbol of naval distinction and honour, for nearly three centuries, and possibly a good deal longer.

Notes

1. Edward C. Russell, "Badges, Battle Honours, Mottoes, Royal Canadian Navy," *The Crowsnest*, 17, No. 6, (Ottawa, Dept. of Public Printing, 1965), p.22.

2. "Second World War Funnel Bands," *The Crowsnest*, 10, No. 5, (Ottawa, Dept. of Public Printing, 1958), p.11.

3. Admiral W.W. Smyth, *The Sailor's Word Book*, (London, n.p., 1867), p.319.

II
Reproductions of Selected HMCS Badges

The Royal Canadian Navy

Blazon: Within an orle of ten maple leaves gold, an oval cartouche azure fimbriated or thereon a foul anchor of the same, the whole ensigned by a representation of the Royal Crown.

Significance: This badge can be clearly read: Royal (the crown) Canadian (the maple leaves) Navy (the foul anchor). For emphasis, the azure of the cartouche is navy blue.

This badge was approved by the Naval Board on 31 March, 1944 and later by Clarenceux King of Arms. It contained nine maple leaves referring to the nine provinces which made up Canada at that time. In 1952 a design, amended to include an additional maple leaf for Newfoundland was approved by her Majesty Queen Elizabeth II. In 1956 the badge was again amended by the replacement of the Tudor Crown by St. Edward's Crown in accordance with Her Majesty's wishes.

Maritime Command

Blazon: Azure, a wooden-stocked anchor, foul of its cable, a dexter fluke and sinister stock-arm foremost, debruised by an eagle volant affronté, the head turned to sinister, all or.

Significance: The blue field refers to the sea, and the combination of the anchor and eagle to the cooperation between the sea and air in the pursuit of the enemy in those elements.

Motto: Ready Aye Ready

HMCS Algonquin

Blazon: Sable, a base barry wavy argent and azure of four, from which issues an Indian's arm embowed proper, wearing arm and wrist bands argent and holding a fish-spear in bend argent transfixing an eel or.

Significance: This was one of the best badge designs produced during the war before ship's badges were officially issued. Of such excellence of design and appropriateness in suggesting this destroyer's activities in anti-submarine warfare, it has been accepted as the official badge.

Ship's colours: Gold and azure blue.

Motto: "A coup sur" (with sure stroke)

Battle honours: Norway 1944; Normandy 1944; Arctic 1944-45.

HMCS Annapolis

Blazon: Gules, a bend wavy argent charged with a like bendlet azure and over all a cypher of the letters AR entwined in ornamental scrip ensigned by an ancient crown, all gold.

Significance: This ship derives its name from the Annapolis River in Nova Scotia, which is symbolized by the white and blue wavy diagonal. The crowned cypher of the letters AR signifies Annapolis Royal, the settlement the river is named after; Annapolis, Maryland, the site of the United States Naval Academy, and Queen Anne, in whose honour these places were named. The original HMCS *Annapolis* in World War II, was formerly the American "four-stacker" Destroyer, USS *Mackenzie*.

Ship's colours: Gold and scarlet

Motto: To excel

Battle honours: Atlantic 1941-43.

HMCS Assiniboine

Blazon: Or, a bend wavy azure charged with two cotises wavy argent over all a bison's head caboshed proper.

Significance: The name "Assiniboine" was applied by the Algonquins to a tribe of the Sioux who cooked their food by dropping heated stones in water. They inhabited the territory between the Missouri and Saskatchewan rivers, and the name "Assiniboine" was given to a tributary of the Red River that flows into Lake Winnipeg.

The buffalo head was chosen in reference to the location of the Manitoba river. The golden background represents the wheat growing region through which the river flows — and the blue and white "bend" is a symbol for the river.

Ship's colours: Black and gold

Motto: "Nunquam non paratus" (Never unprepared)

Battle honours: Atlantic 1939-45; Biscay 1944; English Channel 1944-45.

HMCS Athabaskan

Blazon: On a field argent a North American Indian clad in buckskin breeches, leggings and beaded moccasins, but bare to the waist except for a necklace of bear's claws and blue shells, and ear ornaments of the last. The Indian wears the full-feathered head-dress and is mounted bare-back upon an Indian pony being halted from the trot. The Indian holds a red bow and arrow in the "ready" position, the latter pointing down.

Significance: This badge design is based on one planned by officers of the original *Athabaskan*, but before the design was completed the ship was lost in action. The elements of the original design were retained in the new official badge.

Ship's colours: White and scarlet

Motto: "We fight as one"

Battle honours: Arctic 1943-44; English Channel 1944; Korea 1950-53.

HMCS Chaleur

Blazon: A field pily or and gules above barry wavy azure and azure, and in the centre an equilateral triangle azure bearing a fern leaf or.

Significance: This Canadian ship of war takes her name from the Bay of Chaleur (the Bay of Heat) discovered by Cartier on a humid day in July 1534. The heraldic water in the badge refers to the Bay of Chaleur, and the red and gold shafts in the background convey the impression of heat rising. The triangular device in the centre refers to the Bay being in the heart of the Micmac country and the fern leaf to the Micmac legend in which Glooscap, a Prophet of the Great Spirit, slew his brother with a fern. The triangle on which the fern is displayed symbolizes a wigwam.

Ship's colours: Gold and red

Battle honours: Nil.

HMCS Chignecto

Blazon: Gules, a pile azure fimbriated argent charged with a sprig of bulrush or.

Significance: The word "chignecto" is of Micmac Indian origin, and means "the great marsh district." This badge depicts the V-shaped device associated with bay class ships of the RCN. The representation of a bulrush in gold, suggests the vegetation that grows in marshy lands and the red background the reddish coloured earth of the area.

Ship's colours: Blue and gold

Battle honours: Nil.

HMCS Cowichan

Blazon: On a field barry wavy, argent and azure, a pale argent on which a chief's ceremonial mask traditional of the "Cowichan type" of the Salish, vert.

Significance: Cowichan is an Indian word which means "between streams." Thus the vertical strip or "pale" in the middle of the badge lies between two sections of heraldic "water." The mask depicted is taken from one in the Anthropological Museum, University of British Columbia. It is described as the traditional type produced by the Salish, particularly in the Cowichan district of Vancouver Island.

Ship's colours: White and green

Battle honours: Atlantic 1941-45; Normandy 1944.

HMCS Fraser

Blazon: Azure, a buck's head erased or, attired argent, charged on the shoulder with a maple leaf gules.

Significance: This ship derives its name from the Fraser River in British Columbia, discovered by Alexander Mackenzie in 1793, and explored to its mouth by Simon Fraser in 1803, in whose honour the river was named. The badge design is derived from the crest in the Fraser arms, a buck's head in gold with white antlers. It is charged with a red maple leaf, to show that this Simon Fraser was associated with Canada.

Ship's colours: Blue and gold

Motto: "Je suis prêt" (I am ready)

Battle honours: Atlantic 1939-40.

HMCS Fundy

Blazon: Gules, a pile azure, fimbriated argent charged with a maple leaf between two fleur-de-lis, all conjoined on the one stem, or.

Significance: The blue pile refers to the Bay of Fundy. The red background is primarily for contrast and brightness, but also refers to the reddish earth of the land that borders this Bay. The golden floral device pays tribute to the original white settlers around Fundy who came from France — the present-day Acadians. The gold of the floral device is one of the Royal colours.

Ship's colours: Red and gold

Motto: "Verrimus altum" (We sweep the deep)

Battle honours: Atlantic 1939-45.

HMCS Gatineau

Blazon: Vert, a bend wavy argent charged with two like cotisses bendlets azure, debruised with a sun in splendour or which is charged with a beaver sable.

Significance: This ship is named after the Gatineau River in the Province of Quebec. The Gatineau River was named after Nicolas Gatineau or Gastineau, a notary, civic official and fur-trader of Three Rivers. The wavy white and blue diagonal stripe refers to the Gatineau River, the green background to the forests and recreational areas of the Valley. The little black beaver is in tribute to Mr. Nicolas Gatineau and his fur-trading activities.

Ship's colours: Gold and green

Motto: "In hoc catino potestas" (In this ship lies power)

Battle honours: Atlantic 1943-44; Normandy 1944.

HMCS Huron

Blazon: Or, nicotine bloom gules, seedpod vert, and stamens or.

Significance: The Hurons were known as the Tobacco Indians and this badge design, derived from that plant, shows a representation of the nicotine bloom in keeping with the traditional use of flower and plant forms as fighting emblems.

Ship's colours: Gold and crimson

Battle honours: Arctic 1943-45; English Channel 1944; Normandy 1944; Korea 1951-53.

HMCS Iroquois

Blazon: Or, the head of an Iroquois brave, couped at the base of the neck, properly coloured and wearing two eagle feathers in his hair and a gold ring pendant from the ear.

Significance: An unofficial badge for this ship in the shape of a shield bearing the head of an Iroquois brave was taken from a painting by the late C.W. Jeffries. When a definite policy regarding ship's badges was established the head of an Iroquois, facing the opposite direction for heraldic purposes, was approved for reasons of sentiment and appropriateness.

Ship's colours: Gold and black

Motto: Relentless in chase

Battle honours: Atlantic 1943; Arctic 1943-45; Biscay 1943-44; Norway 1945; Korea 1951-53.

HMCS Kootenay

Blazon: Argent, three cotises in bend wavy azure, over all a crescent sable debruised by an Indian fish spear-head gules, bound around the hilt with thongs argent.

Significance: The Kootenay River was named after the Kootenay Indians who caught fish in its waters and hunted buffalo in the Rocky Mountains. The Kootenay River, for which the ship is named, is symbolized by the three blue diagonal wavy stripes. The black crescent resembles the horns of the bison or buffalo, and the fish spearhead is typical of the kind used by the Indians.

Ship's colours: Red and white

Motto: We are as one

Battle honours: Atlantic 1943-45; Normandy 1944; English Channel 1944; Biscay 1944.

HMCS Mackenzie

Blazon: Gules, a bend wavy argent upon which a like bendlet azure, and over all a lion rampant or, armed and langued of the third, charged on the shoulder with a hurt upon which a representation of a compass rose of eight points argent, the vertical and horizontal pointers extending beyond the perimeter of the hurt.

Significance: This destroyer derives its name from the great Mackenzie River in the Northwest Territories, discovered and explored by Sir Alexander Mackenzie (1789), a native of Scotland. The gold lion is the reverse colouring of the main device in the Royal Arms of Scotland. The compass rose is a symbol of geography, travel and exploration, and is part of the crest in the armorial bearings of the Northwest Territories.

Ship's colours: Gold and scarlet

Motto: By virtue and valour

Battle honours: Nil.

HMCS Margaree

Blazon: Azure, three cotises wavy argent, over all a flower of the marguerite (daisy) proper.

Significance: This ship is named after the Margaree River in Cape Breton. Margaree is a corruption of the name Marguerite, the original name of the river. The badge design displays an heraldic representation of a river over which is depicted a flower of the marguerite or daisy plant.

Ship's colours: White and blue

Battle honours: Atlantic 1940.

HMCS Miramichi

Blazon: On a field of birch bark proper, a pile barry wavy of ten argent and azure and overall an equilateral triangle, apex to the chief gules, charged with a porcupine or.

Significance: This ship is named after Miramichi Bay in New Brunswick, which in turn is from an Indian word 'miramichi' meaning 'Micmac land.' The field or background represents birch bark while the V-shaped compartment is shown as heraldic water and represents the Bay of Miramichi. The equilateral triangle suggests the Indian wigwam, and the porcupine in gold, represents the Indians' livelihood.

Ship's colours: Red and gold

Motto: "Loyal a la mort" (Loyal unto death)

Battle honours: Nil.

HMCS Nipigon

Blazon: Gules, in base a bar fessewise wavy argent charged with a like barrulet azure, out of which leaping, two trout or, one to the dexter chief the other to the sinister chief.

Significance: The famous "Red Rock" on which early Indians painted representations of various objects familiar to them, is situated at the mouth of the Nipigon River, which flows into Lake Superior from the North. This "rock" is referred to by the red background in the badge. The Nipigon River, after which this ship is named, is renowned for its excellent trout fishing, symbolized by two golden trout shown leaping from the river of wavy white and blue horizontal stripe.

Ship's colours: Gold and scarlet

Motto: We are one

Battle honours: Atlantic 1940-45.

HMCS Ojibwa

Blazon: Azure, an escallop shell erect argent irradiated by nine ears of wild rice or, all issuing from two barrulets wavy of the last, in base.

Significance: The design of this badge is derived from an Ojibwa legend concerning the great Megis or sea-shell. When the great Megis rose from out of the waters it reflected the rays of the sun and gave warmth and light to the Redman, bringing prosperity. When it descended into the depths of the waters it brought misery and death to the tribe, causing them to migrate to new regions. The sheafs of rice refer to the wild rice growing in one of the tribe's settlements in Northern Ontario.

Ship's colours: White and blue

Motto: "Ne Ke Che Dah" (Let us be prepared)

HMCS Okanagan

Blazon: Or, issuing out of a base barry wavy of four azure and argent, a marine monster "Ogopogo" gules, langued of the second.
Significance: This design pictures a fanciful heraldic version of the monster reputed to inhabit Lake Okanagan in British Columbia. The monster is purely imaginary, even to the colour red since Ogopogo is said to be green.
Ship's colours: Scarlet and gold
Motto: "Ex imo mari ad victoriam" (From the depths of the sea to victory)

HMCS Onondaga

Blazon: Azure, within a representation of the wampum of the Iroquois nation, another of the head of the mace used at the sitting of the first Parliament of Upper Canada in 1792, both proper.
Significance: This design displays a representation of the Wampum of the Iroquois nation, of which the Onondagas were members and known as the "Keepers of the Wampum." The mace head is an indirect reference to the Schooner *Onondaga* a ship of H.M. Provincial Marine on Lake Ontario, which had a part in the convening of the first Parliament of Upper Canada at Newark in 1792, and also in the founding of York (now Toronto) in 1793.
Ship's colours: White and blue
Motto: "Invicta" (Unconquered)

HMCS Oriole

Blazon: Or, an oriole proper.
Significance: Nothing could be more appropriate for this badge design than the oriole in its natural plumage.
Ship's colours: Black and orange
Battle honours: Dunkirk, 1940.

HMCS *Ottawa*

Blazon: Gules, a bend wavy argent charged with two cotises wavy azure, over all a beaver or, the sinister forepaw resting on a log of silver birch proper.

Significance: This design is derived from the unofficial badge of HMCS *Ottawa*, a beaver on a log of wood. The white and blue wavy 'bend' represents the Ottawa River after which the ship is named. The red field refers to the Outaouas or Ottawas, Indians (redmen) who travelled the river from which the name was derived.

Ship's colours: White and red

Battle honours: Atlantic 1939-45; Normandy 1944; English Channel 1944; Biscay 1944.

HMCS *Preserver*

Blazon: Azure, a life preserver argent, cabled or, charged on the centre chief point with a maple leaf slipped gules, and within the ring a star-burst also argent.

Significance: The life preserver is a rebus on the ship's name and gains Canadian identification with the red maple leaf. The star-burst in the centre symbolizes the flare that is automatically ignited when the life preserver touches the water.

Ship's colours: White and blue

HMCS *Protecteur*

Blazon: Azure, a silver helmet with five grills or, garnished of the last, and bearing a coronet fleur-de-lis also or.

Significance: A helmet is an instrument of protection, and in this instance, having the coronet trimmed with fleurs-de-lis, the device of former Royal France, it becomes a "Protecteur."

Ship's colours: Gold and blue

HMCS *Provider*

Blazon: Azure, an ancient Greek amphora garnished around the base of the neck with maple leaves, and on the main body of the vessel, a foul anchor erect all of gold.

Significance: This badge depicts an ancient Greek amphora, an earthenware vessel used as a storage container. The amphora suggests the ship's function of storing and dispensing supplies; the superimposed maple leaves and foul anchor indicate it is a ship of the RCN. The amphora's gold colour represents the colour of oil, a major item of *Provider's* stores, and the dark blue background is known as "Navy blue."

Ship's colours: Golden yellow and Navy blue

Motto: Ready to serve

Battle honours: Nil.

HMCS *Qu'Appelle*

Blazon: Azure, a bend wavy argent charged with a like bendlet gules, and over all a fox's mask argent.

Significance: The Qu'Appelle River in Saskatchewan, for which this destroyer escort is named, derives its name from an Indian legend concerning a mysterious voice calling. The Indians referred to this river as 'Who Calls?,' the French explorers as 'Qu'Appelle.' To suggest an attitude of intent listening and watching, the face or mask of a white fox is shown for the badge, the large erect ears and keen eyes being indicative of this and of the functions of the ship with its sonar (for listening) and radar (for watching).

Ship's colours: White and blue.

Battle honours: Atlantic 1944; Normandy 1944; Biscay 1944.

HMCS *Restigouche*

Blazon: Or, the head of a five-pronged fish spear erect, azure.

Significance: The gold field is derived from the field in the Arms of New Brunswick, the province through which the Restigouche River flows. The five-pronged fish spear is in reference to the five tributaries of this river. Restigouche is derived from a Micmac word meaning "river with five branches." The fork is blue representing water. This device is also an instrument for hunting fish below the surface of the water; a subtle allusion to anti-submarine activities.

Ship's colours: Blue and gold.

Motto: "Rester droit" (Steer a straight course)

Battle honours: Atlantic 1939-45; North Sea 1940; Mediterranean 1943; Normandy 1944; Biscay 1944.

HMCS Saguenay

Blazon: Sable, a bend wavy argent charged with two like cotises azure, surmounted by an Indian's head facing sinister and couped at the shoulder proper having a fillet gules about the temples, depending therefrom, tips downward, four feathers of the second pied of the last, and pendant from the ear an annulet silver.

Significance: During World War II HMCS *Saguenay* used an unofficial badge displaying a shield with three maple leaves beside an Indian's head, similar to the one shown here. To commemorate this ship's war service, the Indian's head is retained in the official badge design. The wavy white and blue diagonal stripe represents the Saguenay River itself, from which the ship derives her name.

Ship's colours: Red and black

Motto: "A l'erte" (On the lookout for danger — ready to act)

Battle honours: Atlantic 1939-42.

HMCS Saskatchewan

Blazon: Vert, a bend wavy argent charged with a like bendlet gules.

Significance: This design refers to the unofficial war-time badge of HMCS *Saskatchewan*, which displayed a wheat sheaf or garb and was derived from the devices and colours in the Arms of the Province of Saskatchewan: three wheat sheaves upon a green field. The wavy white and red diagonal stripe, termed a 'bend' in heraldry, refers to the river.

Ship's colours: Gold and green

Motto: Ready and confident

Battle honours: Atlantic 1943-44; Normandy 1944; Biscay 1944.

HMCS Skeena

Blazon: Azure, out of a base invected argent, a salmon sinisterwise proper.

Significance: The word 'skeena' is derived from the Indian 'iksh' meaning 'out of' and 'shean' or 'shyen,' the clouds. As the Skeena finds its source far inland among the mountains whose tops are often shrouded in clouds and mists, it is natural that this name should be given to this great river. A salmon appeared on the unofficial badge of the original ship *Skeena* and appears in this badge in its honour.

Ship's colours: White and blue

Motto: Go forth

Battle honours: Atlantic 1939-44; Normandy 1944; Biscay 1944.

HMCS Terra Nova

Blazon: Gules, a bend wavy argent charged with two like cotises azure, debruised with a cross of the second charged with a penguin erect proper.
Significance: The wavy diagonal stripe refers to the River Terra Nova in Newfoundland, after which this ship is named. The white cross is derived from the Arms of Newfoundland. The penguin on the ship's badge is a tribute to Captain Scott, who served in the Antarctic on a whaler named Terra Nova.
Ship's colours: White and dark red
Motto: "Tenax propositi" (Do not falter)
Battle honours: Nil.

HMCS Thunder

Blazon: Gules, a pile vert edged or, charged with a representation of the head of Thor, god of thunderstorms, affronte, wearing a Nordic open crown composed of a circlet with eight arches all plain and meeting together in a point at the pinnacle, his beard formed into nine radiating coils each tapering to a point with a small spearhead at the end.
Significance: Named after Thunder Bay in Lake Superior, Northern Ontario, this badge design carries the V-shaped section associated with RCN ships bearing the names of bays. The red field or background refers to copper which was mined in this region. The name 'Thunder' represents the courage of seafaring warriors of the North.
Ship's colours: Green and gold
Battle honours: Martinique 1762; Havana 1762; Basque Roads 1809; Atlantic 1941-44; Normandy 1944; English Channel 1944-45.

HMCS Yukon

Blazon: Gules, a bend wavy or charged with a like bendlet azure, and overall a malamute sled dog, proper.
Significance: The malamute sled dog is derived from the crest in the Arms of the Yukon Territory. The wavy diagonal in blue and gold is a reference to the River Yukon along the borders of which great gold deposits once existed.
Ship's colours: White and red
Motto: Only the fit survive
Battle honours: Nil.

Bibliography

Atkinson, C.T. *Letters and Papers Relating to the First Dutch War 1652-1654, Vol. VI* London: Naval Records Society, 1930.

Badges of the Canadian Forces - CFP 267 Ottawa: Supply and Services Canada, 1977.

Beckett, W.N.T. *A Few Naval Customs, Expressions, Traditions and Superstitions* Portsmouth: Gieves Ltd., 1953.

Campbell, A.B. *Customs and Traditions of the Royal Navy* Aldershot: Gale and Polden Ltd., 1956.

Campbell, G. and Evans, I.O. *The Book of Flags* London: Oxford University Press, 1960.

Canadian Forces Administration Orders Ottawa: Supply and Services Canada, 1981.

Canadian Forces Dress Manual Ottawa: Supply and Services Canada, 1979.

Canadians at War 1939-1945 The Reader's Digest Association (Canada) Ltd., 1953.

Carr, H.G. *Flags of the World* London: Frederick Warne and Co. Ltd., 1953.

Chappell, E. *The Tangier Papers of Samuel Pepys* London: William Clowes and Sons, Ltd., 1934.

Cobb, D. *Rig of the Day* Harwick, Bernards Printers, 1956.

The Crowsnest Magazine Ottawa: King's and Queen's Printer, Dec. 1948 - June 1965.

Customs and Etiquette of the Royal Navy London: Gieves Ltd., 1950.

"Divisional System (The)" London: *The Naval Review*, 1950.

Dorling, H.T. *Ribbons and Medals* London: George Philip and Son Ltd., 1957.

Eayrs, J. *In Defence of Canada - Appeasement and Rearmament* Toronto: University of Toronto Press, 1967.

Eayrs, J. *In Defence of Canada — From the Great War to the Great Depression* Toronto: University of Toronto Press, 1967.

Ffoulkes, C. and Hopkinson, E.C. *Sword, Lance and Bayonet* Cambridge: n.p., 1938.

Firth, C.H. (ed). *Naval Songs and Ballads* London: Naval Records Society, 1908.

Gardiner, S.R. *Letters and Papers Relating to the First Dutch War 1652-1654, Vol. I & II* London: Naval Records Society, 1889.

Gurney, R. *History of the Northamptonshire Regiment 1742-1934* Aldershot: Gale and Polden Ltd., 1935.

Hampshire, A.C. *No Baton for the Admiral* London: n.p., 1959.

Hartog, J. de. *A Sailor's Life* New York: Harper and Brothers, 1955.

Hellyer, P. *The Canadian Forces Reorganization Act* Ottawa: Queens Printer, 1966.

Hicks, J.S. *The Duchess Wore Blue* London: n.p., 1953.

"Hoisting and Hauling Down the White Ensign," *The Mariner's Mirror* St. Albans: Staples Printers, Nov. 1960.

"Hoisting the Colours," *The Mariner's Mirror* St. Albans: Staples Printers, Feb. 1954.

Howe, Admiral Lord. *Instructions and Standing Orders* London: n.p., 1776.

Instructions of Mary London: Admiralty Library Manuscript, 1558.

"Internal Organization and Administration of Our Warships from the Norman Conquest to the Battle of Trafalgar" London: *The Naval Review*, 1924.

James, Duke of York. *Memoirs of English Affairs, Chiefly Naval 1660-1673* London: n.p., 1729.

Jarret, D. *British Naval Dress* London: J.M. Dent and Sons Ltd., 1960.

Jones, D. *Naval Badges of Rank* London: Navy and Army Illustrated, 1900.

Jones, J.P. *A History of the South Staffordshire Regiment 1765-1923* Wolverhampton: Whitehead Brothers, n.date

Journal of the Society for Army Historical Research n.p., n.p., 1948.

Kihlberg, B. *The Lore of Ships* Gothenburg, Sweden: Crescent Books, 1972.

King, C. *HMS, His Majesty's Ships and their Forebears* London: Studio Publications, 1940.

King's Colours (The) NSC File 1460-25 dated 29 October, 1959.

King's Regulations and Admiralty Instructions London: Eyre and Spottiswood, 1906.

Lawyer, C. *The Naval Sword* London: n.p., 1960.

Lewis, M. *The Navy of Britain - A Historical Portrait* London: George Allen and Unwin Ltd., 1949.

Lloyd, C. *The Naval Miscellany, Vol. I & II* London: The Naval Records Society, 1952.

Lowrey, R.G. *The Origin of Some Naval Terms and Customs - Two Vols* London: Sampson Low, Marston and Co. Ltd., n.date.

Machum, G.C. *Canada's VCs* Toronto: McClelland and Stewart Ltd., 1956.

Mackie, J.D. *The Earlier Tudors 1485-1558* London: Clarendon Press, 1962.

May, W.E. and Kennard, A.N. *Naval Swords and Fire Arms* London: n.p., 1962.

May, W.E. *Notes on the Uniform of Naval Officers* Greenwich: National Maritime Museum, 1951.

May, W.E. "The Sailor's Collar," *The Mariner's Mirror, Vol.48, No. 3* St. Albans: Staples Printers Ltd., 1962.

Merriman, R.D. *Queen Anne's Navy* London: The Naval Records Society, 1961.

Mess Administration - CFP 262 Ottawa: Supply and Services Canada, 1976.

"Military Dress in Former Days," *Canadian Defence Quarterly* Ottawa: Modern Press, 1929.

Milne, G.H. *HMCS* Toronto, Thomas Allen Ltd., 1960.

"One and a Half Stripes," *The Mariner's Mirror, Vol 49, No. 2* St. Albans: Staples Printers, 1963.

Openheim, M. *Naval Accounts and Inventories of the Reign of Henry VII 1485-1488 and 1495-1497* London: The Naval Record Society, 1896.

Petty Officer's Uniform London: Admiralty News, 1961.

Piggott, C.A. "A Brief History of the Divisional System" *The Naval Review* No. 4, Vol 60 London: *The Naval Review*, Oct. 1972.

Queen's Regulations and Orders Ottawa: Queen's Printer, 1961.

Queen's Regulations for the Canadian Navy Ottawa: Queen's Printer, 1961.

Ratcliff, T.P. *News-Chronicle Song Book* London: News-Chronicle Publications, n.date.

Rothwell, D. *The Story of the Stripe* London: n.p., 1956.

Royal Canadian Navy: Badges, Battle Honours, Mottoes Ottawa: Queen's Printer, n.date.

Royal Canadian Navy Manual of Drill and Ceremonial Ottawa: Queen's Printer, n.date.

Royal Canadian Navy Steward's Manual Ottawa: Queen's Printer, 1956.

Russell, E.C. *The Drumhead Service* Ottawa: Office of the Naval Historian, 19 June 1959.

Russell, E.C. *Customs and Traditions of the Canadian Armed Forces* Ottawa: Deneau and Greenburg, 1980.

Russell, E.C. *The Naval Officer's Sword Belt* Ottawa: Office of the Naval Historian, Memo 1440-1 (N/Hist), 1963.

Schomberg, I. *Naval Chronology: An Historical Summary of Naval and Maritime Events* (5 Vols) London: Military Library, 1802.

Schull, J. *The Far Distant Ships* Ottawa: King's Printer, 1950.

"Ship's Cook (The) - A Great Officer," London: *The Naval Chronicle*, 1815.

Smith, T. "The Divisional System in the Eighteenth Century," London: *The Naval Review*, 1930.

Stradling, A.H. *Customs of the Services* Aldershot: Gale and Polden Ltd., 1966.

Tanner, J.R. *A Descriptive Catalogue of the Naval Manuscripts in the Pepysian Library Vol 1* London: The Naval Records Society, 1903-04.

Tanner, J.R. *Samuel Pepys's Naval Minutes* London: William Clowes and Sons, 1926.

Thursfield, H.G. *Five Naval Journals (1789-1817)* Greenwich: n.p., 1950.

Tucker, G.N. *The Naval Service of Canada (2 Vol)* Ottawa: King's Printer, 1952.

Uniform Instructions for the RCN Ottawa: Queen's Printer, 1954.

Wallace, C. *Canadian Etiquette* Winnipeg: Greywood Publishing, 1967.

Warner, O. *Great Sea Battles* London: Weidenfeld and Nicolson, 1963.

Weightman, A.C. *Heraldry in the Royal Navy* Aldershot: Gale and Polden Ltd., 1957.